THE FATHERS
OF THE CHURCH

A NEW TRANSLATION

VOLUME 58

THE FATHERS OF THE CHURCH

A NEW TRANSLATION

EDITORIAL BOARD

ROY JOSEPH DEFERRARI
The Catholic University of America
Editorial Director

MSGR. JAMES A. MAGNER
The Catholic University of America

MARTIN R. P. MCGUIRE
The Catholic University of America

ROBERT P. RUSSELL, O.S.A.
Villanova University

HERMIGILD DRESSLER, O.F.M.
The Catholic University of America

BERNARD M. PEEBLES
The Catholic University of America

REV. THOMAS HALTON
The Catholic University of America

WILLIAM R. TONGUE
The Catholic University of America

REV. PETER J. RAHILL
The Catholic University of America

SISTER M. JOSEPHINE BRENNAN, I.H.M.
Marywood College

SAINT GREGORY OF NYSSA

ASCETICAL WORKS

Translated by
VIRGINIA WOODS CALLAHAN

Howard University
Washington, D C.

THE CATHOLIC UNIVERSITY OF AMERICA PRESS
Washington, D.C. 20017

NIHIL OBSTAT:
>JOHN C. SELNER, S.S.
>*Censor Librorum*

IMPRIMATUR:
>✠ PATRICK A. O'BOYLE, D.D.
>*Archbishop of Washington*

The *Nihil obstat* and *Imprimatur* are official declarations that a book or pamphlet is free of doctrinal or moral error. No implication is contained therein that those who have granted the *Nihil obstat* and *Imprimatur* agree with the contents, opinions, or statements expressed.

Copyright © 1967

THE CATHOLIC UNIVERSITY OF AMERICA PRESS

All rights reserved
Reprinted 1990
First short-run reprint 1999
Library of Congress Catalog Card No.: 66-30561
ISBN 0-8132-0969-2
ISBN-13: 978-0-8132-0969-2 (pbk.)

To the dear memory of the great scholar

WERNER JAEGER

who taught us to know and understand St. Gregory of Nyssa this volume is affectionately and gratefully dedicated.

CONTENTS

	Page
INTRODUCTION	ix
Preface	xx
ON VIRGINITY	3
ON WHAT IT MEANS TO CALL ONESELF A CHRISTIAN	79
ON PERFECTION	93
ON THE CHRISTIAN MODE OF LIFE	125
THE LIFE OF SAINT MACRINA	161
ON THE SOUL AND THE RESURRECTION	195
INDICES	275

INTRODUCTION

OF THE THREE CAPPADOCIAN FATHERS of the Church, St. Basil, St. Gregory of Nazianzus, and St. Gregory of Nyssa, the last is the least well-known and until recently the most neglected. His brother, St. Basil, called the Great, is famous as the founder of monasticism in the East and as a forceful opponent of the Arian heresy. Their close friend, St. Gregory of Nazianzus, is renowned for the glory of his eloquence and the sweetness of his poetry. And yet at the Ecumenical Council of 787, St. Gregory of Nyssa was given the title 'Father of the Fathers.' Modern writers agree that 'he surpassed the other Cappadocians as a philosopher and theologian,'[1] that he was 'more learned and profound'[2] than the others, that he was 'possibly the most versatile theologian of the century,'[3] and that 'as a speculative theologian and mystic he is certainly the most gifted of the three.'[4] The importance of St. Gregory of Nyssa is attested to particularly by the fact that Werner Jaeger, the great Hellenist of our time, devoted much of the last twenty years of his life to the editing of the first critical edition of his complete works and that the distinguished theologian, Jean Daniélou, S.J., has returned again and again to a consideration of his life and work.

In the Christian world of the fourth century, the family of St. Gregory of Nyssa was distinguished for its leadership in civic and religious affairs in the region of the Roman Empire known as the Pontus. Cardinal Newman, in an essay on the

---

1 B. Altaner, *Patrology* (New York 1960) 352.
2 J. M. Campbell, *The Greek Fathers* (New York 1963) 62.
3 H. V. Campenhausen, *The Fathers of the Greek Church* (New York 1955) 109.
4 J. Quasten, *Patrology* 3 (Westminster 1963) 254.

trials of St. Basil, refers to the family circle which produced these two eminent Fathers as 'a sort of nursery of bishops and saints.'[5] From St. Gregory's life of his sister, St. Macrina, a work included in this volume,[6] we learn of the fortitude of the three preceding generations. On her death-bed, St. Macrina, recalling details of their family history, speaks of a great-grandfather martyred and all his property confiscated and grandparents deprived of their possessions at the time of the Diocletian persecutions. Their father, Basil of Caesarea, a successful rhetorician, outstanding for his judgment and well-known for the dignity of his life, died leaving to his wife, Emmelia, the care of four sons and five daughters. St. Gregory praises his mother for her virtue and for her eagerness to have her children educated in Holy Scripture. After managing their estate and arranging for the future of her children, she was persuaded by St. Macrina to retire from the world and to enter a life in common with her maids as sisters and equals. This community of women would have been a counterpart of the monastery founded nearby by St. Basil on the banks of the Iris River. In a moving scene, St. Gregory tells of his mother's death at a rich old age in the arms of her oldest and youngest children, Macrina and Peter. Blessing all of her children, she prays in particular for the sanctification of these two who were, indeed, later canonized as saints. Newman notes the strong influence of the women in the family,[7] and in one of his letters, St. Basil gives credit to his mother and his grandmother, the elder Macrina, for his clear and steadfast idea of God.[8]

Of all the qualities of his oldest sister singled out by St. Gregory, none is more striking than her ability to influence the other members of her family. Betrothed at the age of twelve to a young lawyer who died before they could marry,

---

5 J. H. Newman, *Historical Sketches* 2 (London 1906) 17.
6 Cf. 'The Life of St. Macrina,' p. 159 ff.
7 Newman, *op. cit.*, 18.
8 St. Basil, *Letters*, translated by Sister Agnes Clare Way in *The Fathers of the Church Series*, Vol. 28 (1955), 76.

St. Macrina persuaded her father that it would be wrong for her to consider marriage to another because the young man was not dead but living in God because of the hope of the resurrection. After her father's death, she became the inseparable companion of her mother and led her to what St. Gregory calls the goal of the philosophical life. When St. Basil returned from his studies in Constantinople and Athens, 'puffed up,' as St. Gregory says, because of his intellectual gifts, it was St. Macrina who lured him from the worldliness of the rhetorical profession to the service of God. St. Peter, born after their father's death, had been St. Macrina's special charge from infancy. What she meant to St. Gregory himself as guide and mentor is made clear, not only in the biography, but also in the final work in this volume, a dialogue between St. Gregory and his sister on the condition of the soul after death where it is she who dominates the discussion.[9]

Clearly, the two most influential persons in the forming of St. Gregory's character were St. Macrina and St. Basil. Since he was not educated abroad as St. Basil and St. Gregory of Nazianzus had been, it was to his oldest brother that Gregory looked for instruction in matters secular as well as spiritual. St. Gregory's insights into the thought of Plato and other ancient philosophers prove that he took to heart his brother's views on the profitable use of pagan literature.[10] One can imagine how much the young Gregory must have been impressed by his brother's decision to withdraw from the world and with what interest he must have listened to St. Basil's account of his visits to the centers of asceticism in Egypt which prompted him to establish his monastic community in Neocaesarea. In St. Gregory's earliest ascetical treatise, *On Virginity*, when he wants to set before the monks a model for the ascetic life, it is a portrait of St. Basil that he draws for them.[11]

---

9 Cf. 'On the Soul and the Resurrection,' p. 195 ff.
10 Cf. St. Basil, *Address to Young Men on Reading Greek Literature*, translated by R. J. Deferrari and M. R. P. McGuire in *Loeb Classical Library*, Vol. 4 (London and Cambridge, Mass. 1950) 249-348.
11 Cf. 'On Virginity,' p. 72.

In his encomium of St. Basil after his death in 379, St. Gregory voices his pride in his brother's courage as priest and bishop in the fight against Arianism.[12]

It was St. Basil who had presided at St. Gregory's ordination to the priesthood, and in 371, when St. Basil thought it desirable for the episcopal sees to be safeguarded against Arian intrigue, St. Gregory had allowed himself to be consecrated Bishop of Nyssa. Unfortunately, he seems not to have shared St. Basil's gifts as an administrator, and political enemies, agents of the Arian emperor, were able to bring against him the charge of mismanagement of the diocese. He was deposed in 376 and returned from exile only after Valens' death in 378, not long before St. Basil's death. From then on, he was, as his brother had been, a strong defender of orthodoxy in the councils, at one of which he made the acquaintance of St. Jerome. He was elected Archbishop of Sebaste at the Synod of Antioch in 379 and played a prominent role in the second Ecumenical Council in Constantinople in 381. That he was esteemed by the imperial court is clear, since he was chosen to deliver the funeral orations for the Empress Flaccilla and the Princess Pulcheria in 385. There is no reference to him after 394, in which year he attended a synod at Constantinople.[13]

St. Gregory's writings as well as his activities indicate how persistently he was committed to his brother's interests. Among his dogmatic works, for example, are four treatises against the Arian theologian, Eunomius, who had singled St. Basil out for special attack.[14] Two of his exegetical treatises, *On the Creation of Man* and *On the Hexaëmeron*,[15] are an explication of St. Basil's homilies *On the Hexaëmeron*. The earliest of the

---

12 St. Gregory of Nyssa, *Encomium of St. Basil*, translated by Sister James Aloysius Stein (Washington 1928) 16 ff.
13 For a discussion of St. Gregory's marriage, to which he seems to allude in 'On Virginity' (p. 12), cf. J. Daniélou, 'Le mariage de Grégoire de Nysse et la chronologie de sa vie,' *Revue des Études Augustiniennes* 2 (1956) 71-78.
14 *Contra Eunomium*, ed. W. Jaeger (Leiden 1960).
15 These two works will be published as Volume IV of the Jaeger edition.

ascetical works, *On Virginity*, was written at St. Basil's request and each of the later ascetical writings is a return to the task of giving depth and added substance to his brother's concept of the ascetic ideal. The contents of this volume are a splendid proof of St. Gregory's desire to cooperate with his brother in his efforts to promote monasticism. St. Basil, in his *Rules*,[16] sought to systematize the ascetic life; St. Gregory, in his treatises on virginity and the life of perfect virtue in union with Christ, undertook to interpret the philosophical, theological, and mystical implications of the *Rules*. Related to these are three exegetical treatises: *On the Life of Moses*,[17] *On the Psalms*,[18] and *On the Canticle of Canticles*,[19] which in Jaeger's opinion should be placed among the ascetical writings because they, too, are written as aids to attaining the highest goals of asceticism.[20]

If Jaeger and Daniélou are correct in their dating of the ascetical works from internal evidence, they cover a period of about twenty years beginning with *On Virginity* written about 371.[21] The theme of virginity had probably been suggested to him by St. Basil while he was pursuing his studies in the monastery on the Iris. His approach to it is that of a man whose mind is imbued with the elements of Greek philosophical thought. Although he does not mention Plato by name in this treatise, he does adopt the Platonic psychology, as Cherniss points out,[22] with his emphasis on the dualism of man's nature and the conflict of body and soul, which he illus-

---

16 St. Basil, *Ascetical Works*, translated by Sister Monica Wagner in *The Fathers of the Church Series*, Vol. 9 (1950).
17 Cf. new critical edition and French translation by Daniélou in the series, *Sources Chrétiennes* (Paris 1955).
18 *In Inscriptiones Psalmorum*, Vol. V of the Jaeger edition, edited by J. MacDonough.
19 *In Canticum Canticorum*, Vol. VI of the Jaeger edition, edited by H. Langerbeck (Leiden 1962).
20 W. Jaeger, *Two Rediscovered Works of Ancient Christian Literature* (Leiden 1954) 32.
21 W. Jaeger, *ibid.* 24; J. Daniélou, *From Glory to Glory* (New York 1961) 4.
22 H. Cherniss, *The Platonism of Gregory of Nyssa* (Berkeley 1930) 15 ff.

trates by borrowing the Platonic myth from the *Phaedrus* of the charioteer and the two horses, 'a handy allegory' as Cherniss puts it. Like Plato, St. Gregory stresses the unity of the virtues and defines virtue as the perfection of our nature. In his warning that the ascetic goal is not attained if man goes to the extreme, St. Gregory makes use of the Aristotelian conviction that virtue lies in the mean. Cherniss finds the Platonic reminiscences 'shadowy' and thinks that 'Gregory must have experienced an acute civil war within himself' because of the strong attraction of Greek philosophy. Daniélou, however, maintains that the extent to which St. Gregory uses the Platonic vocabulary without resorting to literal quotations shows us clearly how much he was impregnated by the Platonic imagery, but at the same time not a slave to it.[23] Jaeger, in his numerous discussions of the impact of Greek philosophy on the formation of Christian concepts, looks upon St. Gregory's utilization of the wisdom of the earlier thinkers as the proper working of *paideia*.[24]

In the second of the ascetical treatises, *On What It Means to Call Oneself a Christian*, St. Gregory suggests that he is no longer young, and, since the treatise *On Perfection* is a continuation of this work, it is believed that it was written shortly thereafter. Taken together, these two are a kind of diptych in which the question is asked, what is the nature of the true Christian? But the two analyses of the question differ, the former being philosophical in method and the latter more theological.[25] In *On What It Means to Call Oneself a Christian*, a letter written by St. Gregory to a young friend, he begins by setting up a problem as if he and his correspondent were about to engage in a philosophical dialogue. Like Socrates directing a search for a definition of piety

---

23 J. Daniélou, *Platonisme et théologie mystique* (Paris 1954) 164.
24 W. Jaeger, *Early Christianity and Greek Paideia* (Cambridge, Mass. 1961) 86-89.
25 For the relation of these two treatises, cf. Sister Mary Emily Keenan, '*De professione* and *De perfectione*. A Study of the Ascetical Doctrine of St. Gregory of Nyssa,' *Dumbarton Oaks Papers* 5 (1950) 167-207.

or courage in one of the early works of Plato, St. Gregory seeks to determine the essential meaning of the term 'Christian.' In connection with its etymology, he stresses the need for the person who calls himself a Christian to reflect in his life the nature of Christ whose name he has assumed. He then lists ten expressions which, applied to Christ, reveal his nature to us. It is interesting to note, as an example of St. Gregory's method, that the first seven of the ten are Biblical *testimonia,* but for the last three, there are no literal corresponding references in the Bible. These are terms which would normally be found in the vocabulary of the philosopher. When St. Gregory defines Christianity as 'an imitation of the divine nature,' he has, as Jaeger indicates in his edition of this work, paraphrased Plato's definition of *areté* in the *Theaetetus.* Having offered this definition, he warns that if a Christian's life is not a true reflection of Christ he gives the world a distorted notion of the Archetype, that is, he misrepresents Christ. What man must strive for, therefore, is perfection.

In concluding the treatise, St. Gregory anticipates two objections which might be made to his definition. Someone, he suggests, might wonder how human nature with its limitations can hope to imitate the divine nature of Christ. To this, he answers that the first man, according to Scripture, was 'made in the image of God,'[26] so that anyone who succeeds in imitating the divine nature in his life is merely returning to man's original state. And to those who might doubt that man can hope to attain perfection in an imperfect world, he replies that man has the power of thought which transcends the world and the imperfections of an earthly environment, and he also has the faculty of choosing which makes separation from God not a matter of place but of choice.

In the treatise *On Perfection,* which is also a letter, but much longer and more impersonal, St. Gregory continues to maintain that the true Christian is one whose life is Christ-

---

26 Cf. H. Merki, Ὁμοίωσις θεῷ (Freiburg 1952) and Jaeger's review of it which was reprinted in his *Scripta Minora* (Rome 1960) 469-481.

like. Here, he explores in detail the nature of Christ as it is revealed in some thirty terms applied to Him in the Bible. Since St. Gregory gives a systematic explanation of the implication of each of these terms, the effect is somewhat pedantic; but, despite the didacticism, there is an elation in this treatise which corroborates Daniélou's belief that St. Gregory is rightly referred to as the 'most mystical' of the Fathers and 'the great master of Christian mystical theology.'[27]

These two treatises, together with the one *On Virginity*, form a trilogy preparing the way for the final mature statement on asceticism which was literally rescued and restored to us by Jaeger's reconstruction of the treatise *On the Christian Mode of Life*.[28] Jaeger conceives of it as the great reprise, the ripe fruit, and thinks that it may be his last work.[29] In the period of time between this and the earliest ascetical treatise, lay the distractions and turmoil of the confusion and persecutions of the troubled years and also the large undertaking of the exegetical treatises which were to result in a deeper wisdom and a developed method. St. Gregory's commentaries on various portions of the Old and New Testament are interpretations of Scripture, it is true, but they are never detached from his continuing effort to provide different kinds of illuminations of ways of living a life of virtue. This treatise is a response to a request from a group of monks who wanted a written guide to the ascetic life to which they might have recourse in the future. If it is rightly dated after 390, the year in which St. Gregory of Nazianzus died, the monks would have revered our author as an eloquent spokesman of their ascetic tradition and would, no doubt, have been eager to possess this precious testimony. One senses St. Gregory's consciousness that this is to be an influential statement and his deliberation in selecting topics which will be relevant to the

---

27 J. Daniélou, *Platonisme and théologie mystique*, 6 ff.
28 Cf. the Introduction to this treatise, p. 125.
29 W. Jaeger, *Two Rediscovered Works of Ancient Christian Literature*, 118-119.

spiritual needs of the monks in the years to come. The points of emphasis are an interesting index also of the preoccupations of the religious communities of the eastern Church towards the end of the fourth century. Finally, it is an extremely personal document. Although St. Gregory humbly insists that the seeds of instruction that he is going to give them are to be culled from his earlier works, which he refers to as 'fruits' given to him by the Holy Spirit and supported by Scripture, the treatise is an expressive self-portrait which enables us to see what St. Gregory himself has become in his untiring search for truth which he calls 'the saving medicine of our souls.'

The central questions are still the same, although they are now couched more in the language of St. Paul than of Plato. How can man perfect his nature? How can he know the perfect will of God? Nor are the answers different. There is the same emphasis on virginity as the epitome of the virtues, on the imitation of Christ, on the need to concentrate on the soul. More than in the earlier works, St. Gregory stresses the importance of Baptism as a source of grace, and on prayer as the confirmation of grace in the Holy Spirit. Perhaps because he is writing for a group living in community, he singles out the virtues of humility and charity. The word 'faith' recurs often, but always accompanying it is the conviction that more than faith is required for perfection, that there must be constant toil and struggle. What the monks must have found most comforting and reassuring is St. Gregory's espousal of the concept of *synergia,* the belief that man and God are working together to achieve a common goal.[30]

The second part of the treatise contains practical suggestions on how a group of monks can live together and achieve thereby the spiritual advancement of each individual. St. Gregory discusses not only the relation of the monks to each other, but the relation of the superior to those under his direction. The monks are reminded that a love of God will lead them to a

---

30 W. Jaeger, *ibid.* 92 ff.

love of their brothers, that they must beware of pride in the achievement of virtue, that the soul must be exercised unceasingly, that prayer and fasting are of no use unless the gifts of the Spirit follow along with them. At the end, there is a thoughtful word of comfort to those who are finding it hard to make progress in the ascetic life. What is most striking is the tone of humility and understanding, the bright evidence of St. Gregory's own spiritual development. Here, he has presented himself unwittingly, but convincingly, as the paradigm for the life of virtue.

Although they are not printed among the *Ascetica* in earlier editions of St. Gregory, two other of his works have been included in this volume; his *Life of St. Macrina* and *On the Soul and the Resurrection*. The first of these is included among the *opera ascetica* in Jaeger's edition. Jaeger has explained why, in his opinion, it belongs in this group despite its biographical form. Actually, the question of difference of form provides no difficulty because the biography of St. Macrina is a letter addressed by St. Gregory to a friend, and, in this respect, it would correspond to the treatises *On What It Means to Call Oneself a Christian* and *On Perfection*. Jaeger believed that *The Life of St. Macrina* in which she is presented as 'the very soul' and 'living model' of the monastic community was deliberately written by St. Gregory as 'a perfect contrast to the abstract and austere character of Basil's great *Rules,* in which he appears as lawgiver.'[31] St. Gregory makes it clear that his sister conformed to everything that he advocated in the other ascetical treatises as a means of reaching the goal of the ascetic life. The reader of this biography witnesses her practice of the virtues, her fortitude in adversity, her Christian attitude in the face of death, her immutable faith and unending good deeds, and he recognizes, therefore, that the life outlined by St. Basil and St. Gregory can be lived, since it has already been exemplified in one remarkable human

---

31 W. Jaeger, *ibid.* 18.

being. Daniélou finds interesting parallels between the role of St. Macrina in the biography and that of the Bride in St. Gregory's *Commentary on the Canticle of Canticles*.[32]

It was the somewhat arbitrary decision of the present translator to add to the five works included in Jaeger's edition of the *Ascetica* the dialogue *On the Soul and the Resurrection*. Although it is clearly a dogmatic treatise,[33] it completes the portrait of St. Macrina as the embodiment of asceticism and gives us further insights into the personality of St. Gregory himself. Moreover, since the soul, according to St. Gregory, is to be the focus of the ascetic life and the resurrection the proper end of those who have achieved the perfection of their nature in their pursuit of the ascetic ideal, the subject matter does not lie outside of the scope of this volume.

---

32 J. Daniélou, *Platonisme and théologie mystique*, 328.
33 Cf. H. Cherniss, *The Platonism of Gregory of Nyssa*, 65, who notes that 'Macrina is represented as the ideal champion of orthodox dogma.'

Preface

Until Jaeger's edition of the writings of St. Gregory of Nyssa, the only available edition, except for a number of separate treatises, was the antiquated edition of the Jesuit, Fronto du Duc, ed. J. Gretsen (Paris 1638), reprinted in Migne's *Patrology*. To say that Jaeger spent much of the last twenty years of his life on his edition is to be less than accurate. His devotion to this large task covered a period of fifty years, since it began in 1912, when, having just received his doctor's degree at the University of Berlin, the young scholar was sent to Italy at the instigation of his famous teacher, Ulrich von Wilamowitz Moellendorff. At that time, Monsignor Achille Ratti, later Pope Pius XI, director of the Ambrosian Library in Milan, became aware of the projected edition of Gregory and, in subsequent years, he continued to inquire about its progress. The first two volumes, the *Contra Eunomium*, were published in Germany in 1921.[34] In 1928, G. Pasquali, whose cooperation Jaeger had enlisted, published his edition of the *Epistulae*.[35] In 1939, Jaeger, who had left his homeland under the Hitler regime, founded at Harvard an Institute for Classical Studies, the chief purpose of which was the continuation of the edition. With the assistance of a number of young American and European scholars, most of whom had been his students, he began to carry out his plan for a ten-volume edition. At the time of his death in 1961, seven volumes had appeared and the remaining three were nearing completion.

One of the fascinating results of Jaeger's work, as men-

---

34 Reprinted as Volumes I and II of the Jaeger edition.
35 Reprinted as Volume VIII, part 2, of the Jaeger edition.

tioned previously, was his rediscovery of the treatise *On the Christian Mode of Life,* St. Gregory's most profound exposition of the theoretical and practical aspects of the ascetic life. It was included among the *Ascetica,* the first volume published under the aegis of the Harvard Institute in 1952. The steps leading up to the recognition of that treatise as a work of St. Gregory were disclosed two years later in a book entitled *Two Rediscovered Works of Ancient Christian Literature: Gregory of Nyssa and Macarius* (Leiden 1954). Fortunately, in writing about the authenticity and influence of the 'new' Gregorian treatise, it was necessary for Jaeger to discuss the other ascetical works of St. Gregory, their approximate dates, and their relation to the newly-discovered work. In his last book, *Early Christianity and Greek Paideia* (Cambridge, Mass. 1961), he stressed the contribution of St. Gregory of Nyssa to the development of the Christian heritage.

The translation of all the treatises included in this volume, except *On the Soul and the Resurrection,* is based on Jaeger's edition of the ascetical works: *Gregorii Nysseni Opera Ascetica,* published in Leiden by Brill in 1952. Jaeger himself edited *On What It Means to Call Oneself a Christian, On Perfection,* and *On the Christian Mode of Life. On Virginity* was edited by John P. Cavarnos who most generously read the present translation[36] and offered many suggestions for its improvement, all of which have been incorporated in the final version. *The Life of St. Macrina* was edited by the translator. Unfortunately, Miss H. Polack's edition of *On the Soul and the Resurrection* which is to be published as part of Volume III of Jaeger's edition has not yet appeared, so the present translation of that treatise is based on the edition of J. G. Krabinger (Leipzig 1837).

In addition to Mr. John Cavarnos, thanks must be given to the following good friends for their efforts in helping to

---

36 Since the completion of this translation, Michel Aubineau has published an execellent new edition and French translation of this treatise; cf. Select Bibliography.

bring this volume into being: John Callahan of Georgetown University, Roy J. Deferrari and Bernard M. Peebles of The Catholic University, Father Gerhard Fittkau of the Diocesan Seminary in Essen-Werden, William Heckscher of Duke University, Mrs. Nina Langobardi, Librarian of the American Academy in Rome. A research grant from Howard University provided the opportunity to concentrate on the translation which was completed while I was enjoying the hospitality of the American Academy in Rome.

We gratefully acknowledge the permission of the Brill Publishing House in Leiden to base the translation of the first five treatises on the Jaeger edition. The Scriptural passages follow the Confraternity of Christian Doctrine translation.

SELECT BIBLIOGRAPHY

Texts and Translations:

Sancti Gregorii Nysseni Opera Omnia, Migne, *Patrologia Graeca* 46 (Paris 1863) based on the Morellus edition of 1638.
Gregorii Nysseni Opera Ascetica, ed. W. Jaeger, J. Cavarnos, V. W. Callahan (Leiden 1952). This is Vol. VIII.1 of *Gregorii Nysseni Opera*, edited by W. Jaeger.
Nicene and Post-Nicene Fathers Vol. 5, ed. P. Schaff and H. Wace (New York 1893). This volume contains *On Virginity* and *On the Soul and the Resurrection* translated by W. Moore.
S. Gregorii Episcopi Nysseni De anima et resurrectione, edited with a Latin translation by J. G. Krabinger (Leipzig 1837).
St. Gregory of Nyssa, *The Life of St. Macrina*, translated by W. K. L. Clarke (London 1916).
Grégoire de Nysse, *Traité de la Virginité*, edited with a French translation by Michel Aubineau as No. 119 in *Sources Chrétiennes* (Paris 1966).

General Works:

Altaner, B. *Patrology*, trans. by Hilda Graef (New York 1960).
Balthasar, H. von. *Présence et Pensée: Essai sur la philosophie religieuse de Grégoire de Nysse* (Paris 1942).
Bardenhewer, O. *Geschichte der altkirchlichen Literatur*, Vol. 3 (Freiburg 1924).
Campbell, J. M. *The Greek Fathers* (New York 1963).
Campenhausen, H. von. *The Fathers of the Greek Church* (New York 1959).
Cherniss, H. F. *The Platonism of Gregory of Nyssa* (Berkeley 1930).
Daniélou, J. *Platonisme et théologie mystique* (Paris 1954).

---. 'Le mariage de Grégoire de Nysse et la chronologie de sa vie,' *Revue des Études Augustiniennes* 2 (1956) 71-78.
---. 'La résurrection des corps chez Grégoire de Nysse,' *Vigiliae Christianae* 7 (1953) 154-170.
---. 'Apocatastase chez Saint Grégoire de Nysse,' *Recherches de Science Religieuse* 30 (1940) 347-356.
---. *From Glory to Glory: Texts from Gregory of Nyssa's Mystical Writings*, trans. by H. Musurillo (New York 1961).
---. *Primitive Christian Symbols* (London 1964).
Goggin, Sister Thomas Aquinas. *The Times of St. Gregory of Nyssa as Reflected in the Letters of the Contra Eunomium* (Washington 1947).
Jaeger, W. *Two Rediscovered Works of Ancient Christian Literature: Gregory of Nyssa and Macarius* (Leiden 1954).
---. *Early Christianity and Greek Paideia* (Cambridge, Mass. 1961).
---. 'Von Affen und Wahren Christen,' *Varia Variorum, Festgabe für Karl Reinhardt* (Münster and Cologne 1952) 161-168. Repr. in *Scripta Minora* 2 (Rome 1960) 429-439.
Keenan, Sister Mary Emily. 'De *professione Christiana* and *De perfectione*: A Study of the Ascetical Doctrine of Saint Gregory of Nyssa,' *Dumbarton Oaks Papers* 5 (1950) 167-207.
Leys, R. *Image de Dieu de S. Grégoire de Nysse* (Brussels 1951).
McClear, E. V. 'The Fall of Man and Original Sin in the Theology of Gregory of Nyssa,' *Theological Studies* 9 (1948) 175-212.
Méridier, L. *L'Influence de la seconde sophistique sur l'oeuvre de Grégoire de Nysse* (Rennes 1906).
Merki, H. Ὁμοίωσις θεῷ· *Von der platonischen Angleichung an Gott zur Gottähnlichkeit bei Gregor von Nyssa* (Freiburg 1952). Rev. by W. Jaeger, *Gnomon* (1955) 573-581. Repr. in *Scripta Minora* 2 (Rome 1960) 469-481.
Musurillo, H. 'History and Symbol. A Study of Form in Early Christian Literature,' *Theological Studies* 18 (1957) 357-386.
Newman, John Henry. *Historical Sketches* 2 (London 1906).
Pellegrino, M. 'Il Platonismo di San Gregorio Nisseno nel Dialogo intorno all anima e alla risurrezione,' *Rivista de Filosofia Neoscolastica* 30 (1938) 437-474.
Quasten, J. *Patrology* 3: *The Golden Age of Greek Patristic Literature* (Westminster 1963) 254-296.
Stein, Sister James Aloysius. *Encomium of St. Gregory Bishop of Nyssa on his Brother St. Basil* (Washington 1928).
Stiglmayer, J. 'Die Schrift des heiligen Gregor von Nyssa über die Jungfraülichkeit,' *Zeitschift fur Askese und Mystik* 2 (1927) 334-359.
Völker, W. *Gregor von Nyssa als Mystiker* (Wiesbaden 1955).
---. 'Zur Gotteslehre Gregors von Nyssa,' *Vigiliae Christianae* 9 (1955) 103-128.

ON VIRGINITY

INTRODUCTION

THIS ENCOMIUM OF VIRGINITY, addressed to the monks living under St. Basil's *Rules,* is the earliest of the ascetical works of St. Gregory and is referred to by J. Daniélou as 'the first in date as in importance.'[1] St. Gregory's reference to St. Basil as his 'bishop and father' in the introduction indicates that his brother is still alive, and dates the treatise before 371,[2] the year in which St. Gregory himself was consecrated bishop. Although St. Basil's name occurs nowhere in the treatise, the portrait of him in the final chapter as a model and guide for the young aspirants to the ascetic life which has just been extolled gives a typically Greek climax to the work, since the person of St. Basil provides the ideal paradigm, 'the goal of the divine life as the fixed stars are for the pilots.'[3]

The form of the treatise is the protreptic address used by the philosophers to persuade their listeners to a certain course of action. The usual stylistic and rhetorical devices, e.g., contrast, pathos, similes, and metaphors are skilfully employed in it.[4]

In this eulogy of virginity, there is no need for St. Gregory to be concerned with the specific details of the ascetic life, since these were available to the monks in the *Rules* of their

---

1 J. Daniélou, *Platonisme et théologie mystique,* 12.
2 W. Jaeger (in his *Two Rediscovered Works,* p. 24) dates it before 370 or 371. J. Daniélou (in his *From Glory to Glory,* p. 4) suggests that it was written some years later.
3 P. 72.
4 For a discussion of the variety of forms employed by St. Gregory, cf. H. Musurillo, 'History and Symbol. A Study of Form in Early Christian Literature,' *Theological Studies* 18 (1957) 357-386. For an analysis of his style, cf. L. Méridier, *L'Influence de la seconde sophistique sur l'oeuvre de Grégoire de Nysse* (Rennes 1906).

3

founder. He is free, therefore, to explore the concept of virginity and to approach his subject philosophically rather than pragmatically. Like a philosopher, he seeks, first of all, to define his subject. Virginity is the central virtue through which man perfects himself and reaches his goal which is participation in the purity and incorruptibility of God. It is the mediating force which brings God down to man and lifts man to God. It corrects the catastrophe of man's fall and restores him to the contemplation of the divine nature. St. Gregory stresses the unity of the virtues, insisting that virginity is not confined to bodily purity, but is seen in every activity. He agrees with the Aristotelian idea that virtue lies in the mean and he warns that, although self-discipline is necessary, excess in either direction will deter the soul from achieving its end.

The treatise contains examples of St. Gregory's method of enriching certain well-known Christian concepts by his use of Platonic reminiscences. As illustrations of the self-control to which the monks must aim, St. Gregory chooses two famous passages from Plato, the myth of the charioteer from the *Phaedrus* and the desirability of the harmonious interworking of the faculties of the soul from the *Republic*. An analogy is suggested between the passage in Genesis which teaches that man is made in the image of God and the Platonic theory of ideas. And the parable of the lost coin is Platonized, so to speak, when St. Gregory emphasizes the image of the king on the coin which has been lost sight of because it has been covered with filth, and interprets the neighbors in the parable as the faculties of the soul which not only help to recover the coin, but share in the celebration of its return. When St. Gregory points out that mortal union begets children, whereas those who participate in the spirit beget spiritual children, he fortifies this idea by references to the Bible, but we are reminded also of similar statements in Plato's *Symposium*. Within the Christian point of view, there is a broad extension of the idea of virginity as the monks are reminded that it is a virtue associated with each of the three Persons of the Trinity, the angels, distinguished pairs from the Old and New Testaments, e.g., Elias and St. John the Baptist, St. Basil, and the unmarried saints.

ON VIRGINITY

A letter giving the details which constitute an exhortation to a life of virtue.

HE AIM OF THIS DISCOURSE is to create in the reader a desire for a life of virtue. But because of the many distractions associated with what the divine apostle[1] calls 'the married life,' the treatise suggests, as a kind of door or entrance into a nobler state, the life of virginity. It is not easy for those involved in every day activities also to devote themselves quietly to the more divine life; nor is it easy for those diverted in every way by the business of life to settle down undistractedly and contentedly to higher pursuits. Since advice, in itself, is rather slow to persuade, and since a person who is urging another on to something beneficial does not easily influence him by a mere word, without first exalting that towards which he is urging his listener, our discourse begins with a eulogy of virginity and ends with advice. Because the excellence of each thing somehow becomes necessarily more obvious through contrast, we have made mention, first, of the vexations of the ordinary life. Next, we have introduced a more or less systematic description of the philosophic life and man's inability to achieve it while he is preoccupied with worldly considerations. Then, with regard to those who have rid themselves of idle bodily desire, we have inquired further what the truly desirable thing is, for the sake of which we receive the faculty (of desire) from the Creator of our nature. Once this was revealed, as far as possible, it seemed logical also to suggest some method of attaining this good.

---
1 Cf. 1 Cor. 7.25 ff.

ON VIRGINITY 7

Indeed, true virginity, purified of every stain of sin, has been discovered to be so useful for this purpose, that the entire discourse, even if it seems in part to concern itself with something different, tends to be an encomium of virginity. As for all the particular counsels for such a life, which have been rendered suitable for those who accurately pursue this high excellence, the discourse, avoiding exaggeration, reviews them in outline, and, although it offers advice through more general precepts, it embraces in a certain way the details so that nothing essential is overlooked and excess is avoided. Since it is customary for everyone to participate more eagerly in a pursuit in which he sees someone especially outstanding, we have, of necessity, recalled the glorious unmarried saints; and since descriptions aimed at establishing virtue are not as powerful as the living voice and the actual examples of what is good, we have, perforce, referred at the end of the discourse to our most reverend bishop and father as the only one capable of teaching these things. We did not mention him by name, but the treatise refers to him enigmatically, so that the advice bidding the young to follow in the footsteps of one who has gone before them may not seem incomprehensible to those who have access to the treatise. Asking only who the fitting guide is for such a life, let them select for themselves those who, by the grace of God, point the way to the safeguarding of a life of virtue. For either they will find the one they seek or they will not be ignorant of what kind of person he must be.

The sequence of our thoughts is as follows:

(1) That virginity is beyond praise.
(2) That virginity is the peculiar achievement of the divine and incorporeal nature.
(3) A reminder of the difficulties of marriage and proof that the author of the treatise was not unmarried.
(4) That everything disturbing and bad in life has its beginning in marriage which distracts one from the true life.

(5) That it is necessary that the soul, freed from passions, be the guide to bodily purity.
(6) That Elias and John were concerned with the rigid discipline of this life.
(7) That marriage is not to be despised either.
(8) That it is difficult for the soul which is divided to attain its goal.
(9) That habit in every case is difficult to change.
(10) What is truly desirable.
(11) How one can gain an understanding of the really beautiful.
(12) That the one who has purified himself will see the divine beauty in himself; also on the cause of evil.
(13) That release from marriage is the beginning of caring for oneself.
(14) That virginity is stronger than the power of death.
(15) That true virginity is seen in every activity.
(16) That whatever is outside the realm of virtue is equally dangerous.
(17) That the person who lacks even one of the virtues is imperfect with respect to the good.
(18) That it is necessary for every faculty of the soul to aim at virtue.
(19) Mention of Mariam, the sister of Aaron, as the one who inaugurated this achievement.
(20) That it is impossible to serve the bodily pleasure and, at the same time, to reap the enjoyment of God.
(21) That it is necessary for the one who has chosen a rigid discipline to be estranged from every type of bodily pleasure.
(22) That it is not necessary to exercise self-control beyond the proper measure, and that both carnal indulgence and excessive mortification are opposed to the soul's attaining perfection.
(23) That it is necessary for the one who wishes to learn the

strictness of this life to be taught by one who has achieved it.

(1) *That virginity is beyond praise.*

The lofty form of virginity which is prized by all those who discern the beautiful in purity is present only to those whom the grace of God has kindly assisted in their good inclination. At the same time, it derives befitting praise from the noun with which it is synonymous. The 'incorrupt,' usually spoken of by the multitude in connection with virginity, is significant of the purity in it, so that it is possible to recognize the superiority of this esteemed blessing from its equivalent name, for although many things are accomplished in accordance with virtue, this alone is honored by the title 'the incorruptible.' And, if it is necessary to speak in praise of this great gift of God, the divine apostle succeeds in praising it in a few words by declaring without rhetorical exaggeration that the person adorned with this grace is 'holy and without blemish.'[2] If the achieving of this revered virginity means becoming blameless and holy (but these words are used properly and primarily in praise of the incorruptible God), what greater praise of virginity is there than its being proved that in some way those who have a share in the pure mysteries of virginity become themselves partakers of the glory of God, who is alone holy and blameless, since they participate in His purity and incorruptibility? In my judgment, persons who compose long and detailed panegyrics and think that thus they add something to the wonder of virginity deceive themselves. They effect the opposite of their intention, for what they exalt grandiloquently they render the object of suspicion with their praise. Whatever has greatness in its nature provides wonder of itself and has no need of verbal support. Think, for example, of the sky or the sun or any of the other marvels of the universe. It is for things on a lower level that

---

2 Eph. 5.27.

the word, through its clever praise, adds some fantasy of greatness. As a result, the admiration evoked by encomia is often suspected of being created by man's sophistication. The only sufficient praise of virtue is to make it clear that it is beyond praise and that purity in life is more wonderful than the spoken word. The person who, because of love of esteem, composes an encomium seems to think that a drop of his own sweat is going to make a contribution to a fathomless sea. For if he believes that the human word can exalt such a grace, either he is mistaken about his own ability or he does not understand what he is praising.

(2) *That virginity is the peculiar achievement of the divine and incorporeal nature.*

We need a good deal of intelligence to recognize the superiority of this grace which is perceived in connection with the incorruptible Father. Indeed, it is a paradox to find virginity in a Father who has a Son whom He has begotten without passion, and virginity is comprehended together with the only-begotten God who is the giver of incorruptibility, since it shone forth with the purity and absence of passion in His begetting. And again, the Son, conceived through virginity, is an equal paradox. In the same way, one perceives it in the natural and incorruptible purity of the Holy Spirit. For when you speak of the pure and incorruptible, you are using another name for virginity. Since, by reason of its lack of passion it exists with the whole of other-worldly nature and associates with the superior powers, it neither separates itself from things divine nor does it attach itself to their opposites. For whatever inclines towards virtue by nature and by choice is rendered quite beautiful by the purity of the incorruptible, and whatever rejects virtue for its opposite is referred to as such because of its lack of purity. What power of words can equal such a grace? Or how can one fail to be afraid, lest in his eagerness to praise he besmirch it and decrease the glory of its dignity for his listeners?

It is right, therefore, to forego encomiastic discourse, since it is impossible for the word to rise to the superiority of the subject. However, it is possible always to keep this divine grace in mind and to have this good on our lips. Virginity is exceptional and peculiar to the incorporeal nature, and, through the kindness of God, it has been granted to those whose life has been allotted through flesh and blood, in order that it may set human nature upright once more after it has been cast down by its passionate disposition, and guide it, as if by the hand, to a contemplation of the things on high. It is for this reason, I think, that our Lord Jesus Christ, the source of incorruptibility, did not come into the world through marriage. He wanted to demonstrate through the manner of his becoming man this great mystery, that purity alone is sufficient for receiving the presence and entrance of God, a purity that cannot be otherwise achieved fully, unless one alienates himself entirely from the passions of the flesh. For what happened corporeally in the case of the immaculate Mary, when the fullness of the divinity shone forth in Christ through her virginity, takes place also in every soul spiritually giving birth to Christ, although the Lord no longer effects a bodily presence. For, Scripture says: 'We no longer know Christ according to the flesh,'[3] but, as the Gospel says somewhere, He dwells with us spiritually and the Father along with Him.[4]

Therefore, since the power of virginity is such that it resides in heaven with the Father of spiritual beings, and takes part in the chorus of the supramundane powers, and attains to human salvation, and since, by itself, it brings God down to a sharing in human life and lifts man up to a desire of heavenly things, becoming a kind of binding force in man's affinity to God, and since it brings into harmony by mediation things so opposed to each other by nature, what power of words could be found to equal the grandeur of this marvel?

---
3 Cf. 2 Cor. 5.16.
4 Cf. John 14.23.

However, since it may appear altogether strange that we be silent and insensible in this matter, and one of two things may happen, namely, we may seem not to have recognized the beauty of virginity, or we might be considered to have shown ourselves unresponsive and unmoved by the perception of its beauty, we are disposed to say a few words because of the necessity of establishing in all men a belief in the power of the One who enjoins virginity upon us. However, let no one expect pompous words from me. Perhaps such a thing would be impossible for us, even if we should wish it, since we are unpracticed in such a manner of speech. But even if we possessed this ability, we would prefer what would be to the common advantage rather than what would be esteemed among the few. For I think that every intelligent person must seek, not what will make him more esteemed than others, but those things by which he can benefit himself and others.

(3) *A reminder of the difficulties of marriage and proof that the author was not unmarried.*

If only it were possible for me, too, as I zealously begin my work on this subject, to hand on the treatise with the hope of sharing in the harvest of the ploughing and the threshing. But, as it is now, for me the knowledge of the beauty of virginity is vain and as useless as the grain is to the 'muzzled ox'[5] who goes around the threshing floor, or as the flowing stream is to a thirsty person when the water is out of reach. Blessed are they who have the power to choose the better things and those who are not cut off from them by having chosen the common life previously, so that we are kept as if by an abyss from the boast of virginity to which one cannot return once he has set his foot upon the path of the worldly life. On account of this, we are only spectators of the beauty belonging to others and witnesses of the blessedness of others. And even if we gain some special knowledge of virginity, we have the same experience as cooks and servants who season the delicacies of

---

5 Cf. 1 Cor. 9.9,10.

the rich, but do not themselves partake of what is prepared. How blessed it would be if it were not so, and if we had not come to recognize the beauty in deliberation *post factum*. At any rate, truly enviable are those beyond all prayer and desire who are not barred from the enjoyment of these goods. We are like those who compare their own poverty with the wealth of the rich and are, as a result, the more troubled and annoyed by what they have. In the same way, the more we come to know the wealth of virginity the more we have disdain for the other life, having learned from the comparison how many precious things it lacks. I do not speak only of what is laid up in store for those who have lived virtuously, but also of what they have in the present life. For if someone wishes to examine carefully the difference between this life and the life of virginity, he will find as much difference as there is between the things of heaven and earth. We can learn the truth of this by examining the facts themselves.

But where can one begin in decking out in tragic phrase this burdensome way of life? Or how can anyone bring into view the ordinary evils of the life which all men know from experience? Since men are willingly ignorant of the circumstances in which they exist, nature manages to have these things escape our notice. Do you want us to begin with the most delightful features of married life? Truly, what is chiefly sought after in marriage is the joy of living with someone. Grant that this is so, and let the marriage be described as blessed in every respect: good family, sufficient wealth, harmony in age, the very flower of youth, much affection, and, what is divined in each by the other, that sweet rivalry in subduing one's own will in love. Let there be added to these glory, power, renown, and whatever else you wish, but see the smoldering grief necessarily attendant upon the advantages enumerated. I do not mean the envy which is directed against the prosperous, and the treachery which apparent happiness arouses in men, and the fact that everyone who does not himself have an equal share in the better lot has a natural hatred against the more fortunate. For this reason, the life of those who are seemingly happy is an object of suspicion and brings more grief than pleasure. I pass over these things on the grounds that envy is slothful, and yet it is not easy to find anyone for whom these two circumstances exist being happier than others and escaping envy. But let us assume a life free from all such things, if you like, and let us see if it is possible for men living in such a state of well-being to be happy.

But, you will say then, what grief will there be if not even envy touches them in their happiness? I say that the very sweetness of their life is the fomenting of their grief. For as long as men, these mortal and perishable creatures, exist and look upon the tombs of those from whom they came into being, they have grief inseparably joined to their lives even if they take little notice of it. For the continuous expectation of death is not known through spoken symbols, but because of the uncertainty of the future, inherently frightening, it dissipates our present joy and disturbs our well-being with the fear of what is to come. If only it were possible to know the things of experience before we experience them! If only it were possible to examine things ahead of time, how frequent would be the race of deserters from marriage to virginity! What care and forethought there would be never to be in the power of inescapable snares, the discomfort of which one cannot know accurately if he has never been caught in the net. For you would see, if one could see without taking a risk, a constant mingling of opposites: laughter moistened by tears, grief mingled with joy, death, everywhere present, fastening itself upon each of our pleasures. When the bridegroom looks upon the face of his beloved, the fear of separation immediately comes over him; while he listens to her sweet voice, he is aware that sometime he will not hear it; when he is delighted by the sight of her beauty, then, especially, does he shudder at the expectation of misfortune. When he perceives the qualities in youth sought after by the unthinking, e.g., the shining eye, the lovely eyebrows, the cheeks with their sweet smile, lips blooming with their natural redness, hair golden and heavy, shining about the head with its intricate braid, and all that ephemeral splendor, then, most of all, even if he is not given to brooding, it dawns upon his soul that this beauty will not go on forever, that it will come to nothing, that in place of what he now beholds there will be bones, disgusting and ugly, with no trace, no reminder, no remains of this present blossoming.

Can anyone live happily when such thoughts are in his mind? Will he believe that his present joys will continue forever, or is it not clear from this that he will be at a loss like one in the fantasy of dreams? Will he not be distrustful of his life, as if in attendance upon the goods of others, entirely aware (if he reflects upon reality) that none of the goods of life are what they appear to be, but that life holds out something different to us and deceitfully mocks at those stretching out towards it? Because of the instability of goods, man ignores the facts until all at once, at the moment of reversal, fortune proves to be something quite different from the human expectations of foolish people who have deluded themselves. After thinking about these things, what kind of pleasure can the sweetness of life provide? Will the person aware of them ever be truly pleased and able to enjoy the advantages that seem to be present to him? If he is always disturbed by a fear of the reversal of fortune, will not the enjoyment of what is present go by unperceived?

I omit signs, dreams, omens, and such nonsense which are the product of foolish custom and the cause for suspecting misfortune. Assume that the moment of childbirth is at hand; it is not the birth of the child, but the presence of death that is thought of, and the death of the mother anticipated. Often, the sad prophecy is fulfilled and before the birth is celebrated, before any of the anticipated goods are tasted, joy is exchanged for lamentation. Still burning with affection, still at the peak of desire, without having experienced the sweetest things of life, one is all at once bereft of everything as if in a nightmare. And after this? The house is invaded by relatives as if by the enemy. Instead of a bridal chamber, death provides a tomb. There are senseless invocations and the wringing of hands, recollections of one's former life, curses against those who advised the marriage, complaints against friends who did not prevent it. Parents are severely blamed whether they happen to be present or not. There is vexation with human life, accusations against all of nature, indictments and charges against the divine economy itself, a battle against oneself, a fierce reaction against those offering advice. There is no hesitation about the most unseemly conduct in word and deed. Many times, the end is more bitter tragedy for those overtaken by this sorrow and excessively cast down by grief, and the one left behind is not able to live with his misfortune.

But perhaps this is not the case. Let us assume that conditions are more favorable, that the mother survives the pains of childbirth and a child is born, the very image of the springtime of his parents; what then? Is the supposition of grief lessened because of this, or is it not rather increased? In addition to their earlier fears, they have added those in behalf of the child lest he encounter something unpleasant, lest some disagreeable chance befall him with regard to his upbringing, some unwished-for casualty or suffering or mutilation or danger. These are shared by both parents. But who could enumerate the special worries of the wife? I pass over the ordinary factors known to all, the discomfort of pregnancy, the risk of childbirth, the toil of educating the child, and the special heartbreak caused by a child. And if she becomes the mother of more than one, her soul is divided into as many parts as the number of her children, since she experiences in her own being whatever happens to them. What can we say to all these things we all know so well?

And since, according to the divine plan, the wife does not govern herself, but has her place of refuge in the one who has power over her through marriage, if she is separated from him for even a short time, it is as if she has been deprived of her head. She cannot endure the separation and has a premonition of the life of widowhood and of her husband's departure from the world in a little while. Suddenly, fear makes her despair of her dearest hopes. For this reason, she keeps her eyes glued on the door, full of worry and fright. She pays too much attention to gossip. Her heart, scourged by fear, tortures itself even before any news is brought back. At the door there is only knocking, real or imagined, as if some messenger of evil had suddenly and violently shaken her soul. There are the usual reports, not worth worrying about, but she faints before she receives the message. She keeps her mind away from pleasant matters and dwells upon the opposite. Such is the life of the happy pair! Truly a fine one! Certainly, it cannot be measured against the freedom of virginity.

And yet our brief discourse has not touched upon many of the sadder things. For often, the bride herself, still young in body, still glowing in her bridal splendor, perchance still blushing at the approach of the bridegroom and casting her eyes down with modesty when she encounters desires too ardent to be displayed because of shame, is suddenly bereft of her husband, and, wretched and deserted, she receives in exchange all sorts of appellations that are to be avoided. The misfortune that has fallen upon her subdues, all at once, the girl who was up to this time radiant and bright and enviable, and, despoiling her of her bridal adornment, it envelops her in sadness. In the bridal chamber, there is gloom instead of splendor and dirge singers prolong the wailings, and there is hatred towards those who try to soothe the emotions, scorn of food, wasting away, dejection of spirit, a longing for death, which often increases to the point of death itself. But even if this affliction is somehow taken care of by time, there is another. Either there are children or there are not. If there are orphans, they are piteous because of this and accentuate the grief by their existence; if there are no children, the memory of what has passed disappears completely and the woe is beyond consolation.

I omit the other features of widowhood. For who could enumerate them accurately? The enemies, the relatives, those who become involved in the misfortune, those who are gladdened by the widow's desolation, those who look with pleasure and a bitter eye upon the stricken house, the disdainful servants, and all the other circumstances abundantly attendant upon such misfortunes. Because of these conditions, many women of necessity venture a second time upon the experience of such evils. They cannot endure the bitterness of being laughed at and they marry again as if they were avenging themselves on those grieving for their particular misfortunes. However, many others, because of the memory of what has occurred, withdraw completely rather than fall a second time into a similar misfortune. If you want to learn the disadvantages of the common life, listen to what those say who know this life through experience, how they bless the life of those who chose virginity from the beginning and did not learn afterwards from misfortune which was better, i.e., that virginity is immune to all such troubles. It does not bewail orphanhood, nor does it lament widowhood; it is always accompanied by an incorruptible Bridegroom; it always takes pride in the begetting of reverence; it continuously sees the house truly its own, abounding in the fairest things, because the Master of the house is always present and at home, so that death effects, not a separation, but a union with what is longed for. For, as the apostle says,[6] when one 'dies,' then he is with Christ.

Having examined in detail the circumstances of those who are fortunate, now would be the opportune moment to take

---

[6] Cf. Phil. 1.23.

a look at the other states of life, in which poverty and troubles and the remaining misfortunes of men are fixed, e.g., mutilations, and diseases, and other such human allotments. In the case of all of these, the person living by himself either avoids the experience of them, or he bears the misfortune more easily, because he can concentrate on himself and not be distracted by cares for anything else. Whereas the man whose attention is directed towards wife and children often does not have the leisure to bemoan his own misfortunes, since in his heart resounds the concern for his beloved ones. But perhaps this goes beyond the limits of what we agreed to discuss in this treatise. For if such toil and wretchedness are attached to those who seem to be blessed, what could anyone conjecture about the opposite? Every treatise falls short of the truth if it tries to show us the life of the wretched. However, perhaps it is possible to indicate briefly the sum of unpleasantness in life. Those whose lot is contrary to the ones who seem to be happy have contrary griefs. The life of the prosperous is disturbed by death, present or anticipated; for the wretched, the delay of death is a misfortune. Life divides the two groups diametrically, but despondency with respect to the same end, namely death, afflicts them both.

Thus manifold and varied is the supply of evils that come from marriage. Children born and not born, living and dying, are alike the source of pain. The person who has many children does not have enough to feed them, whereas the one to whom this succession of trouble has not come places the other's misfortune in the category of goods. Each wishes he were the other in respect to the very matter in which he sees the other having difficulty, the one whose beloved child is dead and the one whose uncared-for child still lives. And both are to be pitied, the one lamenting the death of his child and the other the life of his.

I pass over the jealousies and battles arising from real or imaginary causes and the emotions and disasters in which they end. For who could accurately list them all? But you, if you want to learn how human life is filled with such evils, do not go to the old stories which the poets use for the plots of their dramas, for they are considered good mythological material because of their exaggerated unnaturalness: children slain, offspring eaten, husbands murdered, mothers killed, brothers butchered, lawless unions, every kind of confusion of nature, which the story-tellers of old recounted, commencing their story with a marriage and ending it with such misfortunes. Leave all these aside and contemplate the tragedies on the contemporary stage of life whose sponsor is marriage. Come to the law courts, read the marriage laws. See there the abominations of marriage. For just as when you hear doctors describing various diseases, you recognize the wretchedness of the human body, since you learn what evils it can be afflicted with, so when you read the marriage laws and discover the many illegalities of marriage for which fines are inflicted, you perceive clearly the circumstances of marriage. For neither does the doctor cure diseases that do not exist, nor the law punish evil deeds that are not committed.

(4) *That everything wrong in life has its beginning in marriage which distracts one from the true life.*

But why should we treat with contempt the incongruity of such a life by limiting our account of the misfortunes attached to it to adultery, separations, and treachery? For it seems to me that, in the light of higher and truer reason, every evil of life in all matters and pursuits has no power over man's life, unless a person brings it on himself. Thus the truth of our discourse will come to light. The one who perceives the deceitfulness of this life with the pure eye of his soul and rises above the earthly pursuits, and, as the apostle says,[7] sees it all as 'dung' and refrains from marriage during his whole life has no share in human evils, I mean in greed, envy, anger, hatred,

---

7 Cf. Phil. 3.8.

the desire for empty fame, and all such things. Being exempt from these and completely free and at peace in his life, it is not possible for him to be involved in rivalry out of greed or any envious disagreement with his neighbors, since none of these things in which envy thrives is of concern to him. For having elevated his soul above the whole world, and considering his only precious possession to be virtue, he will lead a life that is untroubled and peaceful and without dissension. For the possession of virtue, even if all men share in it, each according to his own ability, is always sufficient for those who desire it. It is different from earthly possessions where those dividing something into pieces, in proportion as they give a part to one, take it from another, and where an abundance for one means a lesser amount for him who shares the whole with him. Whence, also, the contentions for the larger share result for men because of the strong dislike for diminution. But the person who possesses an abundance of virtue will not envy another's greed for property nor, for that reason, incur a penalty from another who thinks himself worthy of an equal amount, for in proportion to the extent of one's withdrawal from the world, his good desires will be fulfilled and the wealth of the virtues is not used up by those who have shared in it previously.

Would the person who looks towards this life and the treasury of virtue which has no human limit set upon it be impelled to incline his soul to anything involving wretchedness and deceit? Will he be overwhelmed by earthly riches or human power, or any of the other things sought after by the foolish? If anyone still disparages this point of view, he is not part of the group we have just mentioned and our discourse is not for him. But if he has his thoughts on high and is making his way up to God, being superior to such people, he will have no common starting point for a discussion about the common cause of error regarding such matters, namely, marriage. For the desire to excel other people, this difficult disease of pride, which someone has reasonably called the seed and root of every thorn connected with sin, has marriage as its original cause.

Indeed, it is not possible for the ambitious man not to blame his children for his misery, or for the man with a mad desire for fame, or a lover of honor, not to refer to his family as the cause of his difficulty, in order not to seem inferior to his ancestors and in order to be considered important in the future, leaving behind accounts of his career for his descendants. And, likewise, the other weaknesses of the soul, envy and malice and hatred and any other such thing, are all derived from this same cause, for all of these go along with the distraught aspects of married life. The person removed from these, looking down from afar from some high vantage point upon such human ills, pities the blindness of those enslaved by such vanity and those who consider the well-being of the flesh important. For when he sees a certain man admired for some feature of his life pluming himself on his honors or wealth or power,. he laughs at the foolishness of those puffed up because of these things, since he measures the longest time of human life by the limited period referred to by the psalmist[8] (i.e., seventy or eighty years). Then, comparing this brief interval of time with the boundless ages, he pities the emptiness of the person whose soul is elated by what is so petty and wretched and ephemeral. For why should one be congratulated for earthly honor, a thing which is eagerly sought by many? What does it add to those who have it? Mortal man remains mortal whether he is honored or not. Or for possessing many acres of land? What useful purpose does this serve aside from the foolish man's thinking that that is his own which does not belong to him? For because of his greediness, he does not know, as it seems, that: 'The Lord's are the earth and its fulness.'[9] For: 'King of all the earth is God,'[10]

---
8 Cf. Ps. 89.10.
9 Ps. 23.1.
10 Ps. 46.8.

and the passion of greed gives man the false name of lordship over what does not belong to him at all. As the wise Ecclesiastes says:[11] 'The earth standeth forever,' serving all generations, begetting them one after the other. Men, not being lords of themselves, but coming into existence they know not when, according to the will of the Maker, and being separated from it when they do not wish to be, think, because of their excessive vanity, that they are lords of it, although they live for a season and are dead for all time, and it remains forever.

Therefore, if one examines these matters and because of this despises whatever is held in honor among men, and longs only for the divine life, knowing that 'all flesh is grass and all the glory of man as the flower of grass,'[12] is he likely to think of grass which exists today and is gone tomorrow as something worth striving for? The one who has examined well the things divine knows that not only human affairs have no stability, but also that the whole world itself has not remained forever unchanged. Therefore, he despises this life as alien and impermanent, since 'heaven and earth will pass away,'[13] according to the word of the Savior, and all things of necessity undergo a transformation. Therefore, as long as he is 'in the tent, burdened'[14] by the present life, as the apostle says to illustrate its impermanence, he laments the lengthening of his stay as the psalmist says in his divine songs.[15] For they truly live in darkness who spend their life in these quarters. Because of this, the prophet groans over the extension of his sojourn here and says: 'Alas, my stay is lengthened.'[16] But he attributes the cause of his dejection to darkness, for in Hebrew darkness is equivalent to $\kappa\eta\delta\acute{\alpha}\rho$, as we learn from the scholars. Is it not true that men overcome by some night-blindness are thus dim-sighted in recognizing de-

---
11 Cf. Eccles. 1.4.
12 Cf. 1 Pet. 1.24.
13 Matt. 24.35.
14 Cf. 2 Cor. 5.4.
15 Cf. Ps. 118.4.
16 Cf. Ps. 118.5.

lusion, not knowing that whatever is considered honorable in this life, or even whatever is assumed to be the opposite, is understood thus only on the assumption of the foolish? Of themselves, they are never anything at all. There is no dishonorable lineage or distinction of birth, no glory or renown, no old legends, no vanity dependent on circumstances, no power over others or subjection to others. Wealth, luxury, poverty, want, all the anomalies of life seem something altogether different to the untaught, since they make pleasure the criterion of such things. But to one who is elevated in thought, all things appear to be of equal honor, and none is preferred to another, because the course of life is run equally by opposites, and there is present in the destiny of each person the power to live well or badly, 'with the armor on the right hand and on the left,' as the apostle says,[17] 'in honor and dishonor.' Accordingly, the one who has purified his mind and rightly examined the truth of reality will go on his way in the time assigned to him from birth to death, not spoiled by pleasures or cast down by austerity, but, in accordance with the custom of travelers, he will be little affected by what he encounters. For it is customary for travelers to hasten on to the end of their journey whether they go through meadows and fertile fields or through deserts and rough terrain; pleasure does not delay them, nor does the unpleasant impede them. So he himself will also hurry on without distraction to the goal before him, turning off into none of the byways, and he will pass through life looking only to heaven, just like some good captain who guides his ship to its lofty destination.

However, the one who is stupid looks downwards and hands his soul over to pleasures of the body, as cattle to pasture, living only for the stomach and the organs nearby, being alienated from the life of God and a stranger to the promise of the covenants, considering nothing else to be good than pleasing the body. This one, and everyone like him, is the

---

17 2 Cor. 6.7,8.

one making his way 'in darkness,' as the Scripture says,[18] which is the inventor of evils in this life. Among these evils are greed and unbridled passions and lack of moderation in pleasure and love of power and desire for empty glory and the rest of the band of afflictions that accompany mankind. Somehow, one or the other of these exists and, if one of them is present, the rest always come as if dragged along on a chain by some natural necessity. If the beginning of a chain is drawn tight, the rest of the links cannot remain unmoved. Each link is always moved along with the part ahead of it and the movement continues throughout. It is thus that human weaknesses are linked together and related to each other, and if one of them gains control, the whole train of passions enters the soul. If we must describe this wretched chain, let us imagine someone weakened by any of the pleasures connected with vanity. The desire for more accompanies vanity, since it is not possible for anyone to become greedy unless vanity has led him to that condition. Next, the desire for more than one's share and to be first excites him to anger against anyone who has as much as he, or to arrogance towards anyone below him, or envy towards anyone excelling him. Envy leads to hypocrisy, hypocrisy to bitterness, bitterness to misanthropy, and the final result of all of these is a condemnation which ends up in hell and darkness and fire. Do you see the succession of evils; how one passion follows upon the heels of another?

We see from the counsel of the divinely inspired scriptures one way out once the sequence of passion has come into life, that is, a withdrawal from the life which has this distressing sequence inherent in it. For it is not possible for anyone who is fond of the life in Sodom to escape the rain of fire, or for the one who has left Sodom, but turns back to the devastation of the city, not to be turned into a pillar of salt. Nor will the one who has not left Egypt be delivered from the slavery of

---

18 Cf. John 12.35.

the Egyptians. I refer not to a crossing of the Red Sea, but to his crossing of the black and gloomy sea of life. But if the truth does not make us free, as the Lord tells us it does,[19] and we remain in the evil condition of slavery, how is it possible for us to exist in truth while we are seeking what is false and being tossed about in our wandering? How will anyone escape from slavery who subjects his life to the necessities of nature? Perhaps the argument about these matters could be made more intelligible to us by an example. Just as a river, made turbulent by winter floods, carrying along with it wood and stones and whatever happens to be near, is dangerous and hazardous and flows heedlessly beyond its boundaries, so also the person who is himself leading a turbulent life and who has become involved in passions in keeping with his own nature and is overflowing with the evils of his own life necessarily seduces those who come into his environment. But if a person should leave this torrent behind him, 'the insupportable water,'[20] as Scripture calls it, he will, according to the rest of the Psalm, escape the 'teeth' of the enemy and avoid the snare like the sparrow flying on wings of virtue.

Since, in keeping with the example of the winter torrent suggested by us, human life is overflowing with disturbances and anomalies and is always pouring forth from the precipitousness of its nature and never restrains itself and is never sated, but contaminates everything it happens upon and runs over everything it touches, never by-passing anything, because it is concentrating on the downward flow, it would, for this reason, be advantageous to keep oneself away from such a stream in order not to slight what is established forever because of our being involved with what has no substance. For how is it possible for anyone passionately in love with anything in this life finally to achieve what he longs for? Which of the special objects of our interests remain what they are? What is the acme of youth? What is the good fortune of power

---
19 Cf. John 8.32.
20 Cf. Ps. 123.4.

or beauty? What is wealth? What is glory? Power? Do not all such things blossom for a short time and then fade away and turn into their opposites? Who has lived an entire life of youthfulness? For whom did power persist until the end? What flower of beauty has nature not made more short-lived than those which come forth in the spring? For the things of the passing season appear, and, flowering for a short time, depart again, and the beauty of the present fades away and rises up again and points to the morrow; but the human flower, once its nature has brought its youth to light in the spring, declines in winter and begets old age. Thus, also, all other things in season, deceiving the perception of the flesh, run past and are covered by forgetfulness.

Since, then, such changes, occurring according to the necessity of nature, distress the human being with this obsession, there is only one escape from this evil, that is not to attach oneself to anything changeable. Since it is possible to be separated from any association with the life of passion and the flesh, most assuredly it is also possible to be beyond any sympathy with one's own body, in order not to be subject to the evils of the flesh. But this means living for the soul alone and imitating, as far as possible, the regimen of the incorporeal powers, among whom there is neither marriage nor giving in marriage. Their work and zeal and success consist in the contemplation of the Father of incorruptibility and in beautifying their own form through imitation of the archetypal beauty.

We say that virginity is given to man as an ally and an aid in this thought and lofty desire, as Scripture suggests. And just as in other pursuits certain skills are devised for the perfection of each of the things sought after, it seems to me that the pursuit of virginity is a certain art and faculty of the more divine life, teaching those living in the flesh how to be like the incorporeal nature.

(5) *That it is necessary that the soul, freed from passions, be the guide to bodily purity.*

In such a life, every effort is made to insure that the loftiness of the soul is not brought low by the insurrection of pleasures, for then the soul turns down towards the passions of flesh and blood instead of occupying itself with lofty things and looking upwards. For how is it possible for the soul, nailed down by the pleasure of the flesh and indulging in a desire for human passions, to look up with a free eye to the natural and intelligible light, when it is inclined toward the material through some sorry and coarse misconception? For just as the eyes of pigs are by nature trained on the ground and have no experience of the wonders of the sky, so the soul pulled down by the body can no longer look towards heaven and the beauties on high, being bent towards what is low and brutish in nature. Whereas if the soul, quite free and relaxed, looks up to the divine and blessed pleasures, it will never turn itself back to any of the earthly things, nor will it exchange them for what are commonly considered pleasures, but it will transfer its power to love from the body to the intelligible and immaterial contemplation of the beautiful. It was for such a disposition of the soul that the virginity of the body was intended, to make the soul forget and become unmindful of the passionate movements of its nature, affording it no necessity to descend to the lowly guilt of the flesh. For once freed from such needs, it no longer runs the risk of turning away from and ignoring the divine and unmixed pleasure which only purity of heart naturally seeks after. This occurs when the soul gradually accustoms itself to what seems to yield to some law of nature.

(6) *That Elias and John were concerned with the rigid discipline of this life.*

Consequently, of special importance for us are Elias, great among the prophets, and one who lived later in the spirit and power of Elias, greater than whom there is no one among those born of woman. If the history of these two hints at anything in a riddle, it is this, that through their own lives they recommended separating one's self from the normal sequence of events in human life and having leisure for the contemplation of the invisible, in order not to fall into confusion and error in judging the truly good, as a result of being accustomed to the deceptions which come to us through the senses. Both of them, right from their youth, alienated themselves from human life and placed themselves beyond human nature by their disdain of the usual food and drink and by living in the desert to make sure that their hearing would not be encompassed by sound, that their sight would be safeguarded against wandering, that their taste would remain plain and simple, their needs being fulfilled by whatever they happened upon. Thus, free from external disturbances, they achieved a condition of deep tranquillity and calmness from external disturbances, and, for this reason, they were lifted up to the height of divine grace that the history of each of them reveals. Elias, as a kind of steward of God's gifts, having his needs supplied from heaven according to his office, was a master in shutting himself off from sinners and in approaching those who were repentant. John, the divine history tells us, performed no such miracles, but the grace in him surpassing every prophet was testified to by the One who sees what is hidden. They quickly dedicated their own desire to the Lord from the beginning to the end, pure and unmixed with any material obsession, devoting no time to the love of children or to the thought of women or to any other human attachment. They did not think it fitting to be concerned with the day's food supply or with proving that they were superior by the adornment of clothes. They dispensed with the need of them by wearing whatever was at hand, the one goatskin, the other camel's hair, and I do not think they would have reached that height if they had grown soft because of the pleasures of the body in marriage. These facts are recorded for us, not for their own sake, but, as the apostle says, 'for our correction,'[21] in order that we may direct our lives in accordance with theirs. What, then, do we learn from this? That, in the light of the examples of the saints, the person desiring to fix his thought upon God indulges in none of the practical things of life. For it is not possible for anyone whose mind is diffused in many things to proceed directly to a knowledge of God and a desire for Him.

I think that this can be made clearer by an example. Let us assume that water pouring from the source is divided by chance into diverse streams. As long as it flows along in this way, it will be of no use for farming, because the division makes each stream small and weak and sluggish. However, if anyone could bring all the disorderly streams together and collect what was previously scattered, he could use the collected water and control it for many practical and helpful purposes. It seems to me that this is also true with the human mind; if it flows in all directions, it scatters itself by running towards what is pleasing to the senses, and has no worthwhile force for its journey to the really good. But if it were called in from all sides, collected unto itself, brought together, it would move with its own natural energy and nothing would prevent it from being borne upwards and fastening itself upon the truth of reality. Just as water in a pipe, when constrained by force, often goes straight up, unable to flow elsewhere, even though its natural movement is downwards; so, also, the human mind being constrained from all directions by self-control, as by a kind of pipe, will somehow be taken up by the nature of the movement to a desire for what is above, there not being any place for it to run to. It is never possible for what has been put into eternal motion by its Creator to stop and to use its motion for useless purposes once it has been controlled and made incapable of not going directly to

---

21 1 Cor. 10.11.

the truth, being kept on all sides from what is not suitable for it. We see travelers on long journeys not missing their way because they have learned from experience to avoid the byways. Just as an experienced vagabond returning to the right road will be careful, so, also, will our mind concentrate on the real truth once it has been diverted from vanities. It seems, therefore, that the memory of these great prophets teaches us not to become entangled with what is longed for in the world, and one of these is marriage, the beginning and root of the desire for vain things.

(7) *That marriage is not to be despised either.*

Let no one think that, for these reasons, we are disregarding the institution of marriage. We are not ignorant of the fact that this also is not deprived of God's blessing. But since there is sufficient support for it and since the common nature of man, bestowed upon all who come to birth through marriage, automatically inclines in this direction, whereas virginity somehow goes against nature, it would be superfluous to go to the trouble of writing a plea for marriage and a eulogy of it emphasizing its indisputable inducement, I mean pleasure, unless there should be need of such words because of some people who tamper with the teachings of the Church on marriage, whom the apostle calls 'those having their conscience branded.'[22] These, forsaking the guidance of the Holy Spirit because of the teaching of demons, engrave scars and brands upon their hearts, detesting God's creatures as abominations, addressing them as evil-bringers, causes of evil, and the like. But He speaks saying: 'What have I to do with judging those outside?'[23] For they are truly outside of the court of the mysteries of the word, being lodged, not in the shelter of God, but in the stable of the wicked one, being captives of his will, according to the voice of the apostle.[24]

---

22 1 Tim. 4.2.
23 1 Cor. 5.12.
24 Cf. 2 Tim. 2.26.

And this is because they do not understand that evil is the turning to extremes, all virtue being looked upon as lying in the mean, since one everywhere distinguishes virtue from evil by taking the mean between the slack and the taut.

But the argument could be made clearer by us through practical examples. Cowardice and rashness are two opposites recognized as evils, the one because of a deficiency, the other because of an excess, and fortitude is the mean between them. Again, the pious man is neither atheistic nor superstitious, for there is the same irreverence in believing in no God and in believing in many. Do you want further clarification? The person who avoids miserliness and profligacy in his withdrawal from opposite passions achieves freedom in his character. For freedom consists of this sort of thing, namely, in not being disposed either to immoderate and useless expense or to stinginess with regard to necessary expenditures. Thus it is in all other matters, but we need not enumerate them. Reason recognizes virtue as the mid-point between opposites. Therefore, temperance, too, is a mean and has clear deviations towards evil in each of the two directions. The person who is deficient in the strength of his soul is an easy prey to the passion of pleasure, and, because of this, he does not go near the path of the pure and moderate life, being sunk down in the passions of dishonor. On the other hand, the person who disregards the accessibility of moderation and goes beyond the mean of this virtue is thrown down by the treachery of the demons as if from a cliff, 'branding their own consciences,' as the apostle says. While he defines marriage as disgusting, he pricks himself with the reproaches of marriage. For, as the Gospel says somewhere: 'If the tree is evil, the fruit of the tree is also evil.'[25] But if man is the offspring and the fruit of the plant in marriage, the disgrace of marriage also belongs to the one who is casting it in our teeth.

However, those culprits, branded in their conscience and

---

25 Cf. Matt. 7.18.

covered with stripes for the strangeness of their belief, are refuted by such arguments. And we, on our part, know this about marriage, that the zeal and the desire for divine things come first, but that one should not scorn the moderate and measured use of the duty of marriage. There was the example of the patriarch, Isaac, who did not marry at the peak of his youth, in order that marriage should not be a deed of passion; but when his youth was already spent, he married Rebecca because of the blessing of God upon his seed.[26] He continued in the marriage until the birth of his twin sons, and later, closing his eyes, he entered again fully the realm of the unseen. This is what the story of the patriarch seems to mean, in my opinion, when it refers to the failing of his sight.[27]

(8) *That it is difficult for the soul which is divided in a multiplicity of things to attain its goal.*

But let these matters be the concern of the experts and let us continue our treatise. What were we saying? That if it is possible, one should neither remain aloof from the more divine desires, nor should one reject the idea of marriage. It is not reasonable to disregard the economy of nature or to slander what is honorable as disgusting. For just as we said before in the illustration of the water and the source, when the farmer directs the water to a certain place and draws it off, there is a need for a small central stream to facilitate the flow in proportion to the amount required for it to be mingled again easily with the main stream. But, if someone imprudently and unskillfully opens up a channel for the water, there is the risk that the whole stream will abandon its straight course and be broken up into gullies. In the same way, since there is need in life also for the succession of one thing from another, if someone uses reproduction similarly, while spiritual considerations hold priority, exercising his desire for such things sparingly and fearfully in accordance with the

---
26 Cf. Gen. 25.20.
27 Cf. Gen. 27.1.

requirement of the situation, that person will be a wise farmer, cultivating himself in wisdom according to the injunction of the apostle.[28] He will never disparage rendering those customary debts, but he will properly keep separate his purity of soul by devotion to prayer, fearing lest, through preoccupation with passion, he become wholly flesh and blood, in which the spirit of God does not reside. But the one who is weak by disposition, so that he is not able to withstand in a manly fashion the onslaughts of his nature, might better hold himself removed from such circumstances rather than enter a contest which is beyond his strength. There is no small danger that such a person, misled by his experience of pleasure, may come to think obsessively that there is no other good than that achieved through the flesh and, turning his mind completely from the desire for the incorporeal goods, he may become wholly flesh, hunting for the pleasure in these things in every way, so that he becomes a lover of pleasure rather than a lover of God. Since, then, because of the weakness of nature, it is not possible for everyone to arrive at such a point of balance, and since the one incapable of it is likely to 'stick in the mire of the deep,' as the psalmist says,[29] it would be profitable, as our treatise suggests, to go through life without the experience of marriage, lest, under the pretext of what has been conceded, the passions should make their entry against the soul.

(9) *That habit in every case is difficult to change.*

Habit in every case is something hard to fight against, because it has great power to lead the soul on and to draw it to itself, and it offers a certain fantasy of beauty once an obsessive condition has been established by habituation. Therefore, nature should avoid accustoming itself to what is not considered desirable and worthy to be sought after.

The life of human beings is an illustration of our argument. Although there are so many nations, the same things are not

---
28 Cf. 1 Cor. 3.9.
29 Cf. Ps. 68.3.

sought after by all of them. Different things are prized by different nations and custom creates the desire and zeal for something in each group. And it is not only among nations that one can observe these differences, where certain things are admired by some and disdained by others, but even in the same nation and the same city and the same family such differences may be seen. For example, twins can be very different from each other in the way they live, and this is not surprising because each man does not generally have the same judgment about the same matter, his disposition towards each thing being determined by custom. And, not to belabor the point, we ourselves have known many who, from an early age, appeared to be lovers of moderation, whose participation in what seemed lawful and acceptable pleasures was the cause of their living a sordid life. For once they have had such an experience, according to our analogy of the stream, the entire concept of the desirable is changed for them; they change the direction of their thought from the more divine to the lowly and the material, and they open up in themselves a wide channel for the passions; their desire for things above stops and is completely dried up, being wholly diverted towards the passions.

On this account, we think it advantageous for the very weak to flee for refuge to virginity as to a safe fortress, not to call down upon themselves temptations that flow in sequence, not to involve their minds because of carnal passions with forces that make war upon the law, and not to run the risk of thinking about the limits of earth or the loss of money or anything else zealously sought for in this life, except the predominant hope. For it is not possible for the one who has turned to this world in his thought, and who worries about it, and busies himself with being pleasing to man to fulfill the first and great commandment of the Lord which says: 'Love God with thy whole heart and strength.'[30] For how will anyone love God

---

30 Cf. Matt. 22.37; Mark 12.30; Luke 10.27.

with his whole heart when he is dividing his heart between God and the world, and stealing in some way the love that is owed to that One alone, and squandering it on human passions? 'He who is unmarried is concerned about the things of the Lord, whereas he who is married is concerned about the things of the world.'[31] And if the battle against pleasures seems difficult, let everyone have courage, for habit is not powerless to produce some pleasure through steadfastness in what seems to be most difficult, and it encompasses the most beautiful and the purest pleasure worthy of the mind's attention, rather than estranging us from what is truly great and beyond our imagination because of our shabby concern with lowly things.

(10) *What is truly desirable.*

What treatise could possibly describe how great the penalty is for falling away from the truly beautiful? What kind of extravagant language could one use? How could the ineffable and the incomprehensible be presented and delineated? If anyone has such purity of mental vision that he is able to see, to some degree, what is promised by the Lord in His beatitudes, he will despise every human voice as having no power to set forth what is meant by them. On the other hand, if anyone still immersed in material matters has the clear vision of his soul blurred by some bleary-eyed condition, so to speak, any treatise will be futile as far as he is concerned. For, in the case of the insensitive, minimizing wonders and exaggerating them in discourse will amount to the same thing, just as in the case of the rays of the sun. Any verbal explanation of light is useless and idle for a person blind from birth, because it is not possible to visualize the brilliance of the sun through the ear. In the same way, each individual needs his own eyes to see the beauty of the true and the intelligible light. The one who does see it through some divine gift and unexplainable

---

31 1 Cor. 7.32,33.

inspiration is astonished in the depths of his consciousness; the one who cannot see will not realize what he has missed. For how can anyone confront him with the very good he has run away from? How can anyone bring the ineffable into his line of vision? We have not devised the particular verbal expressions for that beauty. There are no verbal tokens of what we are seeking. It is even difficult to make it clear by comparison. For who likens the sun to a little spark, or who compares a tiny drop with the boundless sea? The relation of the drop to the sea and the spark to the beam of the sun is similar to the relation between all the beauteous wonders in the world of men and that beauty which is seen with reference to the first Good and to what is beyond every good.

So what power of mind can possibly indicate the enormity of the penalty for those who incur it? The great David seems to me to have illustrated this impossibility well. When he was once lifted up in thought by the power of the Spirit, he was, as it were, divorced from himself and saw that incredible and incomprehensible beauty in a blessed ecstasy. But he did see it as far as it is possible for a man to do so when he is released from the limitations of the flesh and comes to the contemplation of the incorporeal and intelligible through thought alone. When he wanted to say something worthy of what he had seen, he sang out that song which all men sing: 'Every man is a liar.'[32] That is, as our treatise shows, that every man who commits his interpretation of the ineffable light to words is really a liar, not because of any hatred of the truth, but because of the weakness of his description. Perceptible beauty as far as it dwells here below in our life, fancied because of some charm in inanimate matter or living bodies, is within our power to admire and to describe and make known to others in treatises, just as such beauty is also painted on an icon. But how could a treatise, even if it explored every means of description, bring into view that whose archetype eludes

---

32 Cf. Ps. 115.2.

comprehension, being without color or form or size or shape or any such foolishness? How could anyone by means of those things which we grasp by perception alone come to know that which is the altogether invisible, the formless, the sizeless, as far as bodily perception goes? And yet one should not, for this reason, despair of his desire simply because these things seem to be beyond his grasp. Indeed, the treatise has shown that, in proportion to the greatness of what is sought after, it is necessary to elevate the mind in thought and to lift it to the level of what we are seeking, so that we are not excluded entirely from participation in the good. For when we try to observe what we are unacquainted with, there is no small risk that we may slip away entirely from the thought of it.

(11) *How one could gain an understanding of the really beautiful.*

On account of this weakness of knowing things through the senses, it is necessary for us to direct our mind to the unseen. But can one achieve such a thing? Some people, looking at matters superficially and thoughtlessly, when they see a man or whatever they happen upon, are interested in nothing more than what they see. It is enough for them having seen the size of the body to think that the whole concept of the man has been grasped. But the clear-sighted person, who has educated his soul, does not entrust his consideration of things to his eyes alone, nor does he stop at appearances, or reason that what he has not seen does not exist; he shrewdly contrives a nature of a soul; he examines the qualities appearing in the body, both in general and separately; and, after considering each quality for its own merits, he again looks at the general relationship and whole in connection with the underlying plan of composition. Accordingly, in the seeking of the beautiful, the person who is superficial in his thought, when he sees something in which fantasy is mixed with some beauty, will think that the thing itself is beautiful because of its own nature, his attention being attracted to it because of pleasure, and he will be concerned with nothing beyond this. But the man who has purified the eye of his soul is able to look at such things and forget the matter in which the beauty is encased, and he uses what he sees as a kind of basis for his contemplation of intelligible beauty. By a participation in this beauty, the other beautiful things come into being and are identified.

Since the majority of men possess such dense minds, it seems to me difficult for them to distinguish logically and separate the matter from the beauty perceived in it, and to come to know the nature of beauty in itself. And if anyone should want to determine the cause of the misconceptions and fallacious assumptions, I think he would find it in the fact that the faculties of the soul are not sufficiently trained in distinguishing between the beautiful and the not beautiful. For this reason, we falter in our zeal for the truly good. Some sink down into a love of the flesh, others turn to lifeless material things, others confine their idea of beauty to honor, glory, and power, but there are also some who are diverted by the arts and certain kinds of knowledge. The lowest of these make their palate and their stomach the criteria of the good. If they had deserted their material considerations and the obsessions with appearances, and sought after the simple and the immaterial and formless nature of beauty, they would not have been led astray in their choice of the desirable, nor would they have been swept away by deception to such an extent that, although they have seen the ephemeral quality of the pleasure in these things, they have not been led to a disdain for them.

The path leading us to the discovery of beauty would thus come into being for us and we would not squander our power of desire on any of the other things which distract us and which are considered beautiful and, for this reason, worthy of our zeal and praise. We would disregard these as being low and ephemeral, nor would we lazily and idly be limited to them, but, having been cleansed from our obsession with lowly things, our desire would go up to where perception does not reach, so that we would not admire the beauty of the sky or the rays of light or any other beautiful appearance, but, through the beauty seen in all these, we would be led to a desire for that beauty of which the heavens tell the glory and the firmament of all creation proclaims the knowledge.[33] In this way, the soul, rising and leaving behind all notice of unimportant things, arrives at a knowledge of the grandeur beyond the heavens.

But how could anyone whose enthusiasm is directed towards the lowly rise to such heights? How could anyone fly up to heaven unless, equipped with heavenly wings, he be borne upwards because of his lofty way of life? Who is so removed from the mysteries of the Gospel, that he does not know that there is one vehicle for the human soul for the journey to the heavens, and that is by likening itself to the cowering dove whose wings the prophet David longed for.[34] It is customary for Scripture to use this symbol in referring to the power of the Spirit, either because the dove is known for its peacefulness, or because it has an aversion to evil smells, as the specialists tell us. Indeed, the person who removes himself from all hatred and fleshly odor and rises above all low and earthbound things, having ascended higher than the whole earth in his aforementioned flight, will find the only thing that is worth longing for, and, having come close to beauty, will become beautiful himself. Through his participation in the true light, he will himself be in a state of brightness and illumination. For just as at night the multitudinous glowing objects of the air which certain people call 'shooting stars'— the physical scientists say they are nothing else than air poured into the aethereal region by the force of the wind, and they say that this firelike trail is traced in the sky when a wind is enflamed in the aether—just as this earthly air, when it is forced upwards by the wind, becomes light-like, being changed

---

33 Cf. Ps. 18.1.
34 Cf. Ps. 54.7.

in the clarity of the aether, so the mind of man, when, after leaving this muddy and dusty life, it is purified through the power of the Spirit, becomes light-like, and it is mixed with the true and lofty purity, and it glows and is filled with rays and becomes light in accordance with the promise of the Lord who declared that the just will shine like the sun.[35] We see this happen also on earth in the case of a mirror or water or anything that has the power of reflection because of its smoothness. For, when these receive the beam of the sun, they create another beam from themselves, but this would not occur if their clean and shiny surface became dirty. Therefore, either we go up, leaving behind earthly darkness, and become light-like there, because we are near the true light of Christ, or the true Light shining in the darkness comes down to us and we are made light, as the Lord says, somewhere to His disciples,[36] unless some dirt resulting from evil comes into our heart and dims the grace of our light.

Perhaps, then, the treatise has gently led us through examples to the thought of transforming ourselves to something better than we are, and has showed us also that the only way for the soul to be attached to the incorruptible God is for it to make itself as pure as it can. In this way, reflecting as the mirror does, when it submits itself to the purity of God, it will be formed according to its participation in and reflection of the prototypal beauty. If there is only such a person who has already left all human things behind, whether these be bodies or money or pursuits connected with the sciences and the arts, or whatever is considered acceptable to law and custom (in connection with these things there is a misconception of beauty, because the senses have become the criterion), such a person will love and desire that alone which has its beauty, not from another source nor in connection with the things just mentioned, but that which is beautiful of itself and in itself, that which is always beautiful, not some-

---
35 Cf. Prov. 4.18.
36 Cf. John 1.9; 12.36,46; also Matt. 5.14.

times beautiful and sometimes not, that which is above addition and increase and incapable of any kind of change and transformation.

I refer to the person who has purified all the powers of his soul from every form of evil, and I dare say that it is clear that the only thing which is beautiful by nature is that which is the cause of all beauty and all goodness. For, just as the eye cleansed from rheum sees objects shining brightly in the distance in the air, so also the soul through incorruptibility acquires the power to perceive the Light. The goal of true virginity and zeal for incorruptibility is the ability to see God, for the chief and first and only beautiful and good and pure is the God of all, and no one is so blind in mind as not to perceive that even by himself.

(12) *That the one who has purified himself will see the divine beauty in himself; also on the cause of evil.*

Perhaps no one is ignorant of this, but it is likely that certain people will want to discover, if this is possible, what method and mode of life leads us to it. The divine books are filled with pertinent suggestions, and many of the saints set before those on their way to God their own lives as guiding lights. It is possible for each of us to gather a wealth of suggestions from both Testaments. For there is much in the prophets and in the Law and much in the evangelical and apostolic tradition to take in abundance. Following the divine voice, our own opinion on the subject is as follows.

This logical and thinking animal, man, came into being as the work and imitation of the divine and unmixed nature. (For thus it is written of him in the story of creation,[37] that: 'He made him in the image of God.') This creature, man, therefore, did not have the elements of passion and mortality essentially and naturally in himself from the beginning.

---

37 Gen. 1.27. Cf. R. Leys, *op. cit.*, and J. Muckle, "The Doctrine of St. Gregory of Nyssa on Man as the Image of God," *Mediaeval Studies* 7 (1945) 55-84.

For it would not have been possible for the meaning of the word 'image' to be preserved if the copied beauty were different from the archetype. It was only later with the first fall that sin came upon man, and thus it crept in. Man was the image and likeness, as it has been said, of the sovereign power over all beings, and, for this reason, even in the exercise of choice, man is like the One who has power over all things, being enslaved by necessity to none of the things outside of himself, and he acts according to his own judgment of what seems best to him. The misfortune in which man is now involved he caused of his own will, having been swept away by deceit. He himself became the inventor of evil, he did not simply discover it after it had been invented by God. Nor did God create death; man, in a way, is the founder and creator of evil.

For it is possible for all who have the power of seeing to have a share in the sunlight, but someone can, if he wishes, by dimming his eyes, shut off the perception of light, not because the sun has withdrawn to another place and thus brought darkness upon him, but because he has, through the dimming of his sight, cut himself off from the sun's rays. And when the power of vision is thus prevented from functioning, it is entirely possible that this condition of being in a state of darkness will become habitual. It is also possible for someone building himself a house to make no provision for the light to enter; he will necessarily live in a darkness of his own making, since he has prevented the rays of light from entering. In like manner, also, the first man on earth, or rather, the begetter of evil among men, had the beautiful and the good naturally at hand in his power everywhere, but he deliberately estranged himself from them and created the experience of evil by choosing to turn away from virtue. For evil outside of choice and by itself does not exist in the nature of things. Every creation of God is beautiful and not to be despised and whatever God has made is exceedingly beautiful.

But when, as has been said, the sequence of sin ruined the life of man, there gushed forth from a small beginning an endless stream of evil for man, and that godlike beauty of the soul made in imitation of the prototype was darkened like some iron by the rust of evil, and it no longer preserves the grace of its own natural form, but is changed into the sordidness of sin. Like man, this 'great and honored being,' as he was called by Scripture,[38] falling from his own worthiness like those who slip and fall into the mud and, having smeared themselves with mire, become unrecognizable even to their companions, so the one who falls into the mire of sin no longer is the image of the incorruptible God, and he is covered through sin with a corruptible and slimy form which reason advises him to reject. However, if, purged by the water, so to speak, of his way of life, the earthly covering can be stripped off, the beauty of the soul may reappear again. The rejection of what is alien means a return to what is proper and natural to oneself, but this is not possible to achieve, unless one be created anew. For, being like the divine is not our function, nor is it the product of human ability, but it is part of the generosity of God who freely, at the birth of the first man, gave our nature a likeness to Himself.

The human effort extends only to this: the removal of the filth which has accumulated through evil and the bringing to light again the beauty in the soul which we had covered over. It is such a dogma that I think the Lord is teaching in the Gospel to those who are able to hear wisdom when it is mysteriously spoken: 'The kingdom of God is within you.'[39] This saying shows, I believe, that the goodness of God is not separated from our nature, or far away from those who choose to seek it, but it is ever present in each individual, unknown and forgotten when one is choked by the cares and pleasures of life, but discovered again when we turn our attention back to it. If there is need for further support of

---
[38] Cf. Prov. 20.6.
[39] Luke 17.21.

the argument, I think this is what the Lord was suggesting in the search for the lost drachma. The rest of the virtues which the Lord refers to as drachmas are of no use, even if they all be present in the soul, if the soul is bereft of the one that is lost. Consequently, He bids us, first of all, to light a lamp, and by this He means perhaps the word which brings to light that which is hidden. Then, He tells us to look for the lost drachma in our own house, i.e., in ourselves. Through this parable, He suggests that the image of the King is not entirely lost, but that it is hidden under the dirt. We must, I think, interpret the word 'dirt' as the filth of the flesh. Once this is swept away and cleaned off by our caring for our life, that which is being looked for becomes visible, and then the soul can rejoice and bring together the neighbors to share her joy. For in reality, all the faculties of the soul, which is what the Lord means by neighbors, do live together, and when the great image of the King which the Creator implanted in our hearts from the beginning is uncovered and brought to light, then, these faculties turn towards that divine joy and merriment, gazing upon the unspeakable beauty of what has been recovered. For it says: 'Rejoice with me, for I have found the drachma that I had lost.'[40] The neighbors, i.e., the faculties of the soul which dwell together, rejoice at the finding of the divine drachma. Reason and desire and the faculty aroused by grief and anger, and whatever other faculties there are, are looked upon as being connected with the soul, and they are logically considered as friends who rightly rejoice in the Lord when they all look to the beautiful and the good and do everything for the glory of God, for now they are no longer the instruments of sin.

This concern, then, for the finding of what is lost is the restoration to the original state of the divine image which is now covered by the filth of the flesh. Let us become what the first being was during the first period of his existence.

---

40 Luke 15.9.

But what was he? Liberated from the threat of death, looking freely upon the face of God, not yet judging the beautiful by taste and sight, but only enjoying the Lord and using the helpmate given to him for this purpose, as Holy Scripture tells us, because he did not know her earlier, before he was driven out of paradise, and before she was condemned to the punishment of the pains of childbirth for the sin which she committed, having been deceived.[41] Through this sequence of events, we, together with our first father, were excluded from paradise, and now, through the same sequence, it is possible for us to retrace the steps and return to the original blessedness. What was the sequence? It was pleasure brought about through deceit which initiated the fall. Shame and fear followed upon the experience of pleasure and they no longer dared to be in the sight of God. They hid themselves in leaves and shadows and, after that, they covered themselves with skins. And in this way, they came as colonists to this place, which is full of disease and toil where marriage was contrived as a consolation for death.

(13) *That release from marriage is the beginning of caring for oneself.*

If, then, we are going to return thence and be with Christ, we must begin at the point of deviation, just as those who have become separated from their own group on a journey, after they have retraced their steps, talk, first of all, to those who are just leaving the spot at which they went astray. Since the point of departure from the life in paradise was the married state, reason suggests to those returning to Christ that they, first, give this up as a kind of early stage of the journey. Next, they must withdraw from the earthly wretchedness in which man became involved after his fall; in addition, they must put off the coverings of the flesh, the garments made of skin, that is, they must put aside the thought of the flesh, and,

---

41 Cf. Gen. 3.16 ff.

after they have rejected the concealments of their shame, they must no longer stand in the shade of the fig tree of the bitter life; they must cast aside the coverings of these ephemeral leaves of life and be once more under the eyes of the Creator; they must disdain the deceptions of taste and sight; they must no longer have as their guide the poisonous serpent, but only the commandment of God. Fastening upon beauty alone and thrusting aside the taste of evil are one and the same thing, because for us the sequence of evils had its beginning in man's not wishing to be ignorant of evil. It was because of this that the first creatures were forbidden the knowledge of evil along with the good, and made to keep apart from the knowledge of good and evil, partaking only of the pure and unmixed good which has no share in evil. And this is nothing else, as our discourse indicates, than being with God and having this unceasing and continuous fastidiousness and not mixing with the enjoyment of the good those things which draw us in the opposite direction. And, if one may speak boldly, it is perhaps in this way that one could be snatched away from this world which lies in shame and restored to paradise where Paul saw and heard things unheard and unseen, which: 'It is not granted for man to utter.'[42]

But since paradise is a dwelling place of living beings which does not admit those who are dead because of sin, and we are 'carnal and mortal, sold into the power of sin,'[43] how is it possible for one who is ruled by the power of death to dwell in the land of the living? What means and plan could anyone devise to be beyond this power? The advice of the Gospel is altogether sufficient also for this. We have heard the Lord telling Nicodemus: 'That which is born of the flesh is flesh; and that which is born of the Spirit is spirit,'[44] and we know that the flesh because of sin is subject to death, whereas the spirit is of God, incorruptible, life-giving, and immortal.

---
42 Cf. 2 Cor. 12.2-4.
43 Rom. 7.14.
44 John 3.6.

Therefore, just as the power which destroys what is born is begotten along with physical birth, so it is clear that the Spirit bestows a life-giving power upon those born through it. What, then, can be deduced from what we have said? That separating ourselves from life in the flesh which death normally follows upon, we must seek a kind of life which does not have death as its consequence. This is the life of virginity. That this is true will be clearer if we explain a little further. Everyone knows that the function of bodily union is the creation of mortal bodies, but that life and incorruptibility are born, instead of children, to those who are united in their participation in the Spirit. Excellent is the apostolic saying about this, that the mother blessed with such children 'will be saved by child-bearing,'[45] just as the psalmist utters in the divine hymns: 'He establishes in her home the barren wife as the joyful mother of children.'[46] The virgin mother who begets immortal children through the Spirit truly rejoices and she is called barren by the prophet because of her moderation.

(14) *That virginity is stronger than the rule of death.*

Therefore, such a life, because it is stronger than the power of death, ought to be preferred by the intelligent. For the bodily procreation of children (let no one be displeased by this argument) is more an embarking upon death than upon life for man. Corruption has its beginning in birth and those who refrain from procreation through virginity themselves bring about a cancellation of death by preventing it from advancing further because of them, and, by setting themselves up as a kind of boundary stone between life and death, they keep death from going forward. If, then, death is not able to outwit virginity, but through it comes to an end and ceases to be, this is clear proof that virginity is stronger than death. Also, that body can well be called incorruptible which is not functioning in the service of the life which ends in corruption,

---
[45] 1 Tim. 2.15.
[46] Ps. 112.9

inasmuch as it has not become an instrument in the process of mortality. In this way, the unceasing succession of destruction and dying, which began with the first man and which continued until the lifetime of the One born of a Virgin, is interrupted. Death, you see, was never able to be idle while human birth was going on in marriage. After accompanying all the generations and going along with those who were always coming into life, death found in virginity a limit to its own activity which it was powerless to overcome. Just as at the time of Mary, the Mother of God, death who had been king from the time of Adam until then, when she was born, was shattered, being dashed against the fruit of virginity as if against a stone, so in every soul which through virginity rejects life in the flesh, the power of death is somehow shattered and destroyed, since it cannot apply its goad to them. Also, just as fire, if wood and kindling and hay or some other inflammable material are not added to it, does not have the nature to persist by itself, so the power of death will not function if marriage does not furnish it with fuel and provide it with victims who are like condemned prisoners.

If you have any doubt, think of the types of misfortunes which come to men from marriage as we have already discussed them in the beginning of this treatise. Can anyone lament widowhood, orphanhood, calamities concerning children, if he does not marry? The longed-for delights and joys and pleasures and whatever else is hoped for in marriage come to an end with these pains. For as the handle of the sword is smooth and well-fitted and polished and gleaming and adapted to the shape of the palm, but the rest of it is steel, an instrument of death, fearful to see, but more fearful to experience, such, also, is marriage holding out to us the smoothness and superficiality of pleasure like a handle which is adorned with skillful carving, but when it is in the hands of someone under attack, it brings pain with it and becomes the creator of grief and misfortune for men.

Marriage presents us with sights which are piteous and tearful, children bereft at an early age and left as booty to those who have charge of them, children who often smile at their misfortune because of their ignorance of evil. And what other source of widowhood is there but marriage? Giving up marriage means being exempt from participation in all these evil experiences and this is not at all unreasonable. Once the sentence set up from the beginning against sin is removed, no longer are the troubles of mothers 'multiplied,'[47] as it is written, nor does the grief derived from human birth continue. Misfortune is removed entirely from life and 'tears are wiped away from the face,' as the prophet says,[48] no longer is there unlawful pregnancy or conception in sin, birth comes, 'not of blood, nor of the will of the flesh, nor of the will of man, but of God'[49] alone. This occurs when someone through the life-giving quality of the heart takes on the incorruptibility of the Spirit and begets wisdom and justice and holiness and redemption. It is possible for everyone to become a mother in reality in this respect, since the Lord says somewhere: 'The one doing my will is my brother and my sister and my mother.'[50]

What place does death still have in such births? In them, mortality is truly conquered by life and the life of virginity seems to be an image of the blessedness that is to come, bringing with it many tokens of the goods that are stored up through hope. It is possible for those examining this argument to see the truth of what has been said. First of all, once one is dead to sin, he lives the rest of the time for God. Death is no longer his harvest. Having put an end to his carnal life, as far as this is within his power, he awaits the blessed hope and the epiphany of the great God, putting no distance between himself and the presence of God because of the

---
47 Cf. Ps. 24.17.
48 Isa. 25.8.
49 John 1.13.
50 Cf. Matt. 12.50; Mark 3.35.

generations in between. Secondly, he reaps the choicest goods in the resurrection and in the present life. For if the life which is promised to the just by the Lord after the resurrection is similar to that of the angels—and release from marriage is a peculiar characteristic of the angelic nature—he has already received some of the beauties of the promise, having mingled with the splendor of the saints and having imitated the purity of the incorporeal beings in the undefiled character of his life. If virginity is the sponsor of such experience, what word can sufficiently extol this grace? What other goods of the soul will appear so great and honorable, that they can be compared with the grandeur of this gift?

(15) *That true virginity is seen in every activity.*

But if we have exaggerated the grace of virginity, it is fitting for us to add the following. Achieving it is not as simple as one might think, nor is it confined to the body; it pertains to all things and extends even to thought which is considered one of the achievements of the soul. The soul, adhering to its true Bridegroom through virginity, not only keeps itself away from bodily defilements, but begins its purity there, and proceeds to all things in the same way and with equal steadfastness, being fearful lest the heart incline beyond its need to some adulterous participation in something evil and incur some sin in accordance with that part. What do I mean? (For I shall take up the argument again.) The soul, clinging to the Lord for the purpose of becoming 'one spirit'[51] with Him, and having entered into a kind of symbiotic agreement to love Him alone with its whole heart and power, must not become involved in fornication, lest the body become one with it, nor must it become involved in anything else that is opposed to salvation, because there is a common sharing of defilements, and if the soul is stained by even one, it can no longer be spotless.

---

51 1 Cor. 6.18.

It is possible to prove this argument by an example. Just as the water of a lake is smooth and motionless if nothing disturbs it from the outside, but, if a stone falls into it, the entire lake is affected and waves rise from the swell; and whereas the stone sinks to the bottom under its weight, the waves appear in a circle all around and they are pushed to the edge of the water by the movement in the center, and the whole appearance of the lake is made rough; so, also, the calm and quiet of the soul is entirely shaken if one sin falls upon it and it is affected by the part that is harmed. Those who are experts in such matters say that the virtues are not separate from each other and that it is not possible to grasp one of the virtues properly without attaining to the rest of them, but where one of the virtues is present the others will necessarily follow. Therefore, the harm to any of the elements in us extends to the whole life of virtue and truly, as the apostle says, the whole is affected by its parts, and 'if one member suffers anything, all the members suffer with it, or if one member glories, all the members rejoice with it.'[52]

(16) *That whatever is outside of the realm of virtue is equally dangerous.*

But our transgressions in a lifetime are countless and Scripture points out in many ways how numerous they are, for it says: 'Many are my persecutors and they that afflict me,'[53] and 'many fight against me from the height,'[54] and there are many other such passages. Perhaps, then, it is right to say that there are many who are adulterously plotting to destroy this honorable marriage and this pure bed. If it is necessary to recount these adulteries by name, we must say that anger is adultery, greed is adultery, envy is adultery, malice, hatred, slander, enmity, and all the things mentioned by the apostle as being in opposition to wholesome teaching come under

---
52 1 Cor. 12.26.
53 Cf. Ps. 118.157.
54 Cf. Ps. 55.2,3.

this heading.⁵⁵ Let us suppose that there is an exceptionally beautiful and lovable woman, fit to marry a king, but, because of her beauty, she is plotted against by licentious men. As long as she is hostile towards all who are connected with her destruction and condemns them in the presence of her lawful husband, she is wise and looks to the bridegroom alone, and the deceptions of these lawless persons make no impression upon her. But if she gives in to one of her assailants, her chastity in regard to the rest of them will not save her from punishment. Defilement of her bed by one is sufficient for condemnation. In the same way, the soul living for God will find no pleasure in any of the deceptive beauties before it, but if it does take some pollution into its heart because of some sin, it surrenders its rights to marriage with the Spirit, and as Scripture says: 'Into a soul that plots evil wisdom enters not.'⁵⁶ This is the same as saying that the good Bridegroom cannot live with a soul which has anything passionate or malignant or any such fault in it.

What intellect is capable of harmonizing things that are different by nature and have no common elements? Listen to the apostle as he teaches that: 'Light hath no fellowship with darkness and justice no participation with injustice';⁵⁷ nor, in a word, has the person who has chosen all the qualities attributed to the Lord any fellowship with those things which are known to be the opposite of the Lord. If, then, it is impossible for things essentially different to have anything in common, the soul subject to any evil is alienated from fellowship with the good. And what do we learn from these observations? That it is necessary for the wise and thoughtful virgin to remain aloof from every evil which in any way touches the soul and to keep herself pure for the Bridegroom legitimately suited to her, having no stain or spot or any such thing. For there is one straight and narrow path, truly compressed and

---
55 Cf. 1 Cor. 6.9,10.
56 Wis. 1.4.
57 Cf. 2 Cor. 6.14.

without deviations, and whatever is outside of it holds an equal risk of downfall.

(17) *That the person who lacks even one of the virtues is imperfect with respect to the good.*

If these things are so, we must correct, as much as we can, the habit of the multitude, of all those who energetically fight against the more shameful pleasures, but seek pleasure elsewhere in honors and administrative power, like the slave who, desiring freedom, does not make an effort to be released from slavery, but changes masters because he thinks that freedom is an exchange of lords. For we are all equally slaves, even if we do not have the same masters, as long as any sin has power over us and rules us by force. And again, there are those who, by reason of much fighting against pleasures, are somehow easily overcome by an opposite kind of weakness and spend their lives in grievances and irritations and malice and all the other things which are the opposite of the sins connected with pleasure. These are easily acquired and difficult to shake off, and this happens when it is not reason, but emotion which governs our way of life.

For, as Scripture says: 'The command of the Lord is clear, enlightening the eyes of the little ones,'[58] telling us that: 'It is good to adhere to God alone.'[59] God is not pain or pleasure or cowardice or rashness or fear or anger or any other such emotion which lords it over the untutored soul, but, as the apostle says, He is 'very wisdom and sanctification and truth and joy and peace,'[60] and such things. How, then, is it possible for anyone to adhere to the One who is truly these things if he is in the power of the opposite? Or how is it not unreasonable for one who is anxious not to be subject to any one of these sins to think that the opposite of them is virtue? For example, for the soul fleeing from pleasure to be

---
58 Cf. Ps. 18.9.
59 Cf. Ps. 72.28.
60 Cf. 1 Cor. 1.30; Rom. 14.17.

subject to pain, or for the soul inclined towards boldness and rashness to be abased by cowardice, or for the soul impregnable to anger to be eager to be cowed down because of fear? What difference does it make if we sin in one way or another when the important thing is that either way estranges us from God who is perfect virtue? In the case of bodily illnesses, no one would say that it makes any difference if the body is being destroyed by an excess or a deficiency, since the lack of balance will have the same result anyway. Therefore, the person who values the life and health of his soul will keep himself at the mean and will not participate in either of the emotions which deviate in either direction from the virtue in question. This is not my argument, but that of the Divine Voice itself. One can find this theory in the teaching of the Lord when he instructs his disciples, who are sent as sheep among wolves, not only to be doves, but to have also something of the serpent in their character.[61] I mean that thinking with simplicity is not the most praiseworthy activity among men since it comes near to being extreme foolishness. On the other hand, one should not think that the cleverness and cunning that are praised by the multitude are the equivalent of pure and unmixed virtue, but that rather from these opposites one should achieve a single mixed character, the one part surpassing innocence, the other surpassing the wisdom used by the wicked, so that from the two, one fine condition is arrived at combining simplicity of judgment and shrewdness. For, it says: 'Be wise as serpents and guileless as doves.'

(18) *That it is necessary for every faculty of the soul to aim at virtue.*

Therefore, let what has been said here by the Lord be the conviction in the life of everyone, especially among those who are approaching God through virginity. They should not

---

61 Matt. 10.16; Luke 10.3.

concentrate on achieving one thing while they are careless about its opposite, but they should seek out the good for themselves from all sides, so that their life will be secure in every respect. A soldier does not protect part of his body with armor and run the risk of leaving the rest of himself exposed. What good is the part protected by armor if he is wounded in a spot that is not covered? Or who could say that a person is handsome, if one of the features contributing to his handsomeness is mutilated in an accident? The ugliness of the injured part diminishes the grace of the part that is unimpaired.

If that person is ridiculous, as the Gospel says somewhere,[62] who undertakes to build a tower, but stops with the foundations and never completes it, what do we learn from this parable except that we should strive to bring every high aspiration to a conclusion, completing the work of God by an elaborate building up of His commandments? For one stone does not make a complete tower, nor does one commandment bring the perfection of the soul to its desired measure. It is entirely necessary both to erect the foundation and, as the apostle says: 'to lay upon it a building of gold and precious stones,'[63] for that is what the products of the commandments are called by the prophet when he says: 'I have loved your command more than gold and much precious stone.'[64] Let eagerness for virginity, then, be put down as the foundation for the life of virtue, but let there be built upon this foundation all the products of virtue. If this is believed to be precious and god-befitting, as it is, but one's whole life does not conform to it, and is stained by the rest of the soul's disorder, then, this is 'the golden ring in the swine's snout,'[65] or 'the pearl trampled under the feet of the swine.'[66] And there are other pertinent passages.

---

62 Luke 14.28 ff.
63 Cf. 1 Cor. 3.12.
64 Cf. Ps. 118.127.
65 Prov. 11.22.
66 Matt. 7.6.

But if anyone considers it unimportant for the elements in one's life to be in harmony with each other, let him behold the objects in his home and learn from this teaching. It seems to me that, as in a private house, the master does not allow the things in it to be unsuitable and incongruous: the bed overturned, the table full of dirt, valuable objects cast aside into filthy corners, vessels serving the needs of nature in full sight of those who come in, but rather he has everything tidy and in good order with each thing in its proper place, so that he confidently receives guests, not fearing any criticism if people see how things are in his house. Thus I think the master and steward of our dwelling ought to be, I mean the mind, making sure that everything in us is well-disposed, and that each of the faculties of the soul, which the Creator has given us in place of instruments or wares, is properly used and for the purposes of beauty. But if anyone says disparagingly that this argument is foolish and frivolous, let him explain in detail how he would manage his own life to his advantage by using what he has.

We say, then, that it is necessary that desire be founded on the purity of the soul as upon some first fruit or votive offering selected for God, purifying the soul and keeping it untouched and undefiled, never soiled by any of the filth of life. Anger and rage and hatred should be aroused, like dogs guarding gates, only for resistance to sin, and used against the thief or enemy who enters to defile the divine treasury and comes to steal, to storm, and to destroy. Instead of a weapon in the hand, one should have courage and bravery so there would be no need to be afraid and one could withstand the onslaughts of the impious. One should be supported, not by a staff, but by hope and steadfastness, if he should ever be weary from temptations. If the moment of repentance for sins should come, one should then exhibit grief, conscious that it is never useful for any other function. Justice should be for him the standard of uprightness, showing, without clumsiness, in every word and deed how it is necessary for things to be disposed in his soul and how he should manage each element according to its worth. The impulse towards more which lies without limit in the soul of each person should be applied to the desire for God, and thus one will be congratulated for his greed, since he is using force where force is praiseworthy. He should have wisdom and prudence as advisers in all circumstances and as sharers of his life, so that he will not be harmed by ignorance or imprudence. However, if one does not use the faculties we have spoken of in accordance with what is natural and appropriate, but perverts their use by applying desire to the most shameful things, such as directing hatred against one's relatives, loving injustice, playing the brave fellow against his parents, being bold where it is out of place, hoping for vain things, rejecting prudence and wisdom as living companions, becoming the comrade of gluttony and folly, and so forth, he will be absurd and monstrous, so that no one could even adequately describe how ridiculous he is. Is it not just as if a soldier would alternately cover his face and put back the crest of his helmet, place his feet in his breastplate, fit the greaves to his chest, change right to left and left to right? What such a soldier would be likely to experience in war is what a person is likely to experience in life who confuses his judgment and his use of the powers of the soul.

Therefore, we ought to provide for harmony in these matters which true moderation puts by nature into our souls. And if it is necessary to consider the perfect definition of moderation, perhaps it could be said authoritatively that this is what it is: the well-ordered economy of all the movements of the soul with wisdom and prudence. Such a condition of the soul has no need of toil and trouble for participation in lofty and heavenly things, since it quickly and easily achieves what seemed before to be difficult to attain, by rejecting the opposite of what it is seeking. For it is necessary for the one who is not in the dark to be completely in the light, and for the living not to be dead, and, therefore, unless one foolishly distracts his own soul, he will be entirely on the right road. For provision against being led astray and knowledge are the accurate guides for proceeding on the direct path. And just as slaves, when they have been freed and have stopped serving their masters, turn their attention to themselves, thus, I think, the soul, once it has been freed from deception and service to the body, comes to an understanding of what is particularly its own and of its natural functions. Freedom, as we learn from the apostle, is not to be held 'under the yoke of slavery,'[67] and not to be fettered in the bonds of the married life like a fugitive or a criminal.

But, again, the argument returns to the original point, that perfect freedom does not consist in this alone, in abstaining from marriage. Let no one think that virginity is so small and cheap that it can be thought of as attainable through a slight control of the flesh. Since 'everyone who commits sin is a slave of sin,'[68] i.e., turning to evil in any matter and situation somehow enslaves a man and puts the stigma of a runaway slave on him, scars and brands inflicted by the blows of sin, it is fitting for the one aiming at the great goal of virginity to be uniformly virtuous and for purity to be evident in every aspect of his life.

If it is necessary to strengthen our argument through some divinely inspired word, the truth itself in parable and symbols in the Gospel gives us sufficient support. The art of fishing consists in separating the good and edible fish from the bad and harmful ones, so that the enjoyment of the good ones will not be spoiled by one of the bad ones which has fallen into the baskets. This also is the function of true moderation, having selected from all situations what is pure and useful, and having rejected in each case what is unsuitable and useless, to put it back into the common life of the world which is

---

67 Gal. 5.1.
68 John 8.34.

called the sea in the parable.[69] And when the psalmist offers a similar teaching in one of the Psalms,[70] he points out the unsteady and passionate and disturbed life, when he speaks of 'waters coming unto the soul' and 'the depth of the sea' and 'a tempest,' in which every rebellious thought is like a stone drowned in the sea as the Egyptians were.[71] That which is dear to God and has a clear vision of the truth, which is called Israel in the story, this alone comes to dry land and is never enveloped in the bitter brine of the waves of life. As a symbol under the rule of law (Moses was the symbol of the Law), Israel crossed the sea without getting wet and the Egyptians were drowned, each in keeping with their own attitude, the one crossing easily and the other dragged down into the deep. For virtue is something light and exhilarating. All who live according to it 'fly along like clouds,' according to Isaia,[72] and 'like doves' with their young, but sin is heavy, seated, as one of the prophets says, upon 'a talent of lead.'[73] If such an interpretation of Scripture appears to anyone to be forced and unfitting, because he does not think the miracle of the sea was written as an aid to us, let him listen to the apostle saying that he wrote symbolically, both for the men of his own time and 'for our correction.'[74]

(19) *Mention of Mariam, the sister of Aaron, as the one who inaugurated this achievement.*

This reminds us that the prophetess, Mariam, immediately after the crossing of the sea, took a dry, tuneful 'tambourine in her hand'[75] and led a chorus of women. Perhaps by the tambourine Scripture means to suggest the virginity achieved by the first Mary, who was, I think, the prototype of Mary

---

69 Cf. Matt. 13.47 ff.
70 Cf. Ps. 68.2,3.
71 Cf. Exod. 14.21 ff.
72 Cf. Isa. 60.8.
73 Cf. Zach. 5.7.
74 1 Cor. 10.11.
75 Exod. 15.20.

the Mother of God. For, as the tambourine produces a loud sound, having no moisture in it and being quite dry, so also virginity is clear and noised abroad and has nothing in itself of the life-preserving moisture of this life. If it was a tambourine, a dead body, which Mariam used, then virginity is the deadening of the body, and it is perhaps not unlikely that it was being a virgin which set her apart. We suggest from conjecture and assumption and not from proof that the prophetess, Mariam, led a chorus of maidens. Many of the learned affirm clearly that she was unmarried from the fact that there is no mention in Scripture of her marriage or of her children. Also, she would not have been referred to or been known as the sister of Aaron if she were married, since it is the husband who is the head of the woman and not her brother, and it is her husband's name that she is called by. And so if the grace of virginity appeared precious among a people who considered childbearing desirable and lawful, let us, who hear the divine injunctions, not according to the flesh, but according to the spirit, cling to it all the more. The divine injunctions have often revealed to us that childbearing and the begetting of children are a good thing, and they have indicated the kind of procreation sought after among God's saints. The prophet, Isaia, and the divine apostle both indicated this clearly and precisely. The former has said: 'From fear of you, O Lord, we have conceived and been in labor and given birth.'[76] And the latter proudly said that he has been the most prolific of all in offspring, and had filled entire cities and nations with his children; through his own pangs, he formed them in the Lord,[77] and not only brought to light the Corinthians and the Galatians, but also filled the whole inhabited world with his own children which he begot in Christ through the Gospel 'from Jerusalem round about as far as Illyricum.'[78] Thus, even in the Gospel, the womb of

---

76 Cf. Isa. 26.18.
77 Cf. Gal. 4.19; 1 Cor. 4.15.
78 Rom. 15.19.

the holy Virgin which served the unblemished childbirth is blessed on the grounds that the offspring does not destroy virginity and virginity does not stand in the way of such begetting, for, as Isaia says, where 'the spirit of salvation is born the wishes of the flesh are entirely useless.'[79]

(20) *That it is impossible to serve the bodily pleasures and, at the same time, to reap the enjoyment of God.*

There is some such idea also in the apostle where he says that each man is twofold; there is the 'outer man' to whom corruption is natural, and the one who is known in accordance with the hidden places of his heart, that is, the one who undergoes 'a renewal.'[80] If, indeed, this is true (and it is entirely true because of the truth that is speaking in it), it is not at all unlikely that he has in mind a twofold idea of marriage, profitable and suitable for every man among us. And perhaps the bold will dare to say that it is not beyond likelihood that the virginity of the body is the co-worker and sponsor of an inner and spiritual marriage.

For just as it is not possible for the same person to pursue two crafts, that is, he cannot be a farmer and a sailor at the same time, or a smith and a carpenter, but if he is going to take up the one occupation successfully, he has to let the other go; so, also, for us, although two kinds of marriages are possible, the one accomplished through the flesh and the other through the spirit, a desire for the one necessitates the exclusion of the other. For the eye cannot look at two things at one time, unless it is directed to each of them in turn, nor can the tongue utter two different sounds at the same time, for example, Hebrew and Greek. Also the same person cannot listen to a story and an instruction at the same time, for the meaning of what is heard depends on the sound, and if one hears a mixture of sounds, there will be an unintelligible confusion.

---

79 Cf. Isa. 26.18.
80 2 Cor. 4.16.

According to the same argument, the desiring element in us does not by nature serve bodily pleasures and, at the same time, participate in a spiritual marriage. It is not possible to attain each of these goals through similar activities. Self-control and the mortification of the body and a disdain for everything connected with the flesh are the sponsors of the latter, and the opposites of these are the sponsors of the physical union. Therefore, just as where one has a choice of two masters, since he cannot, at the same time, be subject to both (for 'no man can serve two masters,'[81]), the wise man will choose the more helpful one. So, when we have the choice of two marriages, since a person cannot participate, at the same time, in both ('for he who is unmarried is concerned about the things of the Lord, and he who is married about the things of the world.'[82]), it will be wise for us not to make the wrong selection or to be ignorant of the road that leads to the better one, and this we can learn only through some such analogy.

Just as in a physical marriage a person who is eager not to be rejected makes an effort to have a fine appearance, fitting adornment and sufficient wealth, and takes much care not to be a burden because of his way of life or his family background (these are the factors which would especially occur to him), in the same way, the person planning a spiritual marriage will want to present himself as being youthful and intellectually rejuvenated, and he will indicate that he is from a family that is rich in the way that is most desirable, a family not respected because of its earthly possessions, but because of the abundance of its heavenly treasures. That person will not pride himself on having a family that is looked up to because of the good fortune which comes automatically to many, even to the foolish, but the good fortune that is present because of the toil and effort of one's own accomplishments, which only those achieve who are sons

---
81 Matt. 6.24.
82 1 Cor. 7.32,33.

of the light and children of God and called well-born 'from the risings of the sun'[83] through their enlightened deeds. He will not busy himself with his bodily strength or his appearance or with exercising his body or fattening his flesh, but quite the opposite; he will perfect the power of the spirit in the weakness of the body. I know that the dowry in this wedding does not consist of corruptible things, but of what is given us as a gift from the special wealth of the soul. Do you want to know the names of these gifts? Let anyone who introduces himself as a man of wealth listen to Paul, the fair escort of the bride. Listing many other important qualities, he also mentions 'innocence.'[84] And, again, wherever the fruits of the spirit are enumerated,[85] they are the gifts of this marriage. If anyone is going to obey Solomon and take true wisdom as the companion and sharer of his life, concerning which he says: 'Love her, and she will safeguard you,'[86] and: 'Honor her, in order that she may embrace you,'[87] he will worthily prepare himself for this longing, keeping festival in a pure garment, rejoicing with those in this marriage, in order not to be rejected because of being clothed as a married person.

It is clear that the eagerness for this kind of marriage is common to men and women alike, for since, as the apostle says: 'There is neither male nor female,'[88] and Christ is all things for all human beings, the true lover of wisdom has as his goal the divine One who is true wisdom, and the soul, clinging to its incorruptible Bridegroom, has a love of true wisdom which is God. Now, what spiritual marriage is and towards what goal the pure and divine love looks has been sufficiently revealed in what we have said before.

---

83 Cf. Isa. 41.25.
84 2 Cor. 6.6.
85 Cf. Gal. 5.22.
86 Prov. 4.6.
87 Cf. Prov. 4.8.
88 Gal. 3.28.

(21) *That it is necessary for the one who has chosen a rigid discipline to be estranged from every type of bodily pleasure.*

Since it is impossible for anyone to draw near to the purity of God who has not become pure himself, it is necessary for a person to separate himself from pleasures with a large and strong partition, so that the purity of the heart will, in no way, be defiled by coming near them. A safe protective wall is the complete estrangement from everything involving passion. For if one pleasure exists (as we learn from the philosophers), it is like the stream of water from one source which, when it is divided into different streams, spreads to each of the pleasure-loving organs of the senses. Therefore, the one who is weakened by any one of the sensual pleasures, damages his heart, as the voice of the Lord teaches, when He says that the one who has fulfilled the desire of his eyes has already received the wound in his heart.[89] I think that the Lord is speaking of all the senses in this one example, so that those of us who follow His words should add that the one who has heard or touched or employed any faculty in the service of pleasure has sinned in his heart.

To make certain that this does not happen, the following rule should be used by the wise man for his own life: never allow the soul to come near any temptation to pleasure, and be on guard, above all, against the pleasure of taste, because somehow this seems to be the most persistent, being practically the mother of all that is forbidden. Pleasures connected with eating and drinking abound in immoderate consumption, create in the body the necessity for a surfeit of undesirable evils, and this begets many similar sins among men.

Indeed, in order for our body to remain calm and be soiled by none of the sins of satiety, we must provide for a life of greater self-control, by defining not only the limit and boundary of every enjoyment connected with pleasure, but

---

89 Cf. Matt. 5.28.

the limit connected with our individual need. If the pleasant is often mingled with the need (for want knows how to season everything because of the vehemence of the longing, sweetening everything that is discovered through need), one does not have to banish the need because of the enjoyment attendant upon it, nor, however, should one pursue pleasure as a guide. It is fitting, further, to choose from all things that which is useful and to control the sensations of enjoyment.

We see farmers skilfully separating the chaff from the wheat, so that each of them is put aside for a special need, the one for the use of human beings and the other for fuel or the nourishing of animals. Therefore, the cultivator of wisdom distinguishes the need from the pleasure like the wheat from the chaff: the one he will throw aside for the less intelligent 'whose end is to be burnt,' as the apostle says,[90] but he will thankfully partake of what is necessary according to his need.

> (22) *That it is not necessary to exercise self-control beyond the proper measure, and that carnal indulgence and excessive mortification are both opposed to the soul for attaining perfection.*

But since many fall into the other form of immoderation and, through excessive discipline, achieve the opposite effect of what they are aiming for, distracting their soul in a different way from what is lofty and divine, descending to lowly thoughts and occupations, directing their attention to bodily mortifications, so that they no longer soar mentally in freedom or look on high, but incline towards toil and the wearing out of the flesh, it would be well for us to give some importance to this and to guard against an equal lack of moderation in this direction. We should not bury the mind in sensuality, nor, again, should we make it powerless and abject because of the weakness imposed upon it by bodily toil. We should, instead, remember the equally wise advice which

---

90 Heb. 6.8; cf. Matt. 3.12; Luke 3.17.

forbids that one should deviate to things to the right or to the left.

I heard a certain physician explaining professionally that our body is made up of four similar elements which are direct opposites to each other, namely, hot and cold, wet and dry, mixed together. He said that, although the mixture of wet and dry is illogical, they do go together through some intermediary relationship. And he astutely explained the meaning of the natural philosophers by saying that each of these elements is diametrically opposed to the other, but that they fit together by nature through some affinity of the qualities in them, the cold and the hot being present equally in the wet and the dry, and, again, the wet and the dry in the hot and the cold. The identity of the qualities appearing equally in the opposites creates by itself a union of opposites. But why is it pertinent for me to go through the opposites in detail, showing how they are separated from each other because of the opposition of their nature, and then, united again, joined by the relationship of the qualities in them? Only to remind us by what has been said that the person who looks at the body in the light of this theory will be impelled to think about the equality of power in these elements, because health consists in not having one element in us dominate the others.

Therefore, if this argument has any truth in it, we ought to provide for such a condition for the maintenance of our health. We should induce it by having no one of the elements of which we are made too great or too small as a result of any anomaly in our diet. We should always, as it were, imitate the driver of a chariot. For just as he drives his team in harmony, neither urging on with his whip the swift colt nor restraining the slow one with the reins, nor, again, does he allow them to be too slack or refractory and disordered through their own impulses, but he guides them and stops them short and touches them with the whip until they go harmoniously along the race course; in the same way, our mind, which holds the reins of the body, should not continue to inflame it with excessive heat in its youthfulness, nor should it allow it to abound in what is overly cool and weak once it has been chilled by disease and time. And in connection with the other qualities, the mind will likewise listen to Scripture. In order not to have too much or too little, avoiding the immoderate in each case, it will provide for what is lacking and will equally guard against the superfluous in each part of the body. It will not make the flesh slack and flabby through excessive good living, nor ill and wasted and languid in its necessary activity because of immoderate suffering. This is the most perfect goal of self-control: not to concentrate on the suffering of the body, but on the efficient working of the instruments of the soul.

(23) *That it is necessary for the one who wishes to learn the strictness of this life to be taught by one who has achieved it.*

There are many written instructions teaching the particulars: how it is right for the person choosing to live with this philosophy to conduct his life, what to guard against, in what activities he should engage himself, the limits of self-control, the manner of spending one's time, and all the things one must learn once such a goal has been established. However, the guidance of deeds is more effective than instructions in words; nor is this a cause for discontent, since it is necessary for those starting a long trip or an extensive voyage to have a teacher. The apostle says: 'The Word is near thee.'[91] Grace begins at home. Here is the workshop of the virtues in which such a life is purified to the highest point. Great is the power to teach this divine regimen through deeds, both on the part of those who are silent and those who speak out, since every word seen apart from deeds, even if it is beautifully decked out, is like a lifeless icon which portrays a

---

91 Rom. 10.8. The 'written instructions' seem to refer to Basil's *Rules*.

form blooming with paint and color, but 'he that shall do and teach,'[92] as the Gospel says somewhere, this man is truly alive and outstandingly beautiful and effective in his movements.

Indeed, the novice who is going to acquire the habit of virginity in accordance with convincing logic must have this kind of teacher. For just as one eager to learn the language of a certain people cannot teach himself, but is taught by those who know it, and thus comes to speak the foreign tongue, making quick progress because of the habit of hearing the language, in the same way, I think, one's nature does not make progress in this life automatically, since it is foreign to the novelty of the regimen, unless the person is taken in hand and learns the details from someone who has succeeded in it. In everything we do in life, it is better for the one entering upon something to gain a knowledge of whatever he is striving for from teachers than to undertake to learn by himself. This undertaking of ours is not so simple that one can necessarily judge for himself what is advantageous, and when a person dares to try out what he is not familiar with, he takes a risk. Just as men, through experience and close observation, have gradually discovered the previously unknown art of healing, so that the beneficial and the harmful are recognized through the experiments, knowledge is garnered for the profession, and instruction as to what is going to be observed is handed down by those who have learned beforehand, and thus the neophyte does not have to decide the effects of medicines, whether a drug is harmful or helpful through his own experiments, but becomes a successful physician by learning what is known from others; in the same way, it is not necessary to gain a knowledge of the healing art of the soul through conjectures and assumptions (I am speaking of philosophy through which we learn the cure for all diseases touching the soul), but through the

---

92 Cf. Matt. 5.19.

authority of the learning of one who has established the habit through long and extensive experience.

Youth, for the most part, is a precarious counselor in every matter and we do not easily find any success worthy of emulation in one whom gray hair has not brought to a participation in his subject. In proportion, as the goal we are aiming at is greater than that aimed at in other activities, we must be more careful to insure ourselves against risk. In other circumstances, if youth conducts itself unreasonably, it incurs a fine of money or loses some worldly distinction or esteem. But, in the case of this great and lofty desire, it is not merely money or worldly and temporary glory that is risked, or any of the other external things mentioned by us, for which there is little concern among the wise. The thoughtlessness touches the soul itself and the danger of punishment is not the loss of something just happened upon or something which can be recovered, it is the very destruction of oneself and the punishment of one's own soul. The person who has squandered his patrimony does not despair, as long as he lives, of regaining his former prosperity through ingenuity, but the one who fails in this life removes all hope of a change for the better.

Therefore, since the majority of persons who intend to lead a life of virginity are still young and immature, they must concern themselves with this before all, the finding of a good guide and teacher on this path, lest, on account of their ignorance, they enter upon trackless places and wander away from the straight road. For, as Ecclesiastes says: 'Two are better than one.'[93] The one is easily overcome by the enemy lying in ambush on the divine road, and verily: 'Woe to the solitary man, for if he should fall he has no one to lift him up.'[94] In the past, certain people have made an auspicious beginning in their desire for this life, but, although they have attained perfection in their intention, they have been tripped

---
93 Eccles. 4.9.
94 Eccles. 4.10.

up because of their vanity. They deceived themselves, through some craziness, into thinking that that was fair towards which their own thought inclined. Among these, there are those called 'the slothful'[95] in the Book of Wisdom, who strew their path with thorns, who consider harmful to the soul a zeal for deeds in keeping with the commandments of God, the demurrers against the apostolic injunctions, who do not eat their own bread with dignity, but, fawning on others, make idleness the art of life. Then, there are the dreamers who consider the deceits of dreams more trustworthy than the teachings of the Gospels, calling fantasies revelations. Apart from these, there are those who stay in their own houses, and still others who consider being unsociable and brutish a virtue without recognizing the command to love and without knowing the fruit of long-suffering and humility.

Who could enumerate all such deviations into which one is carried because of not wishing to associate himself with those esteemed in the sight of God? Of these, we know also those who starve themselves to death on the grounds that such a sacrifice is pleasing to God, and again, others, completely opposite to these, who practice celibacy in name, but who do not refrain from social life, not only enjoying the pleasures of the stomach, but living openly with women, calling such a living together 'brotherhood,' and thinking that they are avoiding suspicion by this pious term. Because of them, this revered and pure way of life is blasphemed by the pagans.

Indeed, it is advantageous for the young not to regulate the path of this life for themselves. Demonstrations of the goods of this life of ours are not lacking. In fact, now especially, its dignity is flourishing and it is popular, being perfected to the highest degree by gradual additions to it, so that it is possible to walk in such footsteps and have a share in it, and, following after the scent of the perfume, to be filled with the fragrance of Christ. For just as when one candle is lighted the

---

95 Cf. Prov. 15.19.

flame is then distributed to all the candles nearby, and the original light is not lessened, although it is equally present in those lighted from it, so the dignity of this life is distributed by the one who has succeeded in it to those who come near him. For the prophetic word is true that one associating with the holy and the innocent and the elect will take on their characteristics.[96]

Moreover, if you seek tokens through which it is possible not to miss the good example, an outline is easy. If you see the life of a man standing between life and death, choosing philosophically what is useful on either side, neither taking on the negative aspect of death because of his eager attitude towards the divine commandments, nor stamping with both feet upon life because of his alienation from worldly desires, and in those matters in which the life of the flesh is esteemed, remaining more idle than the dead, but in those deeds of virtue by which those living in the spirit are known, being alive and energetic and strong, look to this man as the model of your life. God has made him as a goal for our own lives. Let this one be for you the goal of the divine life as the fixed stars are for the pilots. Imitate the old age and the youth of this one, rather, imitate the old age in his youthfulness and the youthfulness in his old age. For when he is approaching old age, time does not dim the strength and vigor of his soul, nor is his youth distinguished by the activities in which youth usually engages, but there is some wonderful mixture of opposites in each age, a release from what is peculiar to each, his power for good being young in his old age, and his youthfulness in adolescence doing nothing connected with evil. But, even if you are searching for lovers of that age, imitate the steadfastness and fire of the divine love of wisdom which increases from youth and persists to old age.

However, if you are not able to look at him as those who have weak eyes cannot look at the sun, contemplate the

---

96. Cf. Ps. 17.26,27.

chorus of the saints arrayed under it, those shining in life in imitation of those who have come of age, among whom are many, who, although they are young in years, are old in the purity of their self-control, anticipating old age in their logic and, in a way, going beyond time, those who have demonstrated a more steadfast and forceful love of wisdom than of bodily pleasures, not because these were foreign to their nature (for in everybody 'the flesh lusts against the spirit'[97]), but because they listened well to the one who said that wisdom 'is the tree of life to those who grasp her.'[98] Sailing through the wave of youth with that tree as if on a raft, they are moored in the harbor of the will of God, and now, in tranquillity and calm, their soul is not washed by the waves, and they are blessed by smooth sailing; after having moored what they had on good hope as if with a safe anchor, they are calm beyond the reach of disturbing waves, extending the brightness of their life to those following them like beacons on a high promontory. Therefore, having someone to whom we can look, let us sail securely through the storm of temptations.

Why are you so curious about those who have had intentions along these lines, but have faltered, and why, for this reason, do you despair on the grounds that it is not practical? Look rather to the one who has succeeded and, being encouraged by him, dare to undertake the good voyage using the intelligence of the Holy Spirit with Christ as the pilot at the rudder of moderation. Those who go down to the sea in ships and work in many deep waters are not deterred from hope because shipwrecks have occurred, but, projecting their own good hope, they speed on to a successful end. Or would it not be the most ridiculous thing of all for someone to say that failure in the life of perfection is an evil, and, then also, to advise that it is better to grow old making mistakes throughout one's life? If it is a terrible thing to fall into sin once,

---
97 Gal. 5.17.
98 Prov. 3.18.

do you also, for this reason, think it is safe not to attempt a higher goal? Is it not more difficult to make sin one's life occupation, and, because of this, to remain completely without any share of the purer life? How do you, the living, listen to the Crucified One, the Healer of sin, when He orders us to follow Him and to carry the cross as a banner against the Adversary, if you are not crucified to the world and have not taken on the death of the flesh? How does the person 'conformed' to this age and not 'transformed in the newness' of his mind and not walking in the newness of this life, but following instead the sequence of the life of ancient man, obey Paul who commanded you to present your body as a sacrifice, living, holy, and pleasing to God?[99] How are you a priest for God, having been anointed for this very purpose of offering a gift to God, a gift that is not altogether alien or fraudulent, because it is made up of what is external to you, but a gift that is truly yours, which is the man within you helping you to be perfect and blameless according to the word of the Lamb, free from all stain and dishonor? How will you set these offerings before God, if you do not listen to the law which forbids an unholy man to be a priest?[100] And if you are longing for God to appear to you, why do you not listen to Moses who ordered the people to abstain from (the privileges of) marriage in order to be present at the appearance of God?[101] If these things seem unimportant to you, being crucified with Christ, offering yourself as a sacrifice to God, becoming a priest of the highest God, being worthy of the great epiphany of God, why should we consider anything beyond these things for your benefit? Uniting yourself with God comes from being crucified with Him and living with Him and sharing His glory and His kingship; offering yourself to God means transforming human nature and worth into the angelic. Thus Daniel says: 'Thousands upon thousands were minis-

---

99 Rom. 12.1,2.
100 Cf. Exod. 19.22.
101 Cf. Exod. 19.15.

tering to Him.'[102] Once one has taken on the true priesthood and allied oneself with the great High Priest, this alliance continues in every way, and one is a priest forever, unhindered by death from being near Him always. There is no other reward for being worthy to see God than this very thing: seeing Him. For the crown of every hope and the achievement of every desire and the limit and acme of every praise of God and every promise of the ineffable goods believed to be beyond perception and knowledge is this crowning experience which Moses longed for and many prophets and kings desired. Only 'the clean of heart' are worthy of it, and it is for this reason they are truly called 'blessed,' that 'they shall see God.'[103] We want you to be one of those crucified with Christ, to stand beside Him as a pure priest, to become a pure sacrifice in all purity, preparing yourself through your holiness for the presence of God, in order that you yourself may see God in the purity of your heart according to the promise of God and our Savior Jesus Christ, to whom is the glory and the power forever and ever. Amen.

---

102 Dan. 7.10.
103 Matt. 5.8.

ON WHAT IT MEANS TO CALL ONESELF A CHRISTIAN

INTRODUCTION

RITTEN MANY YEARS LATER than the treatise on virginity, this work, in the form of a letter, is addressed to a young admirer of St. Gregory named Harmonius. Its warm personal tone goes beyond the conventional epistolary style and, despite its length, the impression is given that it is a real letter written to a friend for whom the saint had an affectionate regard. We learn that, in the past, the two men had had the pleasure of long and enjoyable discussions about virtue and man's service of God, that during a long separation St. Gregory had neglected to reply to the many letters sent by his friend, that he now intends to pay the debt for the unanswered letters by writing a long letter which will imitate in style and content their former conversations.

He begins, as in a philosophical dialogue, by setting a problem directly related to man's conduct. The question he proposes is: What is meant by the term 'Christian'? Christianity had been the state religion for some decades and it is not unlikely that certain persons were calling themselves Christians for reasons of prestige and personal advantage. In order to illustrate the absurdity of assuming the name of Christian without conforming in one's life to its essential meaning, St. Gregory makes use of a story taken from secular literature about a monkey disguised by a clever entrepreneur as a dancer whose masquerade was revealed when, in the midst of his performance, he was unable to resist the temptation of sweetmeats thrown before him. The same story had been used by Lucian to satirize the philosophers whose lives did not correspond to their precepts. The adaptation is in keeping with St. Gregory's propensity for equating the philosophical life with that of the Christian ascetics.

In his discussion of the etymology of the word 'Christian,' St. Gregory lists a number of qualities mentioned in Scripture as being inherent in the incorruptible nature of Christ, and he maintains that anyone who sincerely calls himself a Christian must reflect these qualities. In this treatise, no effort is made to analyze the appellations applied to Christ in the Bible, but in his later treatise *On Perfection*, he returns to them and explains in detail how each of them can and should be applicable to the person striving to be a Christian. Here, for the time being, he is content merely to define Christianity as 'an imitation of the divine nature.' This, he asserts, can only be achieved by an earnest attempt on man's part to perfect his nature to such an extent that it will resemble the nature of God. The interrelation of man's perfection resulting from a life of virtue and man's assimilation to God is a favorite Gregorian motif. If it is true that becoming a true Christian means the perfecting of oneself through an imitation of God, it is clear that Christianity involves much more than symbol and gesture. It is a deeply personal experience of transformation which can be had only if man alienates himself completely from evil and elevates himself through the impetus of thought to God upon whose generous aid and cooperation Scripture has assured us that we can depend. According to St. Gregory, then, Christianity is equated with the perfection of man's nature and it is the mark of the true Christian that, in his attempt to assimilate himself to God, he is living as far as possible a life of perfect virtue.

ON WHAT IT MEANS TO CALL ONESELF A CHRISTIAN

IN SENDING THIS LETTER to your Reverence, I am behaving like those debtors who happen upon some good fortune and pay the entire amount owed at one fell swoop. For after being constantly in your debt in the matter of letter writing (because for Christians a promise is a debt), I now wish to pay in full the past debt, which I contracted unwillingly, by extending this letter to such a length that it will count as many when it is judged by the customary length of letters. But, in order that I may not go on idly writing at length, I think that it will be good for me to imitate in my epistolary style the conversations we used to have when we were face to face. Indeed, I remember very well that the starting point of our discussions on every occasion was a concern for virtue and exercise related to the service of God. You always reacted attentively to what was said, although you did not accept it without examining it, while I, on account of our having anticipated it, came to a final solution to what we were seeking on each occasion as a consequence of our discussion. Surely, if it were possible, even now, for the impetus to argument to be derived from your presence, it would be better in every way; there would be a mutual benefit from our seeing each other (what in life is sweeter to me than this?) and, under the plectrum of your intelligence, our old lyre would reawaken. But, since the necessity of life causes us to be separated in body, even if our souls are always united, I shall be forced to assume your role also, if some logical conclusion is to develop for us. First of all, however, it would be best to propose a hypothesis profitable to the soul for the scope of our letter, and, then, to direct our argument to what lies before us. Therefore, let us ask as in a logical problem: What is meant by the term 'Christian'?

For surely, a look at this question will not be without profit, since, if what is indicated by this name is determined accurately, we shall have much assistance for a life in accordance with virtue, provided, of course, that we are eager through a lofty discipline to be truly what the name signifies. For just as a person who longs to be called a doctor or an orator or a geometrician is not worthy of a title until he has some education as to what it means, that is, until he discovers from experience what he is being called, and just as the person wishing to be thus addressed in accordance with truth, so that the form of address will not be a misnomer, will want the use of the title to depend on the practice itself; in the same way, if we seek the true meaning of the word 'Christian' and find it, we will not choose not to conform to what the name implies when it is used of us, in order that the story about the monkey in secular literature[1] may not also be applicable to us.

They say that a certain showman in the city of Alexandria, having trained a monkey to dance with some grace, and having dressed him in a dancer's mask and a costume suitable for the occasion, and having surrounded him with a chorus, gained fame by the monkey's twisting himself in time with the music and concealing his nature in every way by what he was doing and what he appeared to be. While the audience was enthralled by the novelty of the spectacle, one of the clever persons present, by means of a trick, showed those watching the performance that the dancer was a monkey. When everyone was crying out and applauding the gesticulations of the monkey, who was moving rhythmically with the music,

---

1 Cf. Lucian *The Fisher* 36. For a discussion of St. Gregory's adaptation of this story, cf. Werner Jaeger, 'Von Affen und Wahren Christen,' *Scripta Minora* II (Rome 1960) 429 ff., and H. W. Janson, *Apes and Ape Lore in the Middle Ages and the Renaissance* (London 1952), 155.

they say that he threw onto the dancing place some of the sweetmeats which arouse the greediness of such animals; whereupon the monkey, without a moment's delay, when he saw the almonds scattered in front of the chorus, forgetting the dancing and the applause and the elaborate costume, ran after them and grabbed what he found in the palms of his hands. And in order that the mask would not get in the way of his mouth, he energetically thrust aside the disguise with his nails and immediately evoked a laugh from the spectators in place of the praise and admiration, as he emerged ugly and ridiculous from the shreds of the mask. Therefore, just as the assumed form was not sufficient for that creature to be considered a man, once his nature was disclosed in the incident of the almonds, so those individuals not truly shaping their own natures by faith will easily be disclosed in the toils of the devil as being something other than what they are called. For, instead of a fig or an almond or some such thing, vanity and love of honor and love of gain and love of pleasure, and whatever else the evil assembly of the devil places before greedy men instead of sweetmeats, easily bring to light the ape-like souls who, through pretense and imitation, play the role of the Christian and then remove the mask of moderation or meekness or some other virtue in a moment of personal crisis. It is necessary, therefore, for us to understand what the name 'Christian' means, for then, perhaps, we will become what the term implies and not be shown up by the one who perceives what is hidden, namely, that we have disguised ourselves by mere assent and by the pretense of the name alone when we are actually something contrary to what we appear to be.

Let us, then, consider, first of all, from the term itself what Christianity is. From those who are wiser it is, of course, possible for us to discover a meaning more profound and more noble in every way, and more in keeping with the dignity of the word. However, what we begin with is this: the word

'Christ,' exchanged for a clearer and more familiar word, means 'the king,' and Holy Scripture,[2] in accordance with proper usage, indicates royal dignity with such a word. But since, as Scripture says, the divine is inexpressible, incomprehensible, exceeding all comprehensive thought[3] the prophets, inspired by the Holy Spirit, and the apostles necessarily contribute with many words and ideas to our understanding of Christ's incorruptible nature, one setting us right about one divine idea and another about another. His dominion over all is suggested by reference to his kingship, and his purity and freedom from every passion and every evil is indicated by the names of the virtues, each being understood as referring to the Almighty. Such expressions are used as 'justice itself' and 'wisdom and power' and 'truth' and 'goodness' and 'life' and 'salvation' and 'incorruptibility' and 'permanence' and 'lack of change' and whatever elevated concept there is, and Christ is and is said to be all of them.[4] If, therefore, every lofty idea is conceived of in the name of Christ (for the other qualities mentioned are included under the higher designation, each of them being implied in the notion of royal power), perhaps some understanding of our interpretation of the term 'Christian' will follow. If we, who are united to Him by faith in Him, are synonymous with Him whose incorruptible nature is beyond verbal interpretation, it is entirely necessary for us to become what is contemplated in connection with that incorruptible nature and to achieve an identity with the secondary elements which follow along with it. For just as by participating in Christ we are given the title 'Christian,' so also are we drawn into a share in the lofty ideas which it implies. Just as in a chain, what draws

---

2 Cf. 1 Tim. 6.15.
3 Cf. 1 Tim. 6.16.
4 Of the nine expressions enumerated, the first six are Biblical: 'justice' (cf. Heb. 7.2), 'wisdom and power' (1 Cor. 1.24), 'truth' (John 14.6), 'goodness' (cf. John 7.12), 'life' (John 14.6), 'salvation' (Acts 4.12); the remaining three, St. Gregory has taken from the language of the philosophers.

the loop at the top also draws the next loops, in like manner, since the rest of the words interpreting His ineffable and multiform blessedness are joined to the word 'Christ,' it would be necessary for the person drawn along with Him to share these qualities with Him.

If, therefore, someone puts on the name of Christ, but does not exhibit in his life what is indicated by the term, such a person belies the name and puts on a lifeless mask in accordance with the model proposed to us. For it is not possible for Christ not to be justice and purity and truth and estrangement from all evil, nor is it possible to be a Christian (that is, truly a Christian) without displaying in oneself a participation in these virtues. If one can give a definition of Christianity, we shall define it as follows: Christianity is an imitation of the divine nature.[5] Now, let no one object to the definition as being immoderate and exceeding the lowliness of our nature; it does not go beyond our nature. Indeed, if anyone considers the first condition of man, he will find through the Scriptural teachings that the definition does not exceed the measure of our nature. The first man was constituted as an imitation of the likeness of God. So Moses, in philosophizing about man, where he says that God made man, states that: 'He created him in the image of God,'[6] and the word 'Christianity,' therefore, brings man back to his original good fortune.

But, if man was originally a likeness of God, perhaps we have not gone beyond the limit in declaring that Christianity is an imitation of the divine nature. Great, indeed, is the promise of this title. Perhaps it would be fitting to investigate also whether not conforming to the definition in one's life is without danger for one who makes use of the word. What is meant might become clear from examples. Assume that a professional painter is given a commission to paint a picture of the king for those living far away. If he draws a ridiculous

---

5 Cf. Plato *Theaet.* 176b; *Rep.* 613b.
6 Gen. 1.27.

and ugly shape on the wood and calls this ungracious figure an image of the king, would it not be likely that the powers that be would be annoyed, on the grounds that the handsome original had been insulted through this bad painting among those who had never seen the king? For people will necessarily think that the original is what the form on the icon shows him to be. If, then, the definition says that Christianity is an imitation of God, the person who has never been given an explanation of this mystery will think that the divine is such as he sees life among us to be, accepting it as a valid imitation of God, so that, if he sees models of complete goodness, he will believe that the divine revered by us is good; but, if someone is emotional and brutal, changing from one passion to another, and reflecting many forms of animals in his character (for it is easily possible to see how the changes in our nature correspond to animals[7]) when such a one calls himself a Christian and it is clear to all that the promise of the name proclaims an imitation of God, then, that person makes the divine, which is believed to be reflected in our private life, an object of blame among unbelievers. Scripture, therefore, utters a kind of fearful threat to such persons, crying: 'Woe to those on account of whom my name is blasphemed among the nations.'[8] and our Lord seems to me to be guiding our thoughts in this direction when He says to those able to hear: 'You are to be perfect, even as your heavenly Father is perfect.'[9] For, in naming the true Father of the faithful, He wishes the Father and those born through Him to be the same in the perfection of the goods contemplated in the Father.

Then you will ask me: 'How could it come about that human lowliness could be extended to the blessedness seen in God, since the implausibility in the command is immediately evident? How could it be possible for the earthly to be like the One in heaven, the very difference in nature proving the

---

7 Cf. Plato *Rep.* 588b ff.
8 Cf. Isa. 52.5.
9 Matt. 5.48.

unattainableness of the imitation? For it is as difficult to make oneself equal in appearance to the heavenly greatness and the beauties in it as it is for man on earth to make himself like the God of heaven.' But the explanation of this is clear. The Gospel does not order nature to be compounded with nature, I mean the human with the divine, but it does order the good actions to be imitated in our life as much as possible. But what actions of ours are like the actions of God? Those that are free from all evil, purifying themselves as far as possible in deed and word and thought from all vileness. This is truly the imitation of the divine and the perfection connected with the God of heaven.

It does not seem to me that the Gospel is speaking of the firmament of heaven as some remote habitation of God when it advises us to be perfect as our heavenly Father is perfect, because the divine is equally present in all things, and, in like manner, it pervades all creation and it does not exist separated from being, but the divine nature touches each element of being with equal honor, encompassing all things within itself. And the prophet teaches this saying, 'even if I am in heaven in my thought, even if I examine what is below the earth in my calculation you are present, even if I extend the intellectual part of my soul to the boundaries of being, I see all things in the power of your right hand,' for the text is as follows: 'If I go up to the heavens, you are there; if I sink to the nether world, you are present there. If I take the wings of the dawn, or settle at the farthest limits of the sea, even there your hand shall guide me, and your right hand hold me fast.'[10] It is possible to learn from these words that not being separated by choice from God is the same as living in heaven. Since the world above is known to be free from evil, Holy Scripture often mentions this to us symbolically, and since experiences connected with evil take place in this more material life below, the inventor of evil, the serpent,

---

10 Ps. 138.8-11.

crawls and creeps through life on earth, as is said of it in the symbolic statement: 'On your belly shall you crawl and dust shall you eat, all the days of your life.'[11] This kind of movement and this type of food explain to us that this refers to the life on earth which accepts the serpent of manifold evil and nurtures this creature that creeps upon it. Therefore, the One who orders us to imitate our Father orders us to separate ourselves from earthly passions, and this is a separation which does not come about through a change of place, but is achieved only through choice. If, then, estrangement from evil is accomplished only in the impetus of thought, the word of the Gospel enjoins nothing difficult upon us. There is no trouble connected with the onrush of thought, since it is possible for us without exertion to be present through thought wherever we wish to be, so that a heavenly sojourn is easy for anyone who wants it even on earth, as the Gospel suggests, by our thinking heavenly thoughts and depositing in the treasury there a wealth of virtue. 'Do not lay up for yourselves treasures on earth,' it says, 'but lay up for yourselves treasures in heaven, where neither moth nor rust consumes nor thieves break in and steal.'[12] In these words, Scripture indicates the incorruptible power that governs blessedness above. For in the midst of the moral filth of life here, we produce many different kinds of evil for ourselves, either we beget through our thoughts a moth, which, because of its corroding and destroying power, renders useless anything it grows upon unless it is shaken off, and creeps towards whatever is lying about, suggesting through its movement a path of destruction for those it comes near; or, if all is secure within, there is a conspiracy of external circumstances. Either the treasure of the heart is shut off through pleasure or the receptacle of the soul is rendered empty of virtue through some other experience, being distracted by desire or grief or some such emotion. But since the Lord says that in the treasures above

---
11 Gen. 3.14.
12 Matt. 6.19; cf. Luke 12.33.

neither moth nor rust is present, nor evil from theft which teaches us to be suspicious, we must transfer our activities to a region where what is stored is not only safe and undiminished forever, but where it also produces many kinds of interest. Because of the nature of the One receiving the deposit, it is altogether necessary that the return be amplified. For just as we, in accordance with our nature, accomplish little in making our deposit because we are what we are, so, also, it is likely that the One who is rich in every way will give to the depositor a return which reflects His nature. So let no one be discouraged when he brings into the divine treasury what is in keeping with his own power, assuming that he will go off with what corresponds to the amount he has given, but let him anticipate, according to the Gospel which says he will receive in exchange large for small, the heavenly for the earthly, the eternal for the temporal, such things as are not able to be grasped by thought or explained by word, concerning which: 'Eye has not seen, ear has not heard, nor has it entered into the heart of man, what things God has prepared for those who love him.'[18]

Thus, O cherished friend, we have given you payment in full, not only for the letters not sent before, but also in advance for the ones which may not be written hereafter. May you fare well in the Lord and may what is pleasing to God be always in your mind and heart and in mine.

---

[18] 1 Cor. 2.9.

ON PERFECTION

INTRODUCTION

THIS TREATISE HAS AN alternate title: 'On What It is Necessary for a Christian to be,' and, in the margin of one of the manuscripts, it is described as 'a letter characterizing the true Christian.' It is clearly related in subject matter to the foregoing letter to Harmonius on what it means to call oneself a Christian. In fact, it is an amplification of the conviction that St. Gregory expressed therein, that the essential activity of the Christian is to imitate the nature of God in whose image he has been created, and that this can only be achieved if man perfects his own nature by living a life of perfect virtue. Because of the enlargement upon this theme, the treatise is thought to be later in date than the letter to Harmonius. It is in every way a more formal work and less revealing of the author, although, in the opening paragraph, there is an appealing personal note when St. Gregory states that he feels that he himself has not advanced sufficiently in virtue to offer his own life as a model. There is some doubt about the identity of the person to whom the letter is addressed since three persons are named in the manuscripts. One of those named is Olympius, the ascetic to whom St. Gregory's biography of his sister, St. Macrina, is addressed.

In the introduction, we are again reminded of the incongruity of a man who calls himself a Christian, but is inconsistent in his practice of Christianity, and St. Gregory warns that the Christian who is not recognized as such in his entirety is a kind of monster not unlike the fabled Minotaur and the centaurs. Despite its title, the work might better have been called 'Christ, the Model of Perfection' since the central portion of it consists of a detailed analysis of some thirty references to Christ in the writings of St. Paul, who, according to St. Gregory, knew more than any other person what Christ is, and transformed his own soul by his imitation of Christ.

The treatise has rightly been referred to as St. Gregory's Christology because in it he provides us with a systematic commentary on each of the terms which St. Paul applied to Christ. There are still echoes of St. Gregory's Platonic way of thinking, as when, in his discussion of the power and wisdom of Christ, he says that one's belief in them should be connected with 'the possession of the good,' and that, in applying to ourselves the idea that Christ is peace, what we must aim at is not only peace with our neighbor, but a harmony of the dissonant parts of our own being. However, emphasis is placed more on the specifically Christian themes, e.g., Christ the Redeemer who has purchased us from death, Christ the paschal victim, Christ as propitiation. There is a soaring toward mysticism in St. Gregory's referring to Christ as 'the brightness of glory and the figure of his substance.' St. Paul's image of Christ as the 'corner stone' provides the author with an opportunity to develop a brilliant passage filled with architectural symbols. Ingenious, also, is St. Gregory's allegory of the Christian as a student of painting who must strive to capture the qualities of his model Christ by the use of the colors of meekness and patience. And finally, lest an objection be made that a human being cannot hope to imitate God whose nature is immutable, St. Gregory extols man's capability of changing which allows for a continuous process of perfection like a kind of 'wing of flight to greater achievements.'

ON PERFECTION

OUR ZEAL TO KNOW HOW ANYONE may become perfect through a life of virtue so that you may achieve a blamelessness in all things is in keeping with your purpose in life. I could have considered it of great importance that patterns for everything that you are striving for be found in my life, so as to furnish you with the instruction you seek through deeds rather than words. In that way, my guidance towards what is good would have been worthy of belief, because my life was in tune with my words. But, although I pray that this may one day be true, I do not yet see myself as one whose life could be offered to you as an example in place of a treatise. Therefore, in order that I may not seem to be completely useless and incapable of making a contribution to your goal, I have decided to set before you an accurate description of the life towards which one must tend, making this the beginning of my discourse.

Our good Master, Jesus Christ, bestowed on us a partnership in His revered name, so that we get our name from no other person connected with us, and if one happens to be rich and well-born or of lowly origin and poor, or if one has some distinction from his business or position, all such conditions are of no avail because the one authoritative name for those believing in Him is that of 'Christian.' Now, since this grace was ordained for us from above, it is necessary, first of all, for us to understand the greatness of the gift so that we can worthily thank the God who has given it to us. Then, it is necessary to show through our life that we ourselves are what the power of this great name requires us to be. The greatness of the gift of which we are deemed worthy through the partnership with the Master becomes clear to us if we recognize the true significance of the name of Christ, so that when in our prayers we call upon the Lord of all by this name, we may comprehend the concept that we are taking into our soul. We must also understand reverently what we believe He is when He is called upon by this name. When we do understand this, we shall, as a consequence, also learn clearly what sort of persons we should be shown to be as a result of our zeal for this way of life and our use of His name as the instructor and the guide for our life. Accordingly, if we make St. Paul our leader in these two undertakings, we shall have the safest guide to the plain truth of what we are seeking. For he, most of all, knew what Christ is, and he indicated by what he did the kind of person named for Him, imitating Him so brilliantly that he revealed his own Master in himself, his own soul being transformed through his accurate imitation of his prototype, so that Paul no longer seemed to be living and speaking, but Christ Himself seemed to be living in him. As this astute perceiver of particular goods says: 'Do you seek a proof of the Christ who speaks in me?'[1] and: 'It is now no longer I that live but Christ lives in me.'[2]

This man knew the significance of the name of Christ for us, saying that Christ is 'the power of God and the wisdom of God.'[3] And he called Him 'peace,'[4] and 'light inaccessible'[5] in whom God dwells, and 'sanctification and redemption,'[6] and 'great high priest,'[7] and 'passover,'[8] and 'a propitation'[9] of souls, 'the brightness of glory and the image of substance,'[10]

---

1 2 Cor. 13.3.
2 Gal. 2.20.
3 1 Cor. 1.24.
4 Eph. 2.14.
5 1 Tim. 6.16.
6 1 Cor. 1.30.
7 Heb. 4.14.
8 1 Cor. 5.7.
9 Rom. 3.25.
10 Heb. 1.3.

and 'maker of the world,'[11] and 'spiritual food'[12] and 'spiritual drink and spiritual rock,'[13] 'water,'[14] 'foundation'[15] of faith, and 'corner stone,'[16] and 'image of the invisible God,'[17] and 'great God,'[18] and 'head of the body of the Church,'[19] and 'the firstborn of every creature,'[20] and 'first-fruits of those who have fallen asleep,'[21] 'firstborn from the dead,'[22] 'firstborn among many brethren,'[23] and 'mediator between God and men,'[24] and 'only-begotten Son,'[25] and 'crowned with glory and honor,'[26] and 'lord of glory,'[27] and 'beginning'[28] of being, speaking thus of Him who is the beginning, 'king of justice and king of peace,'[29] and 'ineffable king of all, having the power of the kingdom,'[30] and many other such things that are not easily enumerated. When all of these phrases are put next to each other, each one of the terms makes its own contribution to a revelation of what is signified by being named after Christ and each provides for us a certain emphasis. To the extent that we take these concepts into our souls, they are all indications of the unspeakable greatness of the gift for us. However, since the rank of kingship underlies all worth and power and rule, by this title the royal power of Christ is authoritatively and primarily indicated (for the anointing of kingship, as we learn in the historical books,

---

11 Heb. 1.2.
12 1 Cor. 10.3.
13 1 Cor. 10.4.
14 John 4.13 ff.
15 1 Cor. 3.11.
16 Matt. 21.42; Mark 12.10; Luke 20.17.
17 Col. 1.15.
18 Tit. 2.13.
19 Cf. Col. 1.18.
20 Col. 1.15.
21 1 Cor. 15.20.
22 Col. 1.18.
23 Rom. 8.29.
24 1 Tim. 2.5.
25 John 3.17.
26 Heb. 2.7; cf. Ps. 8.6.
27 Cf. 1 Cor. 2.8.
28 Col. 1.18.
29 Heb. 7.2.
30 Cf. Luke 1.33.

comes first),[31] and all the force of the other titles depends on that of royalty. For this reason, the person who knows the separate elements included under it also knows the power encompassing these elements. But it is the kingship itself which declares what the title of Christ means.

Therefore, since, thanks to our good Master, we are sharers of the greatest and the most divine and the first of names, those honored by the name of Christ being called Christians, it is necessary that there be seen in us also all of the connotations of this name, so that the title be not a misnomer in our case, but that our life be a testimony of it. Being something does not result from being called something. The underlying nature, whatever it happens to be, is discovered through the meaning attached to the name. What do I mean? If someone calls man a tree or a rock, will he, on this account, be a plant or stone? Of course not. It is necessary for him, first of all, to be a man, and, then, to be addressed thus in keeping with his nature. For titles based on similarities have no validity, as if one could say that a man is a statue or an imitation horse. If anything is named validly and not falsely, his nature completely reveals the form of address as a true one. Wood disguised in any way at all is still called wood, bronze is called bronze, stone is called stone, or any other such substance upon which art, shaping it contrary to expectation, imposes a form.

It is necessary, then, for those calling themselves after Christ, first of all, to become what the name implies, and, then, to adapt themselves to the title. We distinguish a man himself from what is considered a good likeness of him in a picture by noting characteristic differences. The man we call a logical thinking animal, the picture an inanimate piece of wood which has taken on the form of the man through imitation; so, also, shall we distinguish the true Christian from the one merely seeming to be a Christian through the individual

---

31 1 Kings 9.16; 10.1 ff.; 12 ff.

elements in his character. The marks of the true Christian are all those we know in connection with Christ. Those that we have room for we imitate, and those which our nature does not approximate by imitation, we reverence and worship. Thus, it is necessary for the Christian life to illustrate all the interpretative terms signifying Christ, some through imitation, others through worship, if 'the man of God is to be perfect'[32] as the apostle says, and this perfection must never be mutilated by evil.

There are men who fashion mythical creatures in their speeches and writings, constructing bull-headed horses or centaurs or serpent-footed monsters or other such things made up of different species. They do not achieve an imitation in keeping with a natural archetype, and, illogically overstepping nature, they fashion something other than man, fabricating the impossible. We would not say that what they have constructed in this strange synthesis is a man, even if some parts of the figure happen to resemble certain parts of the human body. In the same way, a person cannot accurately be called a Christian if he does not give assent to the faith with his mind, even if he conforms to it in other respects, or if his mind gives assent, but his body is not suited to his way of life, exhibiting the anger of dragons and the bestiality of serpents, or adding to his human character an equine madness for women. In such cases, a man becomes double-natured, a centaur made up of reason and passion. It is possible to see many such people: either they resemble the Minotaur, being bull-headed in their belief in idolatry, although they appear to be leading a good life; or they make themselves centaurs and dragons by combining with a Christian facade a bestial body. Now, since, as in the case of the human body, the Christian should be recognized in his entirety, it is fitting for the characteristics of his life to represent a pledge of all the good qualities connected with Christ. For being in some respects what the name im-

---

32 2 Tim. 3.17.

plies, but in others inclining towards the opposite, is to cut oneself apart into a battleground where there are two factions, one of good and one of evil, and thus one becomes truceless to oneself and inconsistent. For, says the apostle: 'What fellowship has light with darkness?'[33]

Since there is a distinct and irreconcilable contradiction between light and darkness, the person partaking of both has a share in neither, because of the opposition of the parts drawn up against each other at the same time in his mixed life. His faith provides the lighted part, but his dark habits put out the lamp of reason. Since it is impossible and inconsistent for light and darkness to exist in fellowship, the person containing each of the opposites becomes an enemy to himself, being divided in two ways between virtue and evil, and he sets up an antagonistic battle line within himself. And just as it is not possible, when there are two enemies, for both to be victors over each other (for the victory of the one causes the death of his adversary), so, also, in this civil war brought about by the confusion in his life, it is not possible for the stronger element to win without the other becoming completely destroyed. For how will the army of reverence be stronger than evil, when the wicked phalanx of the opponents attacks it? If the stronger is going to win, the enemy must be completely slaughtered. And thus, virtue will have the victory over evil only when the entire enemy gives way to it through an alliance of the reasonable elements against the unsound ones. Then will be fulfilled what was spoken from the mouth of God through prophecy: 'It is I who bring both life and death.'[34] For it is not possible for the good to exist in me, unless it is made to live through the death of my enemy. As long as we keep grasping opposites with each of our hands, it is impossible for there to be participation in both elements in the same being. For, if we are holding evil, we lose the power to take hold of virtue.

---

[33] 2 Cor. 6.14.
[34] Deut. 32.39.

Therefore, let us take up the original argument, namely, that the one road to the pure and divine life for lovers of virtue is knowing what the name of Christ means, in conformity with which we must shape our lives, attuning it to virtue through the emphasis on the other terms which we gathered together in our introduction from the holy voice of Paul. Placing these before us with the prescribed zeal, we shall make them the safest guide for a life of virtue, imitating some of these traits, as we said in the first part, and revering and worshiping others. Let the marshaling of these be a battle line for us. Let us begin with the first: 'Christ,' it says, 'is the power of God and the wisdom of God.'[35] Through this description of Christ, we derive, first of all, notions befitting the divine which make the name an object of reverence for us. Since all creation, both whatever is known through perception and whatever lies beyond observation, came into being through Him and is united with Him, wisdom is necessarily interwoven with power in connection with the definition of Christ, the maker of all things. We know this through the yoking together of the two words, I mean, power and wisdom, because these great and indescribable wonders of creation would not exist if wisdom had not thought of their coming into being, nor would they exist if power, through which thoughts become deeds, had not accompanied wisdom in bringing the thought to completion.

The meaning of Christ is appropriately divided into this double emphasis on wisdom and power in order that, when we behold the greatness of the composition of being, we may recognize His unspeakable power through what we comprehend, and, in order that, when we calculate how all things that did not exist before came into being (the multiform nature in being having been endowed with substance through the divine nod), we then worship the incomprehensible wisdom of the One who thought of these things. Indeed, it is

---

[35] 1 Cor. 1.24.

not useless or without benefit to us to believe in the power
and wisdom of Christ in connection with the possession of
the good. For, when a person prays, he draws to himself
through prayer what he is invoking and looking towards
with the eye of his soul. Thus, the person looking towards
power (Christ is power) 'is strengthened with power unto the
inner man,' as the apostle says,[36] and the person calling upon
the wisdom which the Lord knows of old becomes wise, as our
introduction stated. Indeed, the person synonymous with
Christ, who is power and wisdom, having been empowered
against sin, will also exhibit wisdom in himself by his wise
choice. When wisdom and power are displayed in us, the one
choosing what is fair, and the other confirming the choice, a
perfection of life interwoven with both of these qualities is
achieved.

Recognizing Christ as 'peace,'[37] we shall exhibit the true
title of Christian in ourselves through the peace in our life.
For the One 'has slain enmity,' as the apostle says.[38] Let us
not, therefore, bring it to life in ourselves, but rather show
through our life that it is dead. Let us not raise up against
ourselves through anger and backbiting what has been rightly
deadened for our salvation by God. This would destroy our
soul and bring about an evil resurrection of what is rightly
dead. But, if we have Christ, who is peace, let us also deaden
hatred in ourselves in order to achieve in our life what we
believe is in Him. For that One 'has broken down the inter-
vening wall of the enclosure,'[39] and, out of the two elements
in Himself, has created 'one new man,'[40] and made peace.
Therefore, let us also reconcile, not only those fighting against
us on the outside, but also the elements at variance within us,
in order that no longer may the 'flesh lust against the spirit

---

36 Cf. Eph. 3.16.
37 Eph. 2.14.
38 Eph. 2.16.
39 Eph. 2.14.
40 Eph. 2.15.

and the spirit against the flesh.'[41] Subjecting the spirit of the flesh to divine law, let us live peacefully, having been dissolved into the new and peaceful man and having become one from two. For the definition of peace is the harmony of dissonant parts. Once the civil war in our nature is expelled, then, we also, being at peace within ourselves, become peace, and reveal our having taken on the name of Christ as true and authentic.

Knowing Christ as the 'true light,'[42] 'inaccessible'[43] to falsehood, we learn this, namely, that it is necessary for our lives also to be illuminated by the rays of the true light. But virtues are the rays of 'the Sun of Justice,'[44] streaming forth for our illumination, through which we 'lay aside the works of darkness,'[45] so that we 'walk becomingly as in the day,'[46] and 'we renounce those things which shame conceals.'[47] By doing all things in the light, we become the light itself, so that it 'shines' before others,[48] which is the peculiar quality of light. And if we recognize Christ as 'sanctification,'[49] in whom every action is steadfast and pure, let us prove by our life that we ourselves stand apart, being ourselves true sharers of His name, coinciding in deed and not in word with the power of his sanctification.

And learning that Christ is 'redemption'[50] because He gave Himself as an atonement in our behalf, we are taught this knowledge, that when He furnished us with immortality as our particular possession, as if bestowing a certain honor on each soul, He ransomed us from death with His own life. If, then, we become slaves of the One who redeemed us, we

---
41 Gal. 5.17; cf. Rom. 8.6,7.
42 John 1.9.
43 1 Tim. 6.16.
44 Mal. 3.20.
45 Rom. 13.12.
46 Rom. 13.13.
47 2 Cor. 4.2.
48 Cf. Matt. 5.15,16.
49 1 Cor. 1.30.
50 1 Cor. 1.30.

shall look exclusively towards our Master, on the grounds that we no longer live for ourselves, but for the One who possesses us, because He gave His life for us. For we are no longer lords of ourselves, but the possessions of Him who, having bought us, is the Master of His own. Truly, the will of the Master will be the law of our life. And as 'the law of sin'[51] governed us when death was prevailing, so now, that we have become the property of life, it is necessary for us to conform to the government in power. Let us, therefore, never turn aside from the will of life and desert through sin to the wicked tyrant of souls of old, I mean to death.

We are assimilated to Christ, also, if we hear from Paul that he is the 'passover'[52] and 'high priest.'[53] For Christ was truly sacrificed as the paschal victim in our behalf. But the priest, bringing in the sacrifice to God, is no other than Christ Himself. For it says: 'He delivered himself up for us, an offering and a sacrifice.'[54] Through these words we learn this, that the person looking towards that One delivers himself as an offering and sacrifice and passover, and will show himself to God as a living sacrifice, 'holy, pleasing to God,' becoming a reasonable 'service.'[55] But the rule of this holy office is: 'Be not conformed to this world, but be transformed in the newness of your mind, that you may discern what is the good and acceptable and the perfect will of God.'[56] If the flesh lives and is not sacrificed according to the law of the spirit, it is not possible for the will of God to be displayed in it: 'For the wisdom of the flesh is hostile to God and is not subject to the law of God.'[57] As long as the flesh lives, which was offered up through the life-giving sacrifice by 'mortifying the members upon the earth'[58] from which pas-

---

51 Rom. 8.2.
52 1 Cor. 5.7.
53 Heb. 4.14.
54 Eph. 5.2.
55 Cf. Rom. 12.1.
56 Rom. 12.2.
57 Rom. 8.7.
58 Cf. Col. 3.5.

sions spring, it is not possible for the pleasing and perfect will of God to be achieved expeditiously in the life of the faithful.

So, also, Christ, being known as 'a propitiation by his own blood,'[59] teaches each one thinking of this to become himself a propitiation, sanctifying his soul by the deadening of his members. And when Christ is spoken of as 'the brightness of his glory and the image of his substance,'[60] we get from these words the idea of His greatness in the act of being worshiped. For Paul, truly God-inspired and God-taught, examining, 'in the depth of the riches of the wisdom and of the knowledge of God,'[61] the unclear and hidden aspects of the divine mysteries, revealed through suggestive phrases the illuminations[62] that came to him from God concerning the understanding of what is incomprehensible and unsearchable because the tongue is no match for thought. According to the report of those who heard his interpretation of mystery, he spoke, as well as reason can, in the service of thought. For, comprehending as much as human power can concerning the divine nature, he revealed the unapproachable and incomprehensible Logos of substantial being in human terms.

Accordingly, when speaking of the theories concerning the divine nature as peace and power and life and justice and light and truth and such things, he maintained that an account of that nature itself was completely unattainable, saying that God has not been seen and will not be seen. For he says: 'No man has seen or can see' Him.[63] Because of this, when he was asking how to give a name to what cannot be grasped in thought and did not discover a word expressing an interpretation of the incomprehensible, he called whatever underlies all good, and is not sufficiently known or spoken of, 'glory' and 'substance.' The underlying essence of being, he

---

59 Rom. 3.25.
60 Heb. 1.3.
61 Rom. 11.33.
62 Cf. 2 Cor. 12.4.
63 1 Tim. 6.16.

dismissed as unnamable. However, interpreting the unity and inseparability of the Son and the Father and the Son's being contemplated indefinably and invisibly with the indefinable and unseen Father, he addressed Him as 'effulgence of glory' and 'image of substance,' indicating the unity of their nature by the word 'effulgence' and their equality by the word 'image.' For, in connection with an effulgent nature, there is no middle point in a beam of light, nor is there an inferior part of an image in connection with a substance determined by it. The observer of the effulgent nature will know the effulgence in its entirety, and the person comprehending the size of the substance measures it in its entirety with its accompanying image. So he speaks of the Lord as 'the form of God,'[64] not belittling the Lord by the idea of form, but showing the bigness of God through the word, in which the immensity of the Father is contemplated as never exceeding its own form or being found outside of its specific character. For there is nothing formless or unadorned in respect to the Father which does not rejoice in the beauty of the only-begotten Son. Therefore, the Lord says: 'He who sees me, sees also the Father,'[65] indicating through this that there is no deficiency and no excess. But he also means that He upholds 'all things with the word of His power,'[66] and thus dissolves the difficulty of the busy-bodies who seek the undiscoverable when they look for an account of matter and nowhere check their curiosity, asking how the material is experienced by the immaterial, quantity by that without quantity, form by that without form, color by the unseeable and the finite by the infinite, and how, if there is no quality connected with the simple and the uncomposed, matter is interwoven with it. He solves all such inquiries by saying that the Logos 'upholds all things by the word of His power' from non-existence to existence. For all things, as many as exist in connection with

---

64 Cf. Phil. 2.6.
65 John 14.9.
66 Heb. 1.3.

matter and as many as have received an immaterial nature, have one cause of their substance: the Word of the unspeakable power. From these words, we learn to look to Him as the source of being. If we pass into being from that source and have our existence in Him, there is every necessity to believe that there is nothing outside of the One in whom we exist and from whom we come into being, and back to whom we go. Along with this thought, the blamelessness of our life is likewise established. For what person who believes that he lives 'from Him and through Him and unto Him'[67] will dare to make the One who encompasses in Himself the life of each of us, a witness of a life that does not reflect Him?

The divine apostle also, in calling the Lord 'spiritual food and drink,'[68] suggests that he knows that human nature is not simple, but that there is an intelligible part mixed with a sensual part and that a particular type of nurture is needed for each of the elements in us, sensible food to strengthen our bodies, and spiritual food for the well-being of our souls. And just as in the case of the body, the firm and the fluid, mingling with each other, preserve our nature through digestion, in the same way, by analogy, Paul distinguishes the nurture of the intelligible part, using the same terms, food and drink, and adapting them properly to the needs of those assimilating them. For to those who are exhausted and fainting, bread comes to strengthen the heart of a man, but to those who are weary because of the wretchedness of their life and thirsty because of this, wine comes as a joy to their heart.[69]

Now, it is necessary from what has been said to know the power of the Logos by which the soul is nourished according to its need, having received grace from it according to the riddle of the prophet who points out clearly the relief which comes to the weary from the Logos 'in verdant pastures and in restful waters.'[70] And if someone in examining this mystery

---
67 Rom. 11.36.
68 1 Cor. 10.3,4.
69 Cf. Ps. 103.15.
70 Ps. 22.2.

should say that the Lord is rightly called 'spiritual food and drink,' he is not far from the truth. For His 'flesh is food indeed' and His 'blood is drink indeed.'[71] But, in connection with the thought just mentioned, there is participation in such nourishment for all, since the Logos who becomes food and drink is received and assimilated without distinction by those seeking Him. However, in connection with another idea, the participation in this food and drink is not careless or indiscriminate, for the apostle limits it thus: 'Let a man prove himself and so let him eat of that bread and drink of the cup, for he who eats and drinks unworthily eats and drinks judgment to himself.'[72] The evangelist, also, seems to point this out definitely, at the time of the mystical passion when that good councilor took down the body of the Lord and wrapped Him in spotless and pure linen and placed Him in a new and pure sepulcher.[73] Thus, the command of the apostle and the observation of the evangelist become a law to all to receive the Holy Body with a pure conscience. If there is somewhere some stain from sin, we must wash it out with the water of our tears.

And when Christ is called 'a rock,'[74] this word assists us in the firmness and permanence of our virtuous life, that is, in the steadfastness of our endurance of suffering, and in our soul's opposition and inaccessibility to the assaults of sin. Through these and such things, we also will be a rock, imitating, as far as is possible in our changing nature, the unchanging and permanent nature of the Master. And if the same One is called 'the wise builder and the foundation'[75] of faith and the 'corner stone,'[76] neither will this be shown to be without profit for us in leading a virtuous life. For we

---

71 John 6.56.
72 1 Cor. 11.28.
73 Cf. Luke 23.53.
74 1 Cor. 10.4.
75 1 Cor. 3.10.
76 Eph. 2.20; Luke 20.17.

learn through this that the beginning and end of all good government and good learning and practice is the Lord.

And 'the hope'[77] which we know to be the same as the cornerstone towards which all things tend, if they are zealously pursued in virtue, is that One so named by Paul. The beginning of this high 'tower'[78] of life is our faith in Him, upon which we build, putting down the principles of our life as a kind of foundation, and, through our daily achievements, we erect pure thoughts and actions upon it. Thus, the cornerstone of all becomes our cornerstone, fitting Himself diagonally to the two walls of our life which are built out of our body and soul with elegance and correctness. But if one part of the building is deficient, if the external elegance does not correspond to the correctness of the soul, or if the soul's virtue does not balance the outward appearance, Christ, in fitting Himself to a single portion of a double structure, becomes the cornerstone of a half-completed life. For it is not possible for a cornerstone to exist if two walls do not join. The beauty of the chief cornerstone sets off our building when our dualistic existence, straight and true, is harmoniously set up according to the right rule of life by the plumb line of the virtues, having nothing in itself that is bent or crooked.

But when Paul calls Christ 'the image of the invisible God,'[79] meaning the God over all and the great God (and with these words he proclaims the glory of the true Master, speaking of 'our great God and Savior Jesus Christ'[80] and the One 'from whom is Christ according to the flesh, who is over all things, God blessed forever'[81])—saying these things, then, he teaches us what is the One existing forever. It is that thing which only the existing One knows, and, at all times, it exceeds human comprehension in equal measure, even

---
77 Col. 1.27.
78 Luke 14.28.
79 Col. 1.15.
80 Tit. 2.13.
81 Rom. 9.5.

if the person who always 'minds the things which are above'[82] comes near to it in his moral progress. Accordingly, this Person who is beyond knowledge and comprehension, the ineffable and the 'unspeakable'[83] and the 'inexpressible,'[84] in order that He might again make Himself an 'image of God,' because of His love for man, became Himself an 'image of the invisible God' so that he took on the form which He assumed among you, and again, through Himself, He fashioned a beauty in accord with the character of the Archetype. Therefore, if we also are to become an 'image of the invisible God,' it is fitting that the form of our life be struck according to the 'example'[85] of the life set before us. But what is that? It is living in the flesh, but not 'according to the flesh.'[86] The Prototype, 'the image of the invisible God,' living in His virginity, underwent all temptations because of the similarity of His nature to ours, but He did not share the experience of a single sin: 'Who did no sin, neither was deceit found in His mouth.'[87] Therefore, just as when we are learning the art of painting, the teacher puts before us on a panel a beautifully executed model, and it is necessary for each student to imitate in every way the beauty of that model on his own panel, so that the panels of all will be adorned in accordance with the example of the beauty set before them; in the same way, since every person is the painter of his own life, and choice is the craftsman of the work, and the virtues are the paints for executing the image, there is no small danger that the imitation may change the Prototype into a hateful and ugly person instead of reproducing the master form if we sketch in the character of evil with muddy colors. But, since it is possible, one must prepare the pure colors of the virtues, mixing them with each other according to some artistic

---

[82] Col. 3.2.
[83] 1 Pet. 1.8.
[84] Cf. 2 Cor. 9.15.
[85] Cf. John 13.15.
[86] Rom. 8.12.
[87] 1 Pet. 2.22.

formula for the imitation of beauty, so that we become an image of the image, having achieved the beauty of the Prototype through activity as a kind of imitation, as did Paul, who became an 'imitator of Christ,'[88] through his life of virtue.

If it is necessary to distinguish the individual colors through which the imitation comes about, one color is meekness, for he says: 'Learn from me, for I am meek and humble of heart.'[89] Another color is patience which appears quantitatively in 'the image of the invisible God.' A sword, clubs, chains, whips, slaps in the face, the face spat upon, the back beaten, irreverent judgment, a harsh denial, soldiers mocking, the sullen rejection with jests and sarcasm and insults, blows from a reed, nails and gall and vinegar, and all of these terrible things were applied to Him without cause, nay, rather, in return for innumerable good works! And how were those who did these things repaid? 'Father, forgive them, for they do not know what they are doing.'[90] Was it not possible for Him to bring the sky down upon them, or to bury these insolent men in a chasm of the earth, or to throw them down from their own mountains into the sea, or to inundate the earth with the depths of ocean, or to send down upon them the Sodomitic rain of fire, or to do any other angry deed in revenge? Instead, He bore all these things in meekness and patience, legislating patience for your life through Himself. Thus, it is possible to see all the features of the Prototype, the image of God. Looking towards that image and adorning our own form clearly in accordance with that One, each person becomes himself an 'image of the invisible God,' having been portrayed through endurance.

But learning that Christ is the 'head of the Church,'[91] let this be considered before all else, that every head is of the same nature and the same essence as the body subordinate to

---
88 1 Cor. 4.16.
89 Matt. 11.29.
90 Luke 23.34.
91 Eph. 5.23.

it, and there is a unity of the individual parts with the whole, accomplishing by their common respiration a complete sympathy of all the parts. Therefore, if any part is divorced from the body, it is also altogether alienated from the head. Reason tells us through these words that whatever the head is by nature, this the individual parts become, in order to be in communion with the head. But we are the parts who make up the body of Christ. If, then, anyone removes one of the members of the body of Christ and makes it 'the member of a harlot,'[92] hurling unrestrained madness at Him like a sword, through this evil emotion, he alienates the member completely from the head. So, also, all the other instruments of evil become swords through which the members are cut off from the body and separated from the head by the emotions which effected the cutting. In order for the body, therefore, to remain whole in its nature, it is fitting for the separate parts to be in communion with the head; for example, if we assume purity to be logically an essential quality of the head, it is altogether necessary for the members subordinate to the head to be pure. And if we know that the head is incorruptible, then, the members also must be incorruptible. And thus, all other notions one has about the head must necessarily be applied to the members: peace, holiness, truth, and all such things. These similar qualities in the members testify to their union with the head. The apostle says that One is 'the Head,' but 'from Him the whole body (being closely joined and knit together through every joint of the system according to the functioning in due measure of each single part) derives its increase.'[93] And it is fitting for this to be taught through the word 'head,' for, just as in the case of animals, the impulse towards action is given to the body from the head. The movement of the feet and the action of the hands control each act through sight and hearing and, if the eye is not directing or the ear not receiving guidance, it is not possible for any

---
92 Cf. 1 Cor. 6.15 ff.
93 Eph. 4.16.

of the necessary actions to come about. Thus, it is necessary for us, also, to move our bodies in accordance with the true Head towards every action and undertaking, wherever 'He that formed the eye' or 'He who shaped the ear'[94] leads. Moreover, since the Head looks 'to the things above,' it is entirely necessary for the members being in harmony with Him to follow His lead and to be inclined to the things above.

But, when we hear that He is 'the firstborn of every creature'[95] and 'firstborn from the dead,'[96] and 'the firstborn among many brethren,'[97] let us, first of all, dismiss the heretical assumptions, since the shameful dogmatic implications of these have nothing to do with those phrases. And, after that, let us determine the ethical implication of these words for our life. For when those who are fighting against God say that the 'only-begotten' God, 'the creator of all,' the One 'from whom and through whom and unto whom all things are,'[98] is the work and creation and product of God, and, on this account, interpret the phrase 'the firstborn of every creature' as meaning that He is the brother of every creature, taking precedence because of the rights of the eldest in time, as Reuben[99] does over his own brothers, and that He is placed first, not because of His nature, but because of the rights of the eldest, this must, first of all, be said to them, that it is not possible for the same person to be believed to be the only-begotten and the firstborn. For the only-begotten is not thought of as having brothers and the firstborn is not thought of apart from his brothers, but, if one is only-begotten, he does not have brothers; and, if he is the firstborn of brothers, it is altogether impossible for him to be or to be spoken of as only-begotten. Therefore, these words do not coincide and have no common application to

---
94 Ps. 93.9.
95 Col. 1.15.
96 Col. 1.18.
97 Rom. 8.29.
98 Rom. 11.36.
99 Cf. Gen. 29.32.

the same person, since it is not possible for the same person to be called the two things, only-begotten and firstborn. And yet it is said in the Scripture concerning the Logos that He is an 'only-begotten' God and, again, in Paul, that he is 'the firstborn of every creature.' Therefore, it is fitting to distinguish each of these phrases, analyzing them accurately by the criterion of truth. The Logos existing before time is 'only-begotten'; but, since all creation after this came into being in Christ, the Logos made flesh is 'the firstborn' of creation. And whatever thought comes to us when we learn that He is the 'firstborn from the dead' and the 'firstborn among many brethren,' let us understand it as following upon the concept of Him as 'the firstborn of every creature.' Indeed, 'the firstborn of the dead' becomes the One born as 'the first fruits of those who have fallen asleep,'[100] in order to provide for the resurrection of all flesh. Through His engendering from above, and through His making us 'children of the day and children of light,'[101] born 'of water and the Spirit,'[102] although we are those 'who were by nature children of wrath,'[103] He Himself acts as our guide in this birth in the water of the Jordan, sprinkling on us the grace of the Spirit in accordance with the first fruits of his nature. Thus, all those brought into life by this spiritual rebirth are called brothers of the One born before them 'through water and the spirit.' In the same way, also, thinking of Him as the firstborn of every 'new creature in Christ,'[104] we do not go beyond a reverent interpretation. For when the old creature transgressed and became useless through sin, the new creature necessarily took on the role of those who had disappeared, having been formed through the rebirth and 'the resurrection from the dead.'[105] Because He is considered the leader in

---

100 1 Cor. 15.20.
101 1 Thess. 5.5.
102 John 3.5.
103 Eph. 2.3.
104 2 Cor. 5.17.
105 Cf. Acts 3.15.

this life, He is and He is called 'the firstborn of every creature.' How necessary it is to have truth as a self-sufficient ally could easily be demonstrated to the attentive by the few words that have been said. But, how these words appear to contribute to a virtuous life, we shall now explain briefly.

Reuben[106] was the firstborn of those born after him, and their resemblance to him bore witness to their relationship to him, so that their brotherhood was not unrecognized, being testified to by the similarity of appearance. Therefore, if, through the same rebirth 'by water and the spirit,' we also have become brothers of the Lord, He having become for us 'the firstborn among the many brethren,' it follows that our nearness to Him will show in the character of our life, because 'the firstborn of every creature' has informed our life. But what have we learned from Scripture that the character of His life is? What we have said many times, that: 'He committed no sin, nor was deceit found in his mouth.'[107] Therefore, if we are going to act as brothers of the One who gave us birth, the sinlessness of our life will be a pledge of our relationship to Him and no filth will nullify our union with His purity. But the firstborn is also justice and holiness and love and redemption and such things. So if our life is characterized by such qualities, we furnish clear tokens of our noble birth, and anyone, seeing these qualities in our life, will bear witness to our brotherhood with Christ. For He Himself opened the door of the resurrection and, on this account, became 'the firstborn of them that sleep.' He indicated this, that we shall all rise 'in the twinkling of an eye, at the last trumpet,'[108] and He did this for those who were with Him and the rest who are conquered by death.

Nor in the life after this will there be the same resurrection for all who rise from the tomb of earth, for it says: 'They who have done good shall come forth unto resurrection of life;

---
106 Cf. Gen. 29.32.
107 Cf. 1 Pet. 2.22.
108 1 Cor. 15.52.

but they who have done evil unto resurrection of judgment.'[109] So that if someone's life tends toward the fearful judgment, that person, even if he happened to be numbered among the brethren of the Lord through the birth from on high, belies the name and denies his nearness to the firstborn because of his evil form. But, 'the Mediator between God and men'[110] who through Himself joins the human being to God connects to God only that which is worthy of union with Him. For just as He in Himself assimilated His own human nature to the power of the Godhead, being a part of the common nature, but not being subject to the inclination to sin which is in that nature (for it says: 'He did no sin, nor was deceit found in his mouth'), so, also, will He lead each person to union with the Godhead if they do nothing unworthy of union with the Divine. But, if anyone is truly 'the temple of God,'[111] containing no idol or shrine of evil in himself, this person is given a share in the Godhead by the Mediator, having become pure through the reception of His purity. 'Into a soul that plots, evil wisdom enters not,'[112] as Scripture says, nor does 'the clean of heart'[113] see anything else in himself except God, and, cleaving to Him through incorruptibility, he receives the whole of the good kingdom within himself. What has been said becomes clear to us if we take as an adjunct to it the message of the Lord sent to the apostles through Mary (Magdalene); He says: 'I ascend to my Father and your Father, to my God and to your God.'[114] It is the Mediator between the Father and the disinherited who says this, the One who reconciled the enemies of God to the true and only Godhead.[115] For when, according to the prophetic word,[116] men were alienated from the life-giving womb

---

109 John 5.29.
110 1 Tim 2.5.
111 1 Cor. 3.16; cf. 2 Cor. 6.16.
112 Wis. 1.4.
113 Matt. 5.8.
114 John 20.17.
115 Cf. James 4.4.
116 Cf. Ps. 57.4.

through sin, and went astray from the womb in which they were fashioned, they spoke falsehood instead of truth. Because of this, the Mediator, assuming the first fruit of our common nature, made it holy through His soul and body, unmixed and unreceptive of all evil, preserving it in Himself. He did this in order that, having taken it up to the Father of incorruptibility through His own incorruptibility, the entire group might be drawn along with it because of its related nature, and in order that the Father might admit the disinherited to 'adoption'[117] as sons, and the enemies of God to a share in His own Godhead. And just as the first fruit of the dough was assimilated through purity and innocence to the true Father and God, so we, also, as dough in similar ways will cleave to the Father of incorruptibility by imitating, as far as we can, the innocence and stability of the Mediator. Thus, we shall be a crown of precious stones for the only-begotten God, having become an honor and a glory through our life. For Paul says that: 'Having made himself a little lower than the angels because of his having suffered death, he made those whose nature had previously become thorny through sin into a crown for himself, transforming the thorn through suffering into honor and glory.'[118] And yet, once He has 'taken away the sins of the world'[119] and taken upon His head a crown of thorns, in order to weave a crown of 'honor and glory,' there is no small danger that someone be discovered to be a burr and a thorn, because of his evil life, and then placed in the middle of the Master's crown because of sharing in His body. The just voice speaks directly to this one: 'How didst thou come in here without a wedding-garment?'[120] 'How were you, a thorn, woven in with those fitted into my crown through honor and glory?' 'What harmony is there between Christ and Belial? What part has the

---
117 Cf. Eph. 1.5.
118 Cf. Heb. 2.7-9.
119 John 1.29.
120 Matt. 22.12.

believer with the unbeliever?'[121] 'What has light in common with the darkness?' In order that none of these charges be made against our life, we must take care to avoid every thorny deed and word and thought throughout our entire life, so that having become an honor and glory through a pure and innocent regimen, we ourselves shall crown the Head of all, having become, as it were, a treasure and a possession for the Master. 'The Lord of Glory'[122] cannot be and cannot be called the Lord of any dishonored person. Therefore, the person free from unseemliness and shamelessness in the hidden and visible man makes his own master the One who is and is called 'the Lord of Glory' and not the lord of dishonor.

And He is also a 'beginning.'[123] But a beginning of anything is no different from what comes after itself. If someone defines the beginning as life, what comes afterwards will also be considered life. And if the beginning is light, what comes after the beginning will also be considered light. But what benefit do we derive from believing that He is the beginning? We become ourselves what we believe our beginning to be. For the beginning of darkness is not called the light, nor do we consider death a continuation of what is referred to as the beginning of life. But, unless a person is of the same nature as what produced him, i.e., connected with the beginning through innocence and virtue, the One who is the 'beginning' of being would not be his beginning. 'The ruler of darkness'[124] is the beginning of the dark life, the one having power over death is the beginning of death-bringing sin. Truly, it is not possible for the person who is allied with the beginning of darkness because of his wicked life to say that his own beginning is the beginning of all good. And his being called 'the king of justice and peace'[125] imparts the same notion for those who accept the words of the divine Master for their

---

121 2 Cor. 6.15.
122 1 Cor. 2.8.
123 Col. 1.18.
124 Eph. 6.12.
125 Heb. 7.2.

own good. For, according to the teaching on prayer, the person who prays that the kingdom of God may come to him, once he has learned that the true king is the 'king of justice and peace,' will set up justice and peace completely in his own life, in order that the king of justice and peace may be his king. Every virtue of the king is thought of as part of a military force; for I think it is necessary to think of all virtues in connection with justice and peace. If, then, a person having left his post in God's expedition enlists in the ranks of a different group and becomes a soldier of the inventor of evil, putting off the breastplate of justice and peace and all peaceful armor, how can this one be stationed under the king of peace after having thrown away the shield of truth? For it is clear that the device on one's armor will show who one's king is, and the leader is revealed by the character of one's life, instead of by the emblem sketched on the armor. How blessed is he who is drawn up under the divine generalship and enlisted in the ranks of the thousands and thousands of men armed against evil with virtues which are imprinted with the image of the king.

And why was it necessary to prolong the discourse by bringing in the sequence of phrases by which the name of the Lord is interpreted, those phrases, which can lead the way to a life of virtue, each name, by its particular emphasis, accomplishing something for us in the perfecting of our life? I say that it is good for these things to be remembered and reviewed so that there may be some guidance for us in the scope of the discourse which we proposed in the beginning, when we asked how anyone can achieve perfection in himself. For I think that if a person always keeps this in mind, that he is a participant in the revered name, when he is called a Christian according to the teaching of the apostles,[126] he will also necessarily show in himself the power of

---

126 Acts 11.26.

the other names by which Christ is thought of, since through his life he is a sharer in each of them.

What do I mean? Three things characterize the life of Christ: action, word, thought. For thought is the beginning of every word; second, after the thinking, is the word which reveals through the voice the thought coined in the soul; and action has the third rank after mind and thought, bringing what is thought to action. So, when the sequence of life brings us to any one of these, it is good to examine accurately these divine ideas of every word, deed, and thought by which Christ is known and called, lest our deed or word or thought be carried beyond the power of those high terms. As Paul says: 'All that is not from faith is sin,'[127] as can be shown clearly from the following. Every word or deed or thought that does not look to Christ looks completely to the adversary of Christ. For it is not possible for what is outside of light or life not to be completely in darkness or in death. If, then, what is not done or spoken or thought in accordance with Christ is akin to the adversary of the good, what is revealed through these words is clear to all, namely, that the person outside of Him rejects Christ by what he thinks, does, or says. Therefore, the voice of the prophet speaks the truth when it says: 'I have accounted all the wicked of the earth as dross.'[128] For, just as one who denies Christ in his pursuits is a sinner against the revered name, so, also, if someone rejects truth or justice or holiness and incorruptibility; or if, in the moment of his fight with his passions, he casts from his life any of the other qualities considered virtues, he is called a sinner by the prophecy, sinning through each of these in his life. What, then, is it necessary to do to be worthy of the name of Christ? What else than to distinguish in one's self the proper thoughts and words and deeds, asking whether they look to Christ or are at odds with Christ. Making the distinction is very easy. For whatever is done or thought or said

---
127 Rom. 14.23.
128 Cf. Ps. 118.119.

through passion has no agreement with Christ, but bears the character of the adversary, who smears the pearl of the soul with the mud of the passions and dims the luster of the precious stone. What is free from every passionate inclination looks to the source of passionlessness, who is Christ. Drawing from Him as from a pure and uncorrupted stream, a person will show in his thoughts such a resemblance to his Prototype as exists between the water in the running water or stream and the water taken away from there in a jar. For the purity in Christ and the purity seen in the person who has a share in Him are the same, the One being the stream and the other drawn from it, bringing intellectual beauty to his life, so that there is agreement between the hidden and the visible man, since the graceful bearing of our life coincides with our thoughts which are put into motion in accordance with Christ.

This, therefore, is perfection in the Christian life in my judgment, namely, the participation of one's soul and speech and activities in all of the names by which Christ is signified, so that the perfect holiness, according to the eulogy of Paul, is taken upon oneself in 'the whole body and soul and spirit,'[129] continuously safeguarded against being mixed with evil. But what if someone should say that the good is difficult to achieve, since only the Lord of creation is immutable, whereas human nature is unstable and subject to change, and ask how it is possible for the fixed and unchangable to be achieved in the changeable nature? We reply to such an argument that one cannot be worthily crowned 'unless he has competed according to the rules.'[130] For how can there be a lawful contest if there is no opponent? If there is no opponent, there is no crown. Victory does not exist by itself, without there being a defeated party. Let us struggle, therefore, against this very unstable element of our nature, engaging in a close contest with our opponent, as it were, not becoming victors by de-

---
129 Cf. 1 Thess. 5.23.
130 Cf. 2 Tim. 2.5.

stroying our nature, but by not allowing it to fall. For does man make a change only towards evil? Indeed, it would not be possible for him to be on the side of the good if he were by nature inclined only to a single one of the opposites. In fact, the fairest product of change is the increase of goods, the change to the better always changing what is nobly changed into something more divine. Therefore, I do not think it is a fearful thing (I mean that our nature is changeable). The Logos shows that it would be a disadvantage for us not to be able to make a change for the better, as a kind of wing of flight to greater things. Therefore, let no one be grieved if he sees in his nature a penchant for change. Changing in everything for the better, let him exchange 'glory for glory,'[131] becoming greater through daily increase, ever perfecting himself, and never arriving too quickly at the limit of perfection. For this is truly perfection: never to stop growing towards what is better and never placing any limit on perfection.

---

[131] 2 Cor. 3.18; cf. J. Daniélou, *From Glory to Glory*, p. 69.

ON THE CHRISTIAN MODE OF LIFE

INTRODUCTION

THE COMPLETE TEXT OF THIS TREATISE, *On the Christian Mode of Life,* was printed for the first time in 1952 in the Jaeger edition of the ascetical works. It was literally rediscovered by Jaeger who recognized it as the common source of two works included in Migne's *Patrology,* one a treatise of this name attributed to St. Gregory of Nyssa, the other a long letter attributed to a certain Macarius. The work which had come down to us under St. Gregory's name was actually a Byzantine excerpt of the original and a large portion of the 'Macarius Letter' was a copy of the second part of the original treatise which had been combined with a homily of Macarius of Egypt. It had been thought that the material in the treatise attributed to St. Gregory was a mere copy of Macarius. The history of the scholarly controversy involving the authenticity of the 'Macarius Letter' is a long and complicated one which Jaeger summarized in his book entitled, *Two Rediscovered Works of Ancient Christian Literature: Gregory of Nyssa and Macarius* (Leiden 1954). This book, a description of a fascinating achievement of modern scholarship, presents the philological and theological evidence for the authenticity of the original text which had so long been lost sight of. In his account of his investigation, Jaeger includes an illuminating chapter on the theology in the treatise. He points out that St. Gregory's elaboration of the relation between grace and human effort antedates by only a short time the Pelagian controversy in the Western Church. St. Gregory is himself convinced that the two are required if man is to attain perfection and gives us an early statement of the 'synergia theory,' which affirms the cooperation of the grace of God with the moral effort of man.

The treatise was intended as a guide for a large group of monks who had requested it. The first part is concerned with the goal of the religious life which St. Gregory always equates with the life of the philosopher. The second part discusses a number of practical problems connected with being a monk. St. Gregory stresses the idea that the efficacy of the brotherhood in the monastery will depend on the apostolic spirit of love. There is an interesting section at the end on the relation of the superior to the monks. Since the work contains a reformulation of ideas set forth in four other Gregorian treatises, namely, *On Virginity, On the Psalms, On the Canticle of Canticles,* and *The Life of Moses,* it is believed that it was composed during the last years of the saint's life, i.e., after 390. Although many of the ideas are the same as those set forth in the treatise *On Virginity,* the approach is very different. There is a noticeable change of method in the more extensive use of biblical support for the ideas advocated. As part of the 'Macarius Letter,' this was a work widely known and revered in the tradition of Eastern monasticism.

ON THE CHRISTIAN MODE OF LIFE

F ANYONE WITHDRAWS HIS ATTENTION for a moment from his body and, emerging from the slavery of his passions and his carelessness, looks at his own soul with honest and sincere reason, he will see clearly how its nature reveals God's love for us and His intention in creating us. Reflecting in this manner, he will discover as essential and natural to man an impulse of his will towards the beautiful and the best, and connected with his nature a passionless and blessed love of that intelligible and blessed image of which man is the imitation.[1] However, a certain illusion related to the visible and the changing, caused by unreasonable emotion and bitter pleasure, always deceives and beguiles the soul which is careless and unguarded because of indifference, and drags it to terrible evil, originating in the pleasures of life, begetting death for those who love it. It is for this reason that the knowledge of the truth, the saving medicine for our souls, is, by the grace of our Savior, bestowed as a gift upon those who accept it eagerly. By this grace, the illusion beguiling man is dispelled, the dishonoring preoccupation with the flesh is extinguished, and, by the light of truth, the soul, which received the knowledge, makes its way to the divine and to its own salvation.

You have received this knowledge and divine love worthily and have directed it in accordance with the nature given to the soul. You have assembled zealously, fulfilling together the apostolic ideal in your actions, and you have requested from us, as a guide and leader for your life's journey, a discourse which will direct you to the straight path, indicating ac-

---

[1] Cf. Gen. 1.26,27.

curately what the scope of this life is for those entering upon it, what 'the good and acceptable and perfect will of God'[2] is, what kind of road leads to this end, how it is fitting for those traveling upon it to treat each other, how it is necessary for those in authority to direct the chorus of philosophy, and what suffering must be endured by those who are going to ascend to the peak of virtue and make their own souls worthy of the reception of the spirit. Since, moreover, you demand this discourse of us not just orally, but in writing, in order that you may take it and hold it in reserve for the needs of the moment, as if from the treasury of memory, we shall try to speak to your present zeal according to the grace of the Spirit supplied to us. We know very well that the rule of reverence in you is fixed by the right dogma of the faith which holds the Godhead of the blessed and eternal Trinity, never changing in any way, one in essence, one in glory, known by its will and worshiped under the three substances. On the grounds that we have received it from many witnesses, we make our confession by means of the Spirit which washes us in the stream of the mystery. We know that this reverent and infallible confession of faith abides securely in the depths of your soul, and we know your impulse to ascend to the good and the blessed on high, so we are writing for you brief seeds of instruction, selecting them from the fruits given to us previously by the Spirit, quoting Scripture often to give confidence in what is said and to make manifest our understanding of it. We do this lest, in relying on some foolish and inferior thought-process of our own, we seem to reject grace from on high and, in becoming puffed up with vain pride, we introduce stupidly into our writings types of reverence based on merely extraneous considerations.

It is necessary for the soul and body which are going to move towards God, in accordance with the law of reverence, and render unto Him an unstained and pure service[3] to

---
2 Rom. 12.2.
3 Cf. Rom. 12.1.

take as the guide of life the reverent faith which the voices of the saints proclaim in all their writings. Thus, the obedient and tractable soul gives itself over to a course of virtue, freeing itself, on the one hand, from the fetters of this life and separating itself from the slavery of mean and vain pursuits, and, on the other hand, involving itself wholly in the faith and in the life of God alone, because it sees clearly that where there is faith, reverence, and a blameless life, there is present the power of Christ, there is flight from all evil and from death which robs us of life. For shameful things do not have in themselves sufficient power to vie with the power of the Master, but it is their nature to follow upon a disobedience to His commands. This was experienced of old by the first man, but now it is experienced by all of us when we imitate his disobedience through stubborn choice. However, those who approach the Spirit with guileless intent, in perfect faith with no defilement in their conscience, the power of the Spirit cleanses according to the one who says: 'For our gospel was not delivered to you in word only, but in power also; and in the Holy Spirit and in much fullness, as you know.'[4] And again: 'May your spirit and soul and body be preserved blamelessly in the name of our Lord Jesus Christ,'[5] who has furnished a pledge of immortality through Baptism to those who are worthy, in order that the talent entrusted to each may, through their use of it, produce unseen wealth.[6] For, brethren, holy Baptism is important, important for the things perceptible to the mind of those who receive it with fear; for the rich and ungrudging Spirit is always flowing into those accepting grace, filled with which the holy apostles reaped a full harvest for the churches of Christ.

For those who have taken possession of this gift sincerely, it endures as co-worker and companion in accordance with the measure of faith, the good dwelling in each one in propor-

---
4 1 Thess. 1.5.
5 Cf. 1 Thess. 5.23.
6 Cf. Luke 19.13 ff.

tion to the eagerness of the soul in its deeds of faith, in keeping with the word of the Lord. He says that the one who accepts the coin does so on terms of interest, that is, the grace of the Holy Spirit is given to everyone with the understanding that there is to be an augmenting and increase of what is received. It is necessary for the soul which has been born again by the power of God to be nurtured by the Spirit in proportion to its age of intelligibility, refreshed by the water of virtue and the abundance of grace. Just as the nature of the child newly-born does not continue in the tenderness of age, but when it is nourished by food according to the law of nature it takes its measure in proportion to what is given it, so it is fitting for the recently-born soul whose participation in the Spirit restores to its nature its former beauty, after it has destroyed the sickness which comes over it through disobedience, not to remain always like a child, inactive, leisurely, sleeping unmoved in the state of its birth, but to nourish itself by its own food, and, in proportion to what its nature demands, to rear itself by means of every virtue and labor so that it fortifies itself through the power of the Spirit by its own virtue against the unseen robber attacking it with many devices.

It is necessary, therefore, for us to bring ourselves to perfect manhood as the apostle tells us: 'Until we all attain to the unity of the faith and of the deep knowledge of the Son of God, to perfect manhood, to the mature measure of the fullness of Christ; that we may be now no longer children, tossed to and fro and carried about by every wind of doctrine devised in the wickedness of men, in craftiness, according to the wiles of error. Rather are we to practice the truth, and so grow up in all things in him who is the head, Christ.'[7] And elsewhere the same writer says: 'Be not conformed to this world, but be transformed in the newness of your mind, that you may discern what is the good and acceptable and

---

7 Eph. 4.13-15.

perfect will of God,'[8] meaning that the perfect will of God is that the soul be changed by reverence, the soul having been brought to the full flower of its beauty by the grace of the Spirit which attends upon the sufferings of the person who undergoes the change. The development of the body in its process of growing is not in our hands, for nature does not measure size by man's judgment or pleasure, but by its own impulses and by necessity; the measure of the soul, however, in the renewal of its birth and the beauty which the grace of the Spirit furnishes through the zeal of the one who receives it, depends on our judgment. As far as you extend your efforts in behalf of piety, so far will the greatness of your soul extend through efforts and toils towards what the Lord urges us when He says: 'Strive to enter by the narrow gate.'[9] And again: 'Use force, for the forceful take the kingdom of heaven as their prize';[10] and: 'He who has persevered to the end, will be saved';[11] and: 'By your patience you will win your souls';[12] and the apostle says: 'Let us run with patience to the fight set before us';[13] and he says: 'So run as to obtain';[14] and again: 'As the God's ministers in much patience,' etc.[15] By this, he summons us to run and he urges us to enter the contests eagerly, since the gift of grace is measured by the labors of the receiver. For the grace of the Spirit gives eternal life and unspeakable joy in heaven, but it is the love of the toils because of the faith that makes the soul worthy of receiving the gifts and enjoying the grace. When a just act and grace of the Spirit coincide, they fill the soul into which they come with a blessed life; but, separated from each other, they provide no gain for the soul. For the grace of God does not naturally frequent souls which are fleeing from salvation, and

---

8 Rom. 12.2.
9 Luke 13.24; cf. Matt. 7.13.
10 Cf. Matt. 11.12.
11 Matt. 10.22; Mark 13.13.
12 Luke 21.19.
13 Heb. 12.1.
14 1 Cor. 9.24.
15 2 Cor. 6.4.

the power of human virtue is not sufficient in itself to cause the souls not sharing in grace to ascend to the beauty of life. For it says: 'Unless the Lord build the house and keep the city, he labors in vain that builds it and watches in vain who keeps it.'[16] And again: 'For not with their own sword did they conquer the land; nor did their own arm make them victorious (although they used their swords and arms in their struggles), but it was your right hand and your arm, and the light of your countenance.'[17] What does this mean? It means that the Lord from on high enters into an alliance with the doers, and, at the same time, it means that it is not necessary for men considering human efforts to think that the entire crown rests upon their struggles, but it is necessary for them to refer their hopes for their goal to the will of God.

It is necessary, then, to know what is the will of God towards which one must look eagerly if he is striving towards the blessed life and desirous of making his own life conform to it. It is 'the perfect will of God that the soul be purified, through grace,'[18] of all filth, that it rise above the pleasures of the body, and come to God pure, longing and able to see that intelligible and unspeakable light. Such persons the Lord blesses saying: 'Blessed are the clean of heart, for they shall see God.'[19] And among other things, He urges: 'You, therefore, are to be perfect, even as your heavenly Father is perfect.'[20] To this perfection, the apostle also bids us run: 'that we may present every man perfect in Christ Jesus, wherein I also labor.'[21] David, speaking with spirit, teaches those who wish to determine rightly the path of true philosophy by which it is necessary to walk to the final goal, I mean those asking what the Spirit teaches through David: 'Let my heart

---

16 Cf. Ps. 126.1.
17 Ps. 43.4.
18 Rom. 12.2,3.
19 Matt. 5.8.
20 Matt. 5.48.
21 Cf. Col. 1.28.

be perfect in your statutes, that I be not put to shame.'²² He orders us to fear shame and to put off like a garment whatever stained and dishonorable shame we are clothed in. For again, he says: 'Then should I not be put to shame, when I behold all your commands.'²³ You see how the Spirit places confidence in the fulfillment of the commandments. And again: 'A clean heart create for me, O God, and a steadfast spirit renew within me, and with a guiding spirit sustain me.'²⁴ Elsewhere he asks: 'Who can ascend the mountain of the Lord?'²⁵ Then he answers: 'He whose hands are sinless, whose heart is clean.'²⁶ The person clean in all these respects he leads to the mountain of the Lord, the one who neither in intention or thought or deeds completely defiles his soul by persisting in evils, and the one who, having accepted the guiding spirit, by good deeds and thoughts remakes his own heart which had been destroyed by evil. The holy apostle, speaking on the subject of virginity to those who had chosen this state of life, outlines what such a life must be: 'The virgin,' he says, 'thinks about the things of the Lord, that she may be holy in body and in spirit,'²⁷ telling them to be pure in soul and flesh. And he orders them to flee all sin, as far as possible, both the obvious and the hidden; that is to say, he orders them to be free from all sinful acts and sins committed in thought, for the goal of the soul which honors virginity is to be filled with God and to become the bride of Christ.

Now, it is necessary for anyone desiring to be closely united with another to take on the ways of that person through imitation. Therefore, it is necessary for the one longing to be the bride of Christ to be like Christ in beauty through virtue as far as possible. For nothing can be united with light unless

---

22 Ps. 118.80.
23 Ps. 118.6.
24 Cf. Ps. 50.12-14.
25 Cf. Ps. 23.3.
26 Ps. 23.4.
27 1 Cor. 7.34.

the light is shining upon it. And I hear the Apostle John saying: 'Everyone who has this hope in him makes himself holy, just as he also is holy.'[28] And the Apostle Paul says: 'Be imitators of me, as I am of Christ.'[29] For it is necessary for the soul that is going to ascend to the Divine and be joined to Christ to drive out from itself every sin which it has definitely committed through deeds, I mean theft, plunder, adultery, greed, fornication, slander, and all other obvious kinds of sin, as well as whatever sins lie hidden in the soul escaping the notice of those outside, but bitterly consuming man with most malicious fangs. These are envy, disbelief, malice, guile, desire for what is not right, hate, pretense, conceit, and the whole festering swarm of sins which Scripture hates and abominates as much as the obvious kinds of sins, since they are related to each other and grow from the same evil. Whose bones did the Lord scatter? Was it not those of the man-pleasers? Whom does the Lord abominate as accursed and polluted? Was it not the bloody and the deceitful man? For: 'The bloodthirsty and the deceitful the Lord abhors.'[30] Does not David, with reference to those who speak civilly with their neighbors, curse the evils in their hearts when he cries to God: 'Repay them for their deeds.'[31] And he says: 'You willingly commit crimes on earth.'[32] The Lord calls a secret notion a sinful act. On account of this, He orders us not to pursue fair fame among men nor to be ashamed of dishonor among them. Scripture deprives of the rewards of heaven those who ostentatiously pity the poor and then boast of their charity on earth, for, if you seek to please men and bestow charity in order to be praised, you will be paid in full for your good work by the praises of the men on whose account you exhibited pity. Do not look for reward in heaven, having deposited your deeds below; do not expect honor from God,

---

28 1 John 3.3.
29 1 Cor. 11.1.
30 Ps. 5.7.
31 Ps. 27.3,4.
32 Ps. 57.3.

having gotten it from men. Do you long for immortal glory? Reveal your life secretly to the One who is able to provide what you are longing for. Are you afraid of eternal shame? Fear the One who will uncover this on the day of judgment. How, then, can the Lord say: 'Let your light shine before men, in order that they may see your good works and give glory to your Father in heaven'?[33] This means that He orders the person who is following the precepts of God to do everything with an eye toward God and to be pleasing to God alone, without searching for any reputation among men. In ordering us to flee from the praises and approbation of men on the one hand, and, on the other, to be known to all because of our life and deeds, He does not say that the beholders of these deeds should admire the person who does them, but that they should give glory to our Father in heaven. He orders us to refer all glory and to direct all action to the will of that One with whom lies the reward of virtuous deeds. He bids you flee and turn aside from the fair fame of earthly tongues. The person seeking that and directing his life towards it will not only be robbed of eternal glory, but should even expect punishment. For He says: 'Woe to you when all men speak well of you.'[34] Accordingly, flee from all human honor, the end of which is shame and eternal dishonor, and reach out for the praises from on high which is what David refers to when he says: 'From you is my praise';[35] and: 'Let my soul glory in the Lord.'[36]

And the blessed apostle bids not to partake casually of the food at hand, but to render, first, what is due to the One who gave him the provisions of his life. Thus, as long as he orders us to dishonor glory among men, he orders us to seek it from God. For, in doing this, a man is called faithful by the Lord; but the one who longs for honor here, he numbers among the

---
33 Matt. 5.16.
34 Luke 6.26.
35 Cf. Ps. 21.26.
36 Ps. 33.3.

unfaithful. For He says: 'How can you believe, who receive glory from one another, and do not seek the glory which is from the only God?'[37] And listen to what John says hate is: 'Everyone who hates his brother is a murderer. And you know that no murderer has eternal life abiding in him.'[38] He eliminates from eternal life the one who hates his brother as a murderer. Rather, he openly calls hatred murder. For the persons who withhold and destroy their love towards their neighbors and become an enemy instead of a friend, we would easily count as murderers, regarding the hidden hatred of one's neighbor as the hatred of murderers towards those they are plotting against. And since there is no difference between the evils that are hidden within us and obvious and visible evils, the apostle clearly brings them together through these words: 'And as they have resolved against possessing the knowledge of God, God has given them up to a reprobate sense, so that they do what is not fitting, being filled with all iniquity, malice, immorality, avarice, wickedness; being full of envy, murder, contention, deceit, malignity; being whisperers, detractors, hateful to God, irreverent, proud, haughty, plotters of evil; disobedient to parents, foolish, dissolute, without affection, without fidelity, without mercy. Although they have known the ordinance of God, they have not understood that those who practice such things are deserving of death. And not only do they do these things, but they applaud others doing them.'[39]

Do you see how he intertwines deceit and haughtiness and guile and the rest of the hidden faults with murder and avarice and all such things? But what does the Lord Himself mean when He exclaims: 'That which is exalted in the sight of men is an abomination before God.'[40] And: 'Everyone who exalts himself shall be humbled; and he that humbles himself

---
37 John 5.44.
38 1 John 3.15.
39 Rom. 1.28-32.
40 Luke 16.15.

shall be exalted.'[41] And Wisdom says: 'Every proud man is an abomination to the Lord.'[42] And one could find many passages in other books condemning those things which are hidden in our souls. So wicked and hard to cure and strong are those things possessed in the depths of our souls that it is not possible to rub them out and to remove them through human efforts and virtue alone unless through prayer we take the power of the Spirit as an ally and, in this way, conquer the evil which is playing the tyrant within us, as the Spirit teaches us through the voice of David: 'Cleanse me from my unknown faults, and from wanton sin spare your servant.'[43]

There are two things of which man is composed, a soul and a body, the one part is external and the other remains within him during the whole course of his life. It is necessary to watch over the former diligently as a temple of God, taking care lest one of the obvious sins attack it and overthrow and destroy it. The apostle warns us of this when he says: 'If any man destroys the temple of God, him will God destroy.'[44] But the inner part must also be safeguarded in every way lest some ambush of evil, emerging from the depths of some place or other, destroy the reasoning power of reverence and enslave the soul, filling it stealthily with passions which tear it asunder.

It is necessary, then, to turn to the soul and guard it diligently like a general calling to his men and giving orders: O Man, 'with closest custody guard your heart, for in it are the sources of life.'[45] Now, a garrison for the soul is reasonable reverence fortified by a fear of God and grace of the Spirit, and deeds of virtue. For the one who arms his own soul with these easily routs the attacks of the tyrant, I mean guile and desire and blind rage and envy and whatever shameful impulses of evil exist within us. But it is necessary for the cultivator of virtue to be someone simple and steadfast,

---
41 Luke 14.11.
42 Prov. 16.5.
43 Ps. 18.13,14.
44 1 Cor. 3.17.
45 Prov. 4.23.

knowing only how to cultivate the harvest of reverence and never turning aside to the paths of evil or removing from his faith the reasoning power of reverence. He must be someone devoid of subtlety and straightforward, without experience of passions which lie outside his own path. For it is not possible for the woman married to one man and the prostitute to expect the same reward.

The blessed Moses says: 'You shall not yoke on your threshing floor different kinds of animals for the same task, e.g., the ox and the ass, but yoking the same kind you will thresh your harvest; you shall not weave a garment from two different kinds of thread, wool and linen woven together; you shall not cultivate on your plot of ground two harvests in the same year; you shall not breed any of our domestic animals with others of a different species; you shall yoke together kind with kind.'[46]

What does Scripture mean by these riddles? That it is not right for evil and virtue to grow together in the same soul; nor is it right, dividing one's life between opposites, to reap thorns and grain from the same soul; nor is it right for the bride of Christ to commit adultery with the enemies of Christ, or to bear light in the womb and beget darkness. For it is not natural for these things to go together, just as parts of virtue do not go with parts of evil. What kind of friendship exists between moderation and incontinence? What agreement is there between justice and injustice? What does light have in common with darkness? Does not the one give way to the other and refuse to wait for the battle? It is necessary, therefore, for the wise cultivator to send forth the pure waters of his life from a fresh and good source, unmixed with anything muddy, knowing only the agriculture of God and toiling for this and remaining faithful to it in order that, even if some strange reasoning grows up secretly in the harvest of virtue, seeing your labors, the One who sees all will quickly by His

---

46 Cf. Deut. 22.9-11; Lev. 19.19.

own power cut out that treacherous and festering root of reasoning before it sprouts. For the grace of the Spirit follows quickly upon the person who perseveres in toil, destroying the seeds of evil, and it is not possible for the one abiding with God to fall short of his hope or to be neglected or unavenged.

You know the widow in the gospel who emphasized before the unkindly judge the greatness of the injustice she had suffered and the great persistence of her request finally won him over, so that he called out for the punishment of the wrongdoer. Neither should you ever give up beseeching. For, if her persistence in entreaty influenced the verdict of the pitiless magistrate, how should we despair of the zeal directed towards God whose pity often anticipates those requesting something of Him? The Lord Himself, accepting our steadfastness in prayer, urges us to be zealous. He says: 'Hear what the unjust judge says. And how much more will our heavenly Father avenge those crying to him night and day? I say to you that He will quickly avenge them.'[47] And the apostle expends much energy on the progress of those who are learning reverence, and, at the same time, he clearly establishes the scope of truth for all when he says: 'Admonishing every man and teaching every man in all wisdom, that we may present every man perfect in Christ Jesus. At this, too, I work.'[48] And again, He prays that those who hold in high esteem the seal of the Spirit through Baptism will reach the age of intelligence and grow through the additional help of the Spirit saying: 'Wherefore, hearing of your faith and of your love for all the saints, I do not cease to pray for you, asking that the God of our Lord Jesus Christ, the Father of glory, may grant you the spirit of wisdom and of revelation in deep knowledge of him; the eyes of your heart being enlightened, so that you may know what is the hope of his calling, and what the riches of the glory of his inheritance in the saints, and what the

---

47 Cf. Luke 18.6-8.
48 Col. 1.28,29.

exceeding greatness of his power towards us who believe.'[49] Then, he continues, concerning the manner of the Spirit's participation: 'Its measure is the working of his mighty power, which he has wrought in Christ in raising him up from the dead.' Clearly, he is speaking of the Spirit's participation and the Spirit's activity with respect to those in communion with Him, in order, he says, that you also may receive the same habit, the full assurance of that One in the same way. A little later in the letter, he prays for something greater for them, seeking for the more perfect power of the Spirit to come to them: 'For this reason I bend my knees to the Father of our Lord Jesus Christ, from whom all fatherhood in heaven and on earth receives its name, that he may grant you from his glorious riches to be strengthened with power through his Spirit unto the progress of the inner man; and to have Christ dwelling through faith in your hearts; so that, being rooted and grounded in love, you may be able to comprehend with all the saints what is the breadth and length and height and depth, and to know Christ's love which surpasses knowledge, in order that you may be filled unto all the fullness of God.'[50]

And in another epistle concerning these same matters, he also speaks to his disciples, revealing to them the treasure of the Spirit and calling upon them to share in it. He says: 'Strive after the gifts of the Spirit and I point out to you a yet more excellent way. If I should speak with the tongues of men and of angels, but do not have charity, I have become as sounding brass or a tinkling cymbal. And if I have prophecy and know all mysteries and all knowledge, and if I have all faith so as to remove mountains, yet do not have charity, I am nothing. And if I distribute all my goods and if I deliver my body to be burned, yet do not have charity, it profits me nothing.'[51] And what the profit of charity is, what sort of fruit it produces, from what the possessor of charity is re-

---
49 Cf. Eph. 1.15-19.
50 Eph. 3.14-19.
51 Cf. 1 Cor. 12.31; 13.3.

moved, and what it provides, he makes abundantly clear: 'Charity does not envy, is not pretentious, is not puffed up, is not unseemly, is not self-seeking, is not provoked; thinks no evil, does not rejoice over wickedness, but rejoices with the truth; bears with all things, believes all things, hopes all things, endures all things. Charity never fails.'[52] Altogether wisely and accurately, he says: 'Charity never fails.' But what does it mean? Even if someone receives the other gifts which the Spirit furnishes (I mean the tongues of angels and prophecy and knowledge and the grace of healing), but has never been entirely cleansed of the troubling passions within him through the charity of the Spirit, and has not received the final remedy of salvation in his soul, he is still in danger of failing if he does not keep charity steadfast and firm among his virtues.

Do not acquiesce in His gifts, thinking that because of the wealth and ungrudging grace of the Spirit nothing else is needed for perfection. When these riches come to you be modest in thought, ever submissive and thinking of love as the foundation of the treasure of grace for the soul, struggle against all passion until you come to the height of the goal of reverence to which the apostle himself came first and to which he leads his disciples through prayer and teaching, showing to those who love the Lord the change for the better and the grace which results from love, when he says: 'For neither circumcision nor uncircumcision but a new creation is of any account. And whoever follow this rule, peace and mercy upon them, even upon the Israel of God.'[53] And again: 'If any man is in Christ, he is a new creature, the former things have passed away.'[54] The 'new creation' is the apostolic rule. And what this is he makes abundantly clear in another section, saying: 'In order that I might present to myself the church in all her glory, not having spot or wrinkle or any

---

52 Cf. 1 Cor. 13.4-8.
53 Gal. 6.15,16.
54 2 Cor. 5.17.

such thing, but that she might be holy and without blemish.'[55] A new creature he called the indwelling of the Holy Spirit in a pure and blameless soul removed from evil and wickedness and shamefulness. For, when the soul hates sin, it closely unites itself with God, as far as it can, in the regimen of virtue; having been transformed in life, it receives the grace of the Spirit to itself, becomes entirely new again and is recreated. Thus the injunction: 'Purge out the old leaven, that you may be a new dough,'[56] is made clear, and the exhortation: 'Let us keep festival not with the old leaven, but with the unleavened bread of sincerity and truth.'[57] For, when the tempter places many snares for the soul, tossing his own evil spirit before it, man by himself has not the power to gain the victory, and the apostle commands us to gird our limbs with heavenly armor. He orders us to put on the breastplate of justice and have our feet shod with the readiness of the gospel of peace and to gird our loins with truth; in all things taking up the shield of faith.[58] In this way, he says: 'You may be able to quench all the fiery darts of the wicked one.'[59] The fiery darts are unbridled passions. And he commands us to take: 'the helmet of salvation and the sword of the Spirit.'[60] By the holy sword, he means the powerful word of God with which the right hand of the soul must arm itself and beat off the devices of the enemy.

Now, learn how the arms are to be obtained by us from the apostle himself when he says: 'With all prayer and supplication, pray at all times in the Spirit and therein be vigilant in all perseverance and supplication.'[61] Whence also he prays for all as follows: 'The grace of our Lord Jesus Christ and the charity of God and the fellowship of the Holy

---

55 Eph. 5.27.
56 1 Cor. 5.7.
57 1 Cor. 5.8.
58 Cf. Eph. 6.14-16.
59 Eph. 6.16.
60 Eph. 6.17.
61 Eph. 6.18.

Spirit be with you all.'[62] And again: 'May your spirit and soul and body be preserved sound, blameless in the coming of our Lord Jesus Christ.'[63] Do you see what ways he points out as leading to the one goal of salvation and the one goal of being a perfect Christian? This is the end towards which it is necessary for the lovers of truth to go, and they must walk in pleasure with striving and zeal, through firm faith and steadfast hope. For these, the course of life towards the greatest of the commandments, on which every prophet depends with the law, is easily achieved. What commandments do I mean? 'You shall love the Lord, your God, with all your heart, and with all your soul, and with all your mind, and your neighbor as yourself.'[64]

The goal of reverence, therefore, is such as the Lord Himself and the apostles, who received this knowledge from Him, have handed down to us. But let no one blame us if, having received it from those who are greater than we are, we prolong the discussion, wishing to present the truth rather than to abbreviate what has been said. For it is necessary for those who have determined to philosophize rightly and for the souls cleansed from the filth of evil to know accurately the scope of philosophy, in order that, having learned the toil of the path and the end of the course, they may all cast off stubbornness and pride because of their righteous actions, and in order that, having denied their own soul in accordance with the injunction of Scripture, they may look back to one wealth which God ordained for those who love the contest of love for Christ. He calls to Himself all those who have zealously withstood the struggle, those to whom the cross of Christ is pleasing as *viaticum* for the journey of such a life, the cross which one must bear with joy and good hope in following God the Savior, making His stewardship a law and way of life, as the apostle himself said: 'Be ye imitators of me as I

---
62 2 Cor. 13.13.
63 1 Thess. 5.23.
64 Cf. Deut. 6.5; Matt. 2.36 ff.

am of Christ.'[65] And again: 'Let us run with patience to the fight set before us, looking towards the author and finisher of faith, Jesus, who for the joy set before him, endured a cross, despising shame, and sits on the right hand of the throne of God.'[66] There is reason to fear, lest, lifted up by the gifts of the Spirit and having achieved through virtue a starting point towards wisdom and reverence, we may fall in the attempt before we come to the end of our hopes. This would make those of us who chose the toil useless to ourselves because of stubbornness, and seemingly unworthy of the perfection toward which the grace of the Spirit drew us.

It is necessary, then, never to relax the tension of toil or to stand aside from the struggles at hand or to turn to the past if something good has been accomplished, but to forget 'what is behind'[67] and look to the future, according to the apostle, and wear out our heart with the thoughts of toil, having an insatiable desire for justice for which alone those must hunger and thirst who seek to arrive at perfection, becoming poor and needy like those who are somehow making progress in what has been ordered and have migrated afar to the perfect love of Christ. For the person who desires that love and looks to the promise above does not stand elated because things have been set right by fasting or by keeping watch or by zealously pursuing any of the other virtues. Being full of divine longing and looking anxiously toward the One who is calling, he considers all that he suffers in attaining Him small and unworthy of the prize. He struggles valiantly to the end of his life, matching toil with toil and virtue with virtue, until he establishes himself as an honor to God because of his deeds, not thinking for a minute that he has made himself worthy of God. This is the greatest achievement of philosophy, that it subordinates excellence in deeds to the excellence of the heart, and lays a charge against life, some-

---

65 1 Cor. 11.1.
66 Heb. 12.1,2.
67 Phil. 3.13.

how subordinating intelligence to the fear of God in order that we may enjoy His promise in proportion to our faithful love and not in proportion to our toil and labor. The gifts are so great that it is not possible to find toils worthy of them; rather is there need for great faith and hope that the requital may be measured by these and not by toils. The foundation of faith is poverty of spirit and an unmeasured love of God.

Now, I think that enough has been said to those who have chosen the philosophic life concerning matters related to their life and the attaining of their goal. But it still remains to be said how such persons should live with each other, what kinds of labors they should love, how they should run the course together until they come to the city above. It is necessary to disdain the things that are revered in this life, rejecting the companionship and the opinions here below, and, loving heavenly honor, to adjust oneself spiritually to one's brothers in God. At the same time, one must deny his own soul. Denying one's own soul is not seeking one's own will, but rather making one's will the established word of God and using this as a good pilot which guides the common fulfillment of brotherhood harmoniously to the shore of the will of God. Nor is it necessary to possess or to consider as one's own anything apart from the common store except the garment covering one's body. For, if a person has none of these things and is free of thought concerning himself in this life, he will serve the common need and fulfill zealously with pleasure and hope what has been commanded like a well-disposed and simple servant of Christ, providing for the common needs of his brothers. This is what the Lord wishes and orders when He says: 'Whoever wishes to be first and great among you shall be last of all and the slave of all.'[68]

It is necessary for your service among men to be without pay, bringing no honor and glory to the servant lest one appear as 'serving to the eye as pleasers of men';[69] serve the

---
68 Cf. Mark 10.43; Matt. 23.11.
69 Eph. 6.6.

Lord Himself and enter 'the narrow gate'[70] where you zealously put on His yoke and bear it with pleasure to the end with good hope. It is necessary to be subservient to all and to care for one's brothers as if paying the debt of a loan, depositing in the soul consideration for all and fulfilling the love that is owed. But it is necessary, also, for those in charge of this spiritual band to look to the quality of their own thought and, taking account of the evil that lies in wait for them, to exercise worthily the arts of supervision, not destroying thought with authority. There is the danger that certain persons, knowing that they are in charge of others and directing them to the celestial life, may destroy themselves without realizing it. It is necessary for those in charge in matters of supervision to work harder than the rest, to think humbler thoughts than those under them, and to furnish their own life as an example of servitude to the brothers, looking upon those entrusted to them as a deposit of God.

For, if they are carefully welding together the sacred band and providing instruction according to the need of each for preserving the rank which befits each person, and, at the same time, secretly preserving humility in the faith, like well-disposed slaves, then, they are thereby obtaining for themselves a large reward. Accordingly, care for them as if you were kindly tutors of tender children entrusted to you by their fathers. For these observe the habits of the children and to one they give blows, to another admonition, to another praise, to another something else. They do none of these to get the favor or the enmity of the child, but are concerned with what is pertinent to the situation and what the nature of each child requires if he is to become successful in this life. It is also necessary for you to put aside all hatred and stubbornness towards your brothers and to adapt your word to the ability and judgment of each of them. Censure this one, admonish that one, encourage another, bringing medicine for the need

---

70 Matt. 7.14.

of each like a good physician. He diagnoses the illnesses, prescribes a mild medicine for one and a harsher medicine for another, and he is hated by none of those who ask for his therapy, that is, he adjusts his skill to their souls and bodies. Do you, also, follow the requirements of the situation in order that, having educated well the soul of the disciple looking to you, you may bring its shining virtue to the Father, an heir worthy of his gift.

If you are related to each other in this way, those in charge and those under their instruction, the one obeying commands with joy, the other leading his brothers to perfection with pleasure, and if you outwit each other in honors, then, you will lead on earth the life of the angels. Let vanity not be known among you; rather, let simplicity and harmony and a guileless attitude weld the group together. Let each persuade himself that he is not only inferior to the brother at his side, but to all men. If he knows this, he will truly be a disciple of Christ. For, as the Savior says: 'Everyone who exalts himself shall be humbled and he who humbles himself shall be exalted.'[71] And again: 'If any man wishes to be first among you, he will be last of all';[72] and the servant of all: 'for the Son of man has not come to be served but to serve and to give his life as a ransom for many.'[73] And the apostle: 'For we preach not ourselves, but Jesus Christ as Lord; and ourselves merely as your servants in Jesus.'[74] Knowing, then, the fruits of humility and the penalty of conceit, imitate the Master by loving one another and do not shrink from death or any other punishment for the good of each other. But the way which God entered upon for you, do you enter upon for Him, proceeding with one body and one soul to the invitation from above, loving God and each other. For love and fear of the Lord are the first fulfillment of the law.

---

71 Luke 14.11; Luke 18.14; Matt. 23.12.
72 Mark 9.34.
73 Matt. 20.28; Mark 10.45.
74 2 Cor. 4.5.

It is necessary, indeed, for each of you to put into your souls fear and love as a kind of strong and firm foundation, and to refresh it with good deeds and sufficient prayer. Love of God does not come to us simply or automatically, but through many sufferings and great concern in cooperation with Christ, as Wisdom has said: 'If you shall seek her like silver and like hidden treasures search her out: then will you understand the fear of the Lord: the knowledge of God you will find.'[75] But, once you have found the knowledge of God and understanding fear, you will easily succeed in what follows, I mean loving your neighbor. For the first and the greater is obtained through suffering, and the second and the lesser follows upon the first with less toil. However, if the first is not there, clearly, the second will not be present. For, if one does not love God with all his heart and all his soul,[76] how can he care wholesomely and guilelessly for the love of his brothers, since he is not fulfilling the love of the One on whose account he has a care for the love of his brothers? The person in this condition, who has not given his whole soul to God and has not participated in his love, the craftsman of evil finds disarmed and easily overpowers. He trips him up with evil considerations, now making the command of Scripture appear to be heavy and the care for our brothers burdensome; now leading him on to false pretension and conceit in the very serving of his fellow servants, persuading him that he has fulfilled the injunctions of the Lord and that he will be great in heaven. But this is no small wrong. It is necessary for the well-disposed and earnest servant to allow his master to judge his good will and not become himself the judge and praiser of his own deportment. For, if he himself becomes the judge, pushing aside the true judge, he will have no reward from that One because he has already satisfied himself with his own praises and self-conceit instead of the former's opinion. It is necessary, according to the pronouncement of Paul, for the

---

75 Prov. 2.4,5.
76 Cf. Deut. 6.5.

Spirit of God to 'give testimony to our spirit,'[77] but it is not for us to assess what is ours through our own judgment. He says: 'He who commends himself is not approved, but he whom the Lord commends.'[78] The person who does not wait for the commendation from the Lord, but anticipates his judgment falls into human opinions. He undertakes to honor himself among his brothers for his sufferings and he does as the unbelievers do. For an unbeliever is the one who searches for human honors instead of celestial ones, as the Lord Himself says somewhere: 'How can you believe, who receive glory from one another, and do not seek the glory which is from the only God.'[79]

Whom do these seem to me to resemble? Those who 'clean the outside of the cup and the dish but within are full of all kinds of evil.'[80] Be careful lest you experience some such thing. Give your souls to God on high, having the one thought of pleasing the Lord and never straying from the awareness of heavenly things; do not accept the honors of this life; run in such a way as to conceal your struggles in behalf of virtue lest the devil, finding an opportunity to tempt you with worldly honors and having distracted you from leisure for good, lead you to vanity and error. If he does not find an opportunity or chance for destroying those concentrating on the souls above, he perishes and dies. For evil not done and not carried out is the death of the devil. When the love of God is present among you, the other virtues will necessarily follow along with it: love of one's brother, gentleness, honesty, sufficiency, earnestness in prayer, and simplicity in virtue.

When a possession is great, much toil is required to secure it. There is no need for display before men, but there is a need for pleasing the Lord who knows the things that are hidden. It is necessary to look to Him always and to examine

---

77 Cf. Rom. 8.16.
78 Cf. 2 Cor. 10.18.
79 John 5.44.
80 Cf. Matt. 23.25.

the interior part of the soul and to fence it round with considerations of reverence, lest the Adversary find some loophole as a place of attack. It is necessary, also, to exercise the weakened parts of the soul and to train them to distinguish between the good and the bad. The mind which follows God knows how to do these exercises and it directs the entire soul towards God through love of God and hidden thoughts of virtue and commanded deeds and, thus, it curses what is diseased and makes it strong. Since there is but one safeguard and one care for the soul, namely, to remember always to long for God and for good thoughts, let us not deviate from this concentration by eating or drinking or resting or doing or saying anything which does not contribute to the glory of God, so that our life will not put any stain or reflection on our reputation as a result of a desire for evil.

And especially, for those who love God, the toil of the commandments is easy and sweet, since love for Him makes the struggle light and agreeable. On this account, the wicked one tries in every way to cast out fear of the Lord from our souls and to dissolve our love for Him, striving with lawless pleasures and delightful enticements, in order that, taking the soul without spiritual arms and unprotected, he may destroy our labors. He lures us to earthly rather than to celestial glory and muddies the truly beautiful by mixing it with those things which seem to be beautiful through the fantasy of deceit. If he finds the guards careless, he cleverly takes the opportunity to steal upon the toils of virtue and sow his own weeds in with the grain; I mean abuse and conceit and vanity and desire for honor and strife and the other creators of evil. So it is necessary to be alert and to be on guard against the enemy under all circumstances, in order that, if he tries some shameful trick, it may be warded off before it touches the soul.

Bear in mind constantly the following, also, that Abel

offered to the Lord as sacrifice the firstlings of the flock and their fat, but Cain offered the fruits of the earth, but not the first fruits. And it says that God was pleased with the offerings of Abel, but for the offerings of Cain, he had no regard.[81] What is the value of this story? That it enables us to learn that everything offered with fear and trust is pleasing to God, but not that which is lavish and without love. For Abraham did not receive the praise of Melchisedech for other reasons than for bringing the first fruits and the things in season to the priest of God.[82] By fruits in season is meant the choice parts of what exists, the soul itself and the mind itself, and we are ordered not to offer praise and prayers to God in a mean fashion, nor to bring chance things to our Master, but, if some part of the soul is superior, to offer it up entirely with all love and eagerness, in order that, always nurtured by the grace of the Spirit and taking power from Christ, we may easily run the course of salvation, making light and pleasant the struggle in behalf of justice, with God Himself assisting us in our eagerness for toils and paying us back for our deeds of justice.

So much for that. Concerning the parts of virtue, what sort one must consider the greater, which ones we must pursue rather than the others, what the order of them is, it is not possible to say. For they are of equal honor and lead those exercising them to the heights by means of each other. Simplicity gives way to obedience, obedience to faith, faith to hope, hope to justice, justice to service, service to humility. From this comes gentleness which leads to grace, grace to love, and love to prayer. And thus, attached and dependent on each other, they lead us to the peak of what is desired, just as the crown of wickedness leads its own friends in the opposite direction through its own categories to extreme evil. Moreover, it is necessary for us to persevere in prayer.[83] For prayer

---

81 Cf. Gen. 4.4,5.
82 Cf. Heb. 7.4; Gen. 14.18.
83 Cf. Rom. 12.12.

is like a leader of a chorus of the virtues. Through it, the person is strengthened and has a share in and touches upon the other virtues we ask of God through a mystical holiness and a spiritual energy and an inexpressible disposition. Taking the Spirit as companion and ally, one is inflamed towards a love of the Lord and seethes with longing, not finding satiety in prayer, but always inflamed towards a love of the good and enkindling the soul with desire, as it is said: 'He who eats of me will hunger still, he who drinks of me will thirst for more.'[84] And elsewhere: 'You put gladness into my heart.'[85] And the Lord has said: 'The kingdom of God is within you.'[86]

But what does it mean to say that the kingdom of God is within us? What else than the gladness which comes from on high to souls through the Spirit? For this is like an image and a deposit and a pattern of everlasting grace which the souls of the saints enjoy in the time which is to come. So the Lord summons us through the activity of the Spirit to salvation through our afflictions and to a sharing in the goods of the Spirit and his own graces. For He says: 'Who comforts us in our afflictions, that we also may be able to comfort those who are in any distress.'[87] And: 'My heart and my flesh cry out for the living God.'[88] And: 'As with the richness of a banquet, let my soul be satisfied.'[89] All these things make clear in riddles the gladness and comfort of the Spirit.

Since it has been shown what the scope of reverence is which must be prescribed for those choosing to live the God-loving life which is purity of soul and abiding spiritual progress through good deeds, let each of you, having prepared your soul in accordance with what has been indicated and having made it full of divine love, give yourselves over to prayer

---

84 Sir. (Ecclus.) 24.20.
85 Ps. 4.8.
86 Luke 17.21.
87 2 Cor. 1.4.
88 Ps. 83.3.
89 Ps. 62.6.

and fasting according to His will, remembering the one who advises us to: 'Pray without ceasing.'[90] And: 'Be persevering in prayer,'[91] and the message of the Lord in which He says: 'How much more will God avenge those crying to him night and day.'[92] He has spoken and has given a parable about the necessity of praying at all times and not being fainthearted.[93] That the zeal for prayer brings much grace and that the Spirit itself dwells in souls, the apostle clearly shows when he advises us by saying: 'With all prayer and supplications pray at all times in the Spirit, and therein be vigilant in all perseverance and supplication.'[94] So that if anyone of the brethren gives himself over to this part of virtue, I mean to prayer, he cultivates a fair treasure and desires a great possession. Only let each one do this with a precise and upright conscience, never willingly wandering in thought or unwillingly yielding to some necessity, but, filling the soul with love and longing, let him show to all the good fruits of steadfastness. And it is necessary for the others to give due measure to such a person and to rejoice with him in his perseverance in prayer in order that they themselves may have a share in the harvest of goods, becoming partners in such a life by being pleased by it. The Lord Himself will give to those who ask how one ought to pray according to what has been said: He grants the petition of the one who prays. It is necessary, then, to ask and the one persevering in prayer must know how to contend in the struggle with much zeal and all his power. For great struggles require great sufferings because evil lies in wait, especially for such a person, busying itself on all sides, running around and seeking to upset our zeal. Whence come sleep and heaviness of body and weakness of soul and carelessness and meanness and lack of endurance and the other

---

90 1 Thess. 5.17.
91 Rom. 12.12.
92 Cf. Luke 18.7.
93 Cf. Luke 18.1.
94 Eph. 6.18.

passions and activities of evil through which the soul is plundered and destroyed and made to desert to its own enemy.

It is necessary, therefore, to stand by the soul like a wise pilot who never gives any thought to the disturbances of the unfavorable wind and is never distracted by the waves caused by it, but looks directly toward the harbor above and gives his soul wholeheartedly to the trusting and demanding God. For it is not the falling on one's knees nor the placing of ourselves in an attitude of prayer, which is important and pleasing in the Scripture, while our thoughts wander far from God, but rather the giving of the soul to prayer after rejecting all idleness of thought and every undue preoccupation with the body.

It is necessary, also, for those in charge to assist such a person with all zeal and admonition to nurture his desire for the prescribed prayer and cleanse his soul carefully. The harvest of the virtues achieved by those who pray thus should be indicated to the congregation, not only to the one making progress, but to those who are still foolish and in need of instruction. It encourages them and turns them to an imitation of what they see. The harvest of pure prayer is simplicity, love, humility, strength, lack of evil, and such things, which the toil of the person eager in prayer produces here during the course of his life, even before the eternal fruits. Prayer is crowned by such fruits and, if it is lacking, the toil has been in vain. And not prayer alone, but the whole philosophical road, if it produces such offspring, is truly the road of justice and leads to the right goal; but, if it is barren of these, it leaves an empty name and is like the foolish virgins who have no oil in the bridal chamber at the moment that it is needed.[95] They do not have in their souls the light which is the fruit of virtue, nor do they have the lamp of the Spirit in their thinking. Whence Scripture reasonably calls them foolish, their virtue being extinguished before the Bridegroom comes. For this

---

95 Cf. Matt. 25.1 ff.

reason, the wretched maidens are excluded from the bridal chamber on high. Scripture indicates that they are not eager for virginity because the energy of the Spirit is not in them, and this is a just conclusion. What good is there in a vine that has been toiled over if there are no fruits for which the farmer endured the toil? What gain is there in fasting and prayer and vigils if peace and grace and love and the other fruits of the grace of the Holy Spirit, which the holy apostle enumerates, are absent? The lover of grace on high endures every labor for the sake of those things which attract the Spirit and, having obtained a share in the grace from that source, he produces fruit and enjoys the harvest which the grace of the Spirit cultivates in his own humility and active zeal.

It is necessary to endure the toils of prayer and fasting and the other works with much pleasure and love and hope, and to believe that activities are the flowers of labors and the fruits of the Spirit. If anyone imputes these things to himself and gives himself entire credit for them, in the place of the undefiled fruits, there grows up in such a person false pretension and pride, and these passions, like some blight growing in the souls of those easily satisfied, destroy and nullify the labors.

What, then, is it necessary for the person to do who is living for God and in the hope of that One? He must endure the hardships in behalf of virtue with pleasure, he must keep in mind the redemption of the soul from the passions and the ascent to the highest point of the virtues, he must make good the hope of perfection in Him and trust in His kindness. Being thus equipped and enjoying the grace in which he has trusted, he runs without effort and despises the enemy inasmuch as he is stronger than that one and freed from his passions by the grace of Christ. For just as those who admit evil passions into their souls, and joyfully spend their time on these because of their indifference to the beautiful things, easily achieve some natural and personal pleasure, as it were, by harvesting greed and envy and fornication and other heritages of the adversary, so the husbandmen of Christ and truth, who, through faith and the toils of virtue, have received goods from the grace of the Spirit beyond their nature, harvest with unspeakable pleasure, and without effort they attain a guileless and unshakeable love, unmoveable faith, unfailing peace, true goodness, and the rest of the things through which the soul becomes stronger than itself and more powerful than the evil of the enemy, and furnishes itself as a pure dwelling place for the Holy and adorable Spirit. From the Spirit, it receives the eternal peace of Christ and, through it, unites with and cleaves to the Lord. Having done this, the soul not only easily accomplishes deeds of personal virtue, struggling not at all with the enemy because it has become more powerful than the snares of that one, but, greatest of all, it takes to itself the sufferings of the Savior and revels in these more than the lovers of this life do in the honors and glories and powers among men. For the Christian who has advanced by means of good discipline and the gift of the Spirit to the measure of the age of reason, after grace is given to him, being hated because of Christ, being driven, enduring every insult and shame in behalf of his faith in God, experiences glory and pleasure and enjoyment that is greater than any human pleasure. For such a person, whose entire life centers on the resurrection and future blessings, every insult and scourging and persecution and the other sufferings leading up to the cross are all pleasure and refreshment and surety of heavenly treasures. For He says: 'Blessed are you when men reproach you, and persecute you, and, speaking falsely, say all manner of evil against you, for my sake rejoice and exult because your reward is great in heaven.'[96] And the apostle: 'And not only this, but we exult in tribulations also';[97] and elsewhere: 'Gladly therefore I will glory in my infirmities, that the strength of Christ may dwell in me. Wherefore I am satisfied

---
96 Matt. 5.11,12; cf. Luke 6.22,23.
97 Rom. 5.3.

with infirmities, with insults, with hardships, with persecutions. For when I am weak, then I am strong.'[98] And again: 'As God's ministers in much patience.'[99] For this is the grace of the Holy Spirit, possessing the entire soul and filling the dwelling place with gladness and power, making sweet for the soul the sufferings of the Lord, and taking away the perception of the present pain because of the hope of the things to come.

So, govern yourselves thus as you are about to ascend to the highest power and glory through your cooperation with the Spirit; endure every suffering and trial with joy with a view toward appearing to be worthy of the dwelling of the Spirit within you and worthy of the inheritance of Christ. Never be puffed up or enfeebled by indifference to the point of falling yourselves or being the cause of another's sin. But, if certain persons never reach the peak of prayer or the zeal and power required for action and are lacking in this virtue, let them in other matters be obedient according to their ability, ministering zealously, working energetically, serving with pleasure, not for the reward of honor nor for the sake of human glory, not giving in to sufferings because of softness or indifference, ministering not to alien bodies and souls, but to the servants of Christ and to our own hearts, in order that your work may appear pure and guileless to the Lord. Let no one offer as an excuse for his lack of zeal for fair deeds that he is not able to achieve the deeds that will save his soul. God never enjoins upon his servants what is impossible, but shows the love and goodness of his Godhead as something rich and poured out like water upon all, so that He furnishes to each person according to his will the ability to do something good, and none of those eager to be saved is lacking in this ability. He says: 'Whoever gives but a cup of cold water to drink because he is a disciple, he shall not lose his reward.'[100]

---
98 2 Cor. 12.9,10.
99 2 Cor. 6.4.
100 Matt. 12.42; cf. Mark 9.40.

What is more powerful than this injunction? A heavenly reward follows upon a cool drink. Consider also with me the boundlessness of His love of man. 'As long as you did it for one of these, you did it for me.'[101] The command is small, the profit from obedience is given generously and richly by God, so that He asks nothing beyond our power, but, whether you do something small or large, the reward comes to you according to your choice. If it is done in the name and fear of God, the gift comes shining and irrevocable; but, if it is done for display and reputation among men, hear what the Lord Himself asserts: 'Amen, I say to you, they have received their reward.'[102] In order that we may not have this experience, He announces to his disciples and to us through them: 'Take heed that you do not do your alms-giving, nor your praying, nor your fasting before men; otherwise you will not have your reward from your Father in heaven.'[103] He bids you to turn aside from mortals and from the praises of mortals and the reputation that wastes away and eludes us, and to seek that glory alone of whose beauty it is not possible to tell and whose end it is not possible to find, through which we also shall be able to glorify the Father and the Son and the Holy Spirit, now and forever. Amen.

---

101 Matt. 25.40.
102 Matt. 6.2; cf. Matt. 6.5; 6.16.
103 Cf. Matt. 6.1 ff.

THE LIFE OF
SAINT MACRINA

INTRODUCTION

THIS PERSONAL PORTRAIT of his sister as an impressive exponent of the ascetic ideal is an illuminating supplement to St. Gregory's more objective treatises on the ascetic life. Together with his Panegyric on St. Gregory Thaumaturgus, it provides an early example of Christian hagiography. Despite its biographical character, the author refers to it as a letter and it is addressed to his friend, Olympius, to whom the treatise *On Perfection* was also directed. It is an important source of our knowledge of the regimen of an early community of Christian women in the East. To it, we are indebted for much of the information that we have about the distinguished Christian family to which St. Gregory belonged and for many autobiographical details. As he describes his sister's childhood and spiritual development, the atmosphere of the home in which they were reared, his affection for St. Macrina and the other members of the family, he reveals, even more than in his other epistles, the warmth and simplicity of his own personality.

St. Macrina is depicted as a woman of extraordinary strength in her decision not to marry after the death of her betrothed, her ability to lead her mother to the contemplative life, her energetic education of her younger brothers. It is to her that St. Gregory gives credit for St. Basil's conversion from the worldly life of the rhetorician to the asceticism of the priesthood, and he leaves no doubt of the influence that she had upon his own life. In the other treatises in this volume, the rigors of the ascetic life are referred to only in general terms. Here, St. Gregory discloses some of the details of St. Macrina's disciplined existence, the single outfit of clothing, the worn sandals, the board on which she slept even in her last illness. What St. Macrina meant to the women who shared this austere life with her is movingly conveyed by their expression of grief at her death. The picture of St. Macrina is enlarged upon in St. Gregory's work *On The Soul and the Resurrection*, a dialogue between himself and his sister just before her death. In their discussion, St. Macrina defines the Christian view of the nature of the soul and of man's condition after death and refutes the objections offered to it by St. Gregory who assumes the role of antagonist. In his final tribute to his sister's sanctity, therefore, St. Gregory adds the dimension of intellectuality. The two works should be read together. They are believed to have been written not long after 380, the year of St. Macrina's death.

THE LIFE OF ST. MACRINA

Gregory, Bishop of Nyssa, to Olympius

FROM THE HEADING OF THIS WORK, you might think that it is a letter, but it has extended itself into a rather lengthy monograph. My excuse is that you ordered me to write on a subject that goes beyond the scope of a letter. In any case, you will recall our meeting in Antioch, where we happened to come across each other as I was on my way to Jerusalem to fulfill a vow to see the evidence of our Lord's sojourn in the flesh in that region of the world. We talked of all sorts of things (indeed, seeing you precipitated so many topics of conversation that it was not likely to be a silent encounter) and, as often happens, the flow of our conversation turned to the life of an esteemed person. We spoke of a woman, if one may refer to her as that, for I do not know if it is right to use that natural designation for one who went beyond the nature of a woman. We did not have to rely on hearsay since experience was our teacher, and the details of our story did not depend on the testimony of others. The maiden we spoke of was no stranger to my family so that I did not have to learn the wondrous facts about her from others; we were born of the same parents, she being, as it were, an offering of first fruits, the earliest flowering of our mother's womb. At that time, you suggested that a history of her good deeds ought to be written because you thought such a life should not be lost sight of in time and, that having raised herself to the highest peak of human virtue through philosophy, she should not be passed over in silence and her life rendered ineffective. Accordingly, I thought it right to obey you and to write her life story as briefly as I could in an artless and simple narrative.

The maiden's name was Macrina. She had been given this name by her parents in memory of a remarkable Macrina earlier in the family, our father's mother, who had distinguished herself in the confession of Christ at the time of the persecutions. This was her official name which her acquaintances used, but she had been given another secretly in connection with a vision which occurred before she came into the light at birth. Her mother was extremely virtuous, following the will of God in all things and embracing an exceptionally pure and spotless way of life, so that she had chosen not to marry. However, since she was an orphan and flowering in the springtime of her beauty, and the fame of her loveliness had attracted many suitors, there was danger that, if she were not joined to someone by choice, she might suffer some unwished-for violence, because some of the suitors maddened by her beauty were preparing to carry her off. For this reason, she chose a man well known and recommended for the dignity of his life, and thus she acquired a guardian for her own life. In her first pregnancy, she became Macrina's mother. When the time came in which she was to be freed from her pain by giving birth to the child, she fell asleep and seemed to be holding in her hands the child still in her womb, and a person of greater than human shape and form appeared to be addressing the infant by the name of Thecla. (There was a Thecla of much fame among virgins.) After doing this and invoking her as a witness three times, he disappeared from sight and gave ease to her pain so that as she awoke from her sleep she saw the dream realized. This, then, was her secret name. It seems to me that the one who appeared was not so much indicating how the child should be named, but foretelling the life of the child and intimating that she would choose a life similar to that of her namesake.

So the child grew, nursed chiefly by her mother although

she had a nurse of her own. Upon leaving infancy, she was quick to learn what children learn, and to whatever learning the judgment of her parents directed her, the little one's nature responded brilliantly. Her mother was eager to have the child given instruction, but not in the secular curriculum, which meant, for the most part, teaching the youngsters through poetry. For she thought that it was shameful and altogether unfitting to teach the soft and pliable nature either the passionate themes of tragedy (which are based on the stories of women and give the poets their ideas and plots), or the unseemly antics of comedy, or the shameful activities of the immoral characters in the *Iliad*, defiling the child's nature with the undignified tales about women. Instead of this, whatever of inspired Scripture was adaptable to the early years, this was the child's subject matter, especially the Wisdom of Solomon and beyond this whatever leads us to a moral life. She was especially well versed in the Psalms, going through each part of the Psalter at the proper time; when she got up or did her daily tasks or rested, when she sat down to eat or rose from the table, when she went to bed or rose from it for prayer, she had the Psalter with her at all times, like a good and faithful traveling companion.

Growing up with these and similar pursuits and becoming extraordinarily skilled in the working of wool, she came to her twelfth year in which the flowering of youth begins especially to shine forth. Here, it is worth marveling at how the young girl's beauty did not escape notice, although it had been concealed. Nor did there seem to be anything in all that country comparable to her beauty and her loveliness, so that the hand of the painters could not reproduce its perfection, and the art that devises all things and dares the greatest things, even to the fashioning of planets through imitation, was not powerful enough to imitate the excellence of her form. Consequently, a great stream of suitors for her hand crowded round her parents. Her father (he was wise and considered outstanding in his judgment of what was good) singled out from the rest a young man in the family known for his moderation, who had recently finished school, and he decided to give his daughter to him when she came of age. During this period, the young man showed great promise and brought to the girl's father (as a cherished bridal gift, as it were) his reputation as an orator, displaying his rhetorical skill in lawsuits in defense of the wronged. But envy cut short this bright promise by snatching him from life in his piteous youth.

The girl was not unaware of what her father had decided, and when the young man's death broke off what had been planned for her, she called her father's decision a marriage on the grounds that what had been decided had actually taken place and she determined to spend the rest of her life by herself; and her decision was more firmly fixed than her age would have warranted. When her parents talked of marriage (many men wated to marry her on account of the reputation of her beauty), she used to say that it was out of place and unlawful not to accept once and for all a marriage determined for her by her father and to be forced to look to another, since marriage is by nature unique, as are birth and death. She insisted that the young man joined to her by her parent's decision was not dead, but living in God because of the hope of the resurrection,[1] merely off on a journey and not a dead body, and it was out of place, she maintained, for a bride not to keep faith with an absent husband. Thrusting aside the arguments of those trying to persuade her, she settled upon a safeguard for her noble decision, namely, a resolve never to be separated for a moment from her mother, so that her mother often used to say to her that the rest of her children she had carried in her womb for a fixed time, but this daughter she always bore, encompassing her in her womb at all times and under all circumstances. Certainly, the companionship of her

---

[1] Cf. Acts 23.6.

daughter was not burdensome or disadvantageous for the mother, because the care she received from her daughter surpassed that of many of her maidservants and there was an exchange of kindly offices between them. The older woman cared for the young woman's soul and the daughter for her mother's body, fulfilling in all things every desirable service, often even making bread for her mother with her own hands. Not that this was her principal concern, but when she had anointed her hands with mystic services, thinking that it was in keeping with her way of life, in the remaining time she furnished food for her mother from her own labor, and, in addition, she shared her mother's worries. Her mother had four sons and five daughters and was paying taxes to three governors because her property was scattered over that many provinces.

In a variety of ways, therefore, her mother was distracted by worries. (By this time her father had left this life.) In all of these affairs, Macrina was a sharer of her mother's toils, taking on part of her cares and lightening the heaviness of her griefs. In addition, under her mother's direction, she kept her life blameless and witnessed in everything by her, and, at the same time, because of her own life, she provided her mother with an impressive leadership to the same goal; I speak of the goal of philosophy, drawing her on little by little to the immaterial and simpler life. After the mother had skilfully arranged what seemed best for each of Macrina's sisters, her brother, the distinguished Basil, came home from school where he had had practice in rhetoric for a long time. He was excessively puffed up by his rhetorical abilities and disdainful of all great reputations, and considered himself better than the leading men in the district, but Macrina took him over and lured him so quickly to the goal of philosophy that he withdrew from the worldly show and began to look down upon acclaim through oratory and went over to this life full of labors for one's own hand to perform, providing for himself, through his complete poverty, a mode of living that would, without impediment, lead to virtue. But his life and the outstanding activities through which he became famous everywhere under the sun and eclipsed in reputation all those conspicuous in virtue, would make a long treatise and take much time, and my attention must be turned back to the subject at hand. When there was no longer any necessity for them to continue their rather worldly way of life, Macrina persuaded her mother to give up her customary mode of living and her more ostentatious existence and the services of her maids, to which she had long been accustomed, and to put herself on a level with the many by entering into a common life with her maids, making them her sisters and equals rather than her slaves and underlings. But here, I want to insert something into the narrative and not to leave unrecorded an incident which testifies so well to Macrina's exalted character.

The second of the four brothers after the great Basil was named Naucratius, surpassing the others in the excellence of his nature and the beauty of his body and strength and swiftness and adaptability. When he was twenty-one years old and had given such displays of his talent in a public audience that the whole theater was moved, through divine providence and some great inspiration of thought, he was impelled to despise all the opportunities at hand, and he turned to a life of monasticism and poverty, taking no one with him, but going alone. One of his housemen named Chrysaphius followed him because he was used to taking care of him and because he had decided upon the same choice of life. So Naucratius went off to live by himself, having found a remote point on the Iris River. The Iris flows through the middle of Pontus, has its source in Armenia, makes its way through our regions, and empties into the Black Sea. Here, the young man found a spot bristling with deep forest and hidden in a hollow with a rocky cliff overhead, far from the noises of the city, military activities, and the business of rhetoric in the lawcourts. Having freed himself from all the usual distractions of human life, with his own hands, he cared for a group of old people living together in poverty and infirmity, judging it to be in keeping with his life to be occupied with such an activity. Having special skills in matters pertaining to all kinds of hunting, he used to go hunting to procure food for the old people and, at the same time, he tamed his youthful vigor. He also zealously carried out his mother's wishes if she asked anything for herself, and, in these two ways, he charted his life's course, controlling his young manhood by his labor and caring for his mother; and thus he made his way to God by following divine injunctions.

He lived this way for five years, philosophizing and making his mother's life a blessed one because of the way that he regulated his own life through moderation and put all his energy into fulfilling her every wish. Then, there occurred for the mother a grave and tragic experience, planned, I think, by the Adversary, which brought the entire family to misfortune and lamentation. He was unexpectedly snatched from life. It was not illness, which prepares one to anticipate the distaster, nor any of the usually anticipated things that brought the young man to death. He went out to hunt, which was his means of furnishing provisions for the old people. He was brought home dead, he and Chrysaphius, his companion. His mother was a three-day journey away from the scene and someone came to her to report what had taken place. She was perfectly schooled in virtue, but nature won out even over her. She became breathless and speechless on the spot and fainted, reason giving way to passion, and she lay there under the impact of the terrible news like a noble athlete felled by an unforeseen blow.

At this point, the great Macrina's excellence was evident. By setting reason against passion, she kept herself in hand, and, becoming a bulwark of her mother's weakness, she lifted her out of the abyss of grief, and, by her own firmness and unyielding spirit, she trained her mother's soul to be courageous.

Consequently, her mother was not carried away by her misfortune, nor did she react in an ignoble and womanish fashion so as to cry out against the evil or tear her clothes or lament over her suffering or stir up a threnody of mournful melodies. Instead, she conquered her natural impulses and thrust them aside with her own arguments or those suggested by her daughter for the healing of the pain. Then, especially, did the maiden's lofty and exalted soul shine forth because her nature had been subject to the same experience. It had been her brother, and her dearest brother, whom death snatched away in such a manner. Nevertheless, transcending her nature, she lifted her mother up with her own line of reasoning and put her beyond what had happened, directing her by her own example to patience and fortitude. In particular, Macrina's life, always exalted by virtue, did not give the mother an opportunity to grieve for the one who was absent and caused her to rejoice rather in the good that was present.

When the care of rearing the children and the responsibility of educating them and establishing them in life was over, and most of the resources connected with the more material life were divided up among younger members of the family, then, as I said before, Macrina's life became for her mother a guide towards the philosophical and unworldly way of life, and, turning her aside from all that she was used to, she led her to her own standard of simplicity. She prepared her to put herself on a level with the community of virgins so that she shared with them the same food and lodging and all other things one needs in daily life, and there was no difference between her life and theirs. The arrangement of their life, the high level of their philosophy, the lofty regimen of their activities night and day was such that it transcends description. Just as by death souls are freed from the body and released from the cares of this life, so their life was separated from these things, divorced from all mortal vanity and attuned to an imitation of the existence of the angels. Among them was seen no anger, no envy, no hatred, no arrogance, or any such thing; neither was there in them longing for foolish things like honor and fame and vanity, nor a contempt for others; all such qualities had been put aside. Continence was their luxury and not being known their fame; their wealth consisted in their poverty and the shaking off of all worldly abundance like dust from the body. They were not occupied with the concerns of this life; that is, they were not preoccupied. Rather, their one concern was the Divine; there was constant prayer and an unceasing singing of hymns distributed throughout the entire day and night, so that this was for them both their work and their rest from work. What human word could bring this kind of life before your eyes? Their existence bordered on both the human and the incorporeal nature. On the one hand, a nature freed from human cares is more than human, whereas, to appear in the body and to be embraced by form and to live with the senses is to have a nature less than angelic and incorporeal. Perhaps some daring person might say the difference was negligible because, although living in the flesh because of their affinity to the bodiless powers, they were not weighted down by the allurements of the body, but, borne upwards in midair, they participated in the life of the celestial powers. Not a little time was spent in this way and, in time, their successes increased and always their philosophy gave them additional aids for discovering goods leading them to greater purity.

Macrina had a brother who was a great help towards this fine goal of life; he was named Peter and he was the youngest of us, the last offspring of our parents called at once both son and orphan, for as he came into the light of life his father departed from it. His eldest sister, the subject of our story, took him almost immediately from his nurse's breast and reared him herself and led him to all the higher education, exercising him from babyhood in sacred learning so as not to give him leisure to incline his soul to vanities. She became all things to the boy; father, teacher, attendant, mother, the counselor of every good, and she held him in check so that, even before his flowering in the tenderness of youth, he was raised to the high goal of philosophy, and, by some good fortune of nature, he had such skill in every form of handicraft that without instruction he arrived at a complete mastery of skills upon which most people expend much time and energy. So, scorning extraneous instructions and having nature as an adequate teacher of all good learning and always looking to his sister and making her the focal point of every good, he became so virtuous that he was no less esteemed than the great Basil for the excellent qualities of his later life. But then, he was above all a co-worker with his sister and mother in every phase of their angelic existence. Once, when there was a terrible famine and many people came pouring in to our region because of the fame of its prosperity, he furnished so much nourishment through his foresight that the large numbers going to and fro made the hermitage seem like a city.

At this time, our mother, having come to a rich old age, went to God, taking her departure from life in the arms of these two of her children. Worth recording is the blessing she gave to each of her children, suitably remembering each of the absent ones so that none would be without a blessing, and through prayer entrusting especially to God the two who were with her. As they were sitting beside her bed, she touched each of them with her hand and said to God in her last words: 'To you, O Lord, I offer the first and tenth fruit[2] of my pains. The first fruit, my eldest daughter here, and this my tenth, my last-born son. Both have been dedicated to you by law and are your votive offerings. May sanctification, therefore, come to this first and tenth.' And she indicated specifically

---

2 Cf. Luke 1.42.

her daughter and her son. Having finished her blessing, she ended her life, instructing her children to place her body in our father's tomb. These two, having fulfilled her command, attained to a higher level of philosophy, always struggling in their individual lives and eclipsing their early successes by their later ones.

At this time, Basil, distinguished among the holy, was made Bishop of Caesarea. He led his brother to the holy vocation of the priesthood, and consecrated him in the mystical services himself. And through this also, their life progressed to a loftier and higher degree, seeing that their philosophy was enhanced by the consecration. Eight years later, Basil, renowned throughout the entire world, left the world of men and went to God, and his death was a common source of grief for his country and the world. When Macrina heard the report of his distant death, she was greatly disturbed by such a loss. (How could this fail to touch her when even the enemies of truth were affected by it?) But, just as they say gold is tested in many furnaces, that if it gets through the first firing and is tested in the second and, in the last is finally cleansed of all extraneous matter (this is the most accurate proof of true gold if, after all this firing, no impurity remains), something similar happened in her case. When her lofty understanding had been tried by the different attacks of grief, the genuine and undebased quality of her soul was revealed in every way; previously, by the departure of her other brother, then, by the separation from her mother, and, in the third instance, when Basil, the common honor of the family, departed from human life. She remained like an undefeated athlete, in no way overcome by the onslaught of misfortunes.

About nine months after this disaster, there was a synod of bishops in the city of Antioch, in which I participated. And when each of us was leaving to return to his own diocese before the year was out, I, Gregory, thought often of visiting Macrina. For a long time had elapsed during which the circumstances of my trials had prevented our coming together, since I was exiled time and again by the leaders of heresy. When I counted up the time during which these troubles prevented our coming face to face, it added up to almost eight years. When I had almost finished the journey and was about one day away from my destination, a vision, appearing in my sleep, aroused fearful forebodings about the future. I seemed to be carrying the relics of martyrs in my hand and a light seemed to come from them, as happens when the sun is reflected on a bright mirror so that the eye is dazzled by the brilliance of the beam. That same night, the vision occurred three times. I was not able to interpret its meaning clearly, but I foresaw some grief for my soul and I was waiting for the outcome to clarify the dream. When I came near the outskirts of the place where that lady was leading her angelic and celestial life, I asked one of the workmen, first, if my brother happened to be there. He replied that he had gone out to meet us about four days earlier, and this was true, but he had taken a different road. Then, I inquired about the Superior and, when he said that she was ill, I was more eager than ever to complete the trip, for a certain fear, an omen of the future, was disturbing me. As I made my way (rumor had announced my presence beforehand to the community), a line of men streamed toward us. It was customary for them to welcome guests by coming out to meet them. However, a group of women from the convent waited modestly at the entrance of the church for us.

When the prayer and blessing were finished and the women had responded to the blessing by bowing their heads, they removed themselves from our presence and went off to their own quarters. Since not one of them remained with me, I correctly surmised that their Superior was not among them. An attendant led me to the house where the Superior was and opened the door, and I entered that sacred place. She was already very ill, but she was not resting on a couch or bed, but upon the ground; there was a board covered with a coarse cloth, and another board supported her head, designed to be used instead of a pillow, supporting the sinews of her neck slantwise and conveniently supporting the neck. When she saw me standing at the door, she raised herself on her elbow; her strength was already so wasted by fever that she was not able to come towards me, but she fixed her hands on the floor and, stretching as far forward as she could, she paid me the honor of a bow. I ran to her and, lifting her bowed head, I put her back in her accustomed reclining position. But she stretched out her hand to God and said: 'You have granted me this favor, O God, and have not deprived me of my desire, since you have impelled your servant to visit your handmaid.' And in order not to disturb me, she tried to cover up her groans and to conceal somehow the difficulty she had in breathing, and, through it all, she adjusted herself to the brighter side. She initiated suitable topics of conversation and gave me an opportunity to speak by asking me questions. As we spoke, we recalled the memory of the great Basil and my soul was afflicted and my face fell and tears poured from my eyes. But she was so far from being downcast by our sorrow that she made the mentioning of the saint a starting point towards the higher philosophy. She rehearsed such arguments, explaining the human situation through natural principles and disclosing the divine plan hidden in misfortune, and she spoke of certain aspects of the future life as if she was inspired by the Holy Spirit, so that my soul almost seemed to be lifted up out of its human sphere by what she said and, under the direction of her discourse, take its stand in the heavenly sanctuaries.

And just as we hear in the story of Job,[3] that when the man was wasting away and his whole body was covered with erupting and putrefying sores, he did not direct attention to his pain but kept the pain inside his body, neither blessing

---

3 Cf. Job 2.8; 7.5.

his own activity nor cutting off the conversation when it embarked upon higher matters. Such a thing as this I was seeing in the case of this Superior also; although the fever was burning up all her energy and leading her to death, she was refreshing her body as if by a kind of dew, she kept her mind free in the contemplation of higher things and unimpeded by the disease. If my treatise were not becoming too long, I would put down everything in order: how she was lifted up by her discourse on the soul; how she explained the reason for life in the flesh, why man exists; how he is mortal, whence death comes; and what release there is from death back again into life. In all of this, she went on as if inspired by the power of the Holy Spirit, explaining it all clearly and logically. Her speech flowed with complete ease, just as a stream of water goes down a hill without obstruction.

When the conversation was finished, she said: 'Now, brother, it is time for you to rest your body awhile because the trip must have been tiring.' For me, just seeing her and hearing her noble words was truly a great source of relaxation, but, since it was pleasing and desirable to her, in order to seem obedient to her as my teacher in all things, I found a pleasant resting place in one of the gardens nearby and rested in the shade of the vine-clad trees. However, I was unable to enjoy myself because my soul was overwhelmed by the anticipation of sorrows. For the vision in my dream seemed to have been explained by what I had seen. Truly, this was what had appeared, the remains of a holy martyr had been 'dead to sin,'[4] but illuminated by the grace of the indwelling spirit. I explained this to one of those to whom I had previously told the dream. Guessing, I know not how, that we were dejected by the grief that was to come, Macrina sent a message bidding us to cheer up and to be more hopeful about her condition for she perceived a turn for the better. This was not said to deceive us, but was actually the truth, although we did not

---

4 Cf. Rom. 6.11; 8.10,11.

recognize it at the time. For just as a runner who has outrun his rival and comes to the end of the course when he nears the judges' stand and sees the victor's crown, as if he has already obtained the prize, he rejoices within himself and announces his victory to the cheering onlookers, in the same way, Macrina led us to hope for greater good for herself, for she was already looking towards the prize of her high calling and, in her words, almost echoed the words of the apostle: 'Now there is laid up for me the crown of Justice which the just Judge will give me since I have fought the good fight, finished the race, kept the faith.'[5]

Reassured by this message, we began to enjoy what was put before us and the offerings were varied and pleasurable since the great lady was very thoughtful also in such matters. When we returned to her presence (for she did not allow us to idle away the time by ourselves), she took up the story of her life from infancy as if she were putting it all into a monograph. She told what she remembered of our parents' life, both what happened before my birth and afterwards. What she concentrated on in her story was thanksgiving to God, for what she stressed in the life of our parents was not so much their being outstanding among their contemporaries because of their prosperity, but their having been enhanced by divine favor. Our father's parents had been deprived of their possessions because of the confession of Christ; our mother's grandfather was killed by the anger of the emperor and all his property handed over to other masters. Nevertheless, their life was so exalted on account of their faith that no one had a greater reputation among the men of that time. Later, when their property was divided nine ways in accordance with the number of the children, the share of each had been so bountifully increased that the children lived more prosperously than their parents. Macrina did not accept the amount that was assigned to her in the equal distribution, but gave it all into

---

5 Cf. 2 Tim. 4.7,8.

the hands of the priest in accordance with the divine command. By divine dispensation, her existence was such that she never stopped using her hands in the service of God, nor did she look to men for help or any opportunity for living a life of comfort. She never turned away anyone who asked for something, nor did she look for benefactors, but God, in His blessings, secretly made her little resources of activity grow as seeds, as it were, into a full-flowering harvest.

I told her about the difficulties in which I had been involved; first, how the Emperor Valens drove me into exile for the faith, then, the confusion in the churches which called me to disputes and disagreements. She said: "Will you ever stop ignoring the good things that come from God? Will you not remedy the thanklessness of your soul? Compare your lot with that of our parents, although, as far as this world is concerned, it is true that we are proud of being well born and coming from a good family. Our father in the past was well thought of because of his education, and his reputation was established in the local law courts. Later, although he surpassed the rest in rhetoric, his fame did not go beyond the Pontic region, but he was satisfied to be looked up to in his own land. Whereas you,' she continued, 'are known in the cities, among the peoples and the tribes; churches send you forth and summon you as ally and advocate, and do you not see the grace in it? Do you not realize the cause of such blessings, namely, that the prayers of your parents are lifting you to the heights, since you have little or nothing within yourself by which to achieve this?'

As she went on this way, I kept wishing that the day might be lengthened so that we could continue to enjoy the sweetness of her words. But the sound of the choir was calling us to vespers and, having sent me off to the church, the Superior withdrew to God in prayer and the night was devoted to it. When dawn came, it was clear to me that this day was to be the last for her in the life of the flesh, for the fever had consumed all her natural strength. When she saw our concern about her weakness, she tried to rouse us from our downcast hopes by dispersing again with her beautiful words the grief of our souls with her last slight and labored breathing. At this point, especially, my soul was in conflict because of what it was confronted by. My disposition was naturally made gloomy by the anticipation of never again hearing such a voice, but actually I had not yet accepted the idea that she was going to leave this mortal life, and my soul was so exalted by appearances that I secretly thought that she had transcended the common nature. For the fact was that, in her last breath, she experienced nothing strange in the expectation of the change and displayed no cowardice towards the departure from life. Instead, she philosophized with high intelligence on what had been decided upon by her about this life from the beginning up to her last breath, and this made her appear to belong no longer to the world of men. It was as if an angel had by some providence taken on human form, an angel who had no relation with or similarity to the life of the flesh and for whom it was not at all unreasonable to remain detached since the flesh was not part of her experience. For this reason, she seemed to me to be making clear to those present the divine and pure love of the unseen Bridegroom which she had secretly nourished in the depths of her soul, and she seemed to be communicating the disposition in her heart to go to the One she was longing for, so that, once loosed from the chains of the body, she might quickly be with Him. Truly, her race was towards the Beloved and nothing of the pleasure of life diverted her attention.

The day was almost over and the sun was beginning to set, but the zeal in her did not decline. Indeed, as she neared her end and saw the beauty of the Bridegroom more clearly, she rushed with greater impulse towards the One she desired, no longer speaking to those of us who were present, but to that very One toward whom she looked with steadfast eyes.

Her couch was turned to the East and, stopping her conversation with us, for the rest of the time she addressed herself to God in prayer, beseeching Him with her hands and speaking in a low soft voice so that we barely heard what she said. This was her prayer and there is no doubt that it made its way to God and that it was heard by Him.

She said: 'O Lord, You have freed us from the fear of death;[6] You have made the end of life here the beginning of a true life for us. For a time, You give rest to our bodies in sleep and You awaken us again with the last trumpet.[7] The dust from which You fashioned us with Your hands You give back to the dust of the earth for safekeeping, and You who have relinquished it will recall it after reshaping with incorruptibility and grace our mortal and graceless substance. You redeemed us from the curse[8] and from sin, having taken both upon Yourself; You crushed the heads of the serpent[9] who had seized us with his jaws in the abyss of disobedience. Breaking down the gates of hell[10] and overcoming the one who had the empire of death,[11] You opened up for us a path to the resurrection. For those who fear You, You gave as a token the sign of the holy cross for the destruction of the Adversary and the salvation of our life. O God everlasting, towards whom I have directed myself from my mother's womb, whom my soul has loved[12] with all its strength, to whom I have dedicated my body and my soul from my infancy up to now, prepare for me a shining angel to lead me to the place of refreshment where is the water of relaxation[13] near the bosom of the holy Fathers.[14] You who broke the flaming sword[15] and

---

6 Cf. Heb. 2.15.
7 Cf. 1 Cor. 15.52.
8 Cf. Gal. 3.13.
9 Cf. Ps. 73.13,14.
10 Cf. Matt. 16.18.
11 Cf. Heb. 2.14.
12 Cf. Cant. 1.7.
13 Cf. Ps. 22.2.
14 Cf. Luke 16.22.
15 Cf. Gen. 3.24.

compassionately gave Paradise back to the man crucified with You,[16] remember me also in Your kingdom, for I, too, have been crucified with You, having nailed my flesh through fear of You and having feared Your judgments. Let the terrible abyss[17] not separate me from Your chosen ones; let the Slanderer not stand in my way or my sins be discovered before Your eyes if I have fallen and sinned in word or deed or thought because of the weakness of our nature. Do You who have power on earth to forgive sins[18] forgive me so that I may be refreshed and may be found before You once I have put off my body, having no fault in the form of my soul, but blameless and spotless may my soul be taken into Your hands as an offering before Your face.' As she said this, she made the sign of the cross upon her eyes and mouth and heart, and little by little, as the fever dried up her tongue, she was no longer able to speak clearly; her voice gave out and only from the trembling of her lips and the motion of her hands did we know that she was continuing to pray.

Then, evening came on and the lamp was brought in. Macrina directed her eye toward the beam of light and made it clear that she was eager to say the nocturnal prayer and, although her voice failed her, with her heart and the movement of her hands, she fulfilled her desire and moved her lips in keeping with the impulse within her. When she had completed the thanksgiving and indicated that the prayer was over by making the sign of the cross, she breathed a deep breath and with the prayer her life came to an end. From then on, she was without breath and movement, and I recalled an injunction she had given me when I arrived, saying that she wanted my hands to be placed upon her eyes and the customary care of the body to be taken by me. So I placed my hand, deadened by grief, upon her holy face so as not to seem to disregard her request. Actually, her eyes required no

---
16 Cf. Luke 23.42.
17 Cf. Luke 16.26.
18 Cf. Matt. 9.6; Mark 2.10.

attention; it was as if she was asleep with her eyelids becomingly lowered; her lips were set naturally and her hands rested naturally on her breast and the whole position of her body was so spontaneously harmonious that there was no need for any arranging hand.

My soul was disquieted for two reasons, because of what I saw and because I heard the weeping of the virgins. Until now, they had controlled themselves and kept in check the grief in their souls and they had choked down the impulse to cry out for fear of her, as if they were afraid of the reproach of her voice already silent; lest, contrary to her order, a sound should break forth from them and their teacher be troubled by it. But when their suffering could no longer be controlled in silence (their grief was affecting their souls like a consuming fire within them), suddenly, a bitter, unrestrained cry broke forth, so that my reason no longer maintained itself, but, like a mountain stream overflowing, it was overwhelmed below the surface by my suffering and, disregarding the tasks at hand, I gave myself over wholly to lamentation. The cause of the maidens' grief seemed to me to be just and reasonable. They were not bewailing the deprivation of some ordinary bond or carnal attraction or any other such thing for which one mourns. But, as if they were torn away from their hope in God or the salvation of their souls, they cried out and loudly bewailed as follows:

'The lamp of our life has been extinguished; the light that directed the path of our souls has been taken away; the safety of our lives has been destroyed; the seal of our incorruptibility has been removed; the bond of our union has been demolished; the support of the feeble has been shattered; the care of the weak taken away. With you even our night was illuminated like day by the pure life, but now even the day is turned into darkness.' The ones who called her mother and nurse were more seriously distraught than the rest. These were those she had nursed and reared after finding them prostrate along the highway at the moment of starvation and she led them to the pure and uncorrupted life.

But when I recalled my soul from the depths, gazing intently at the holy head, and, as if I were rebuked for the disorderly conduct of the women, I said: 'Look at her,' shouting at the maidens in a loud voice, 'and be mindful of the instructions she gave you for order and graciousness in everything. Her divine soul sanctioned one moment of tears for us, commanding us to weep at the moment of prayer. This command we can obey by changing the wailing of our lamentation into a united singing of psalms.' I said this with a loud voice to drown out the noise of the wailing. Then, I bade them withdraw a little to their quarters nearby and to leave behind a few of those whose services she accepted during her lifetime.

Among these, there was a woman outstanding for her wealth and birth and the beauty of her body, and admired in her youth for her other attributes. She had been married to a distinguished man and, after having been with him for a short time, she was released from marriage while still quite young. She made Macrina the guardian and director of her widowhood, and, spending much of her time with the women, she learned from them the life of virtue. The woman's name was Vetiana, whose father was Araxius, one of the senators. I told her that now, at least, it was suitable to put brighter raiment on the body and to adorn with shining ornament that pure and unsullied flesh. She replied that it was necessary to learn what decisions had been made by the holy one about these matters, for it would not be right for us to do anything to her contrary to what would be pleasing to her. But what was dear and pleasing to God was also desirable to her.

There was a certain woman, a deaconess in charge of a group of the women, whose name was Lampadium, and she said she knew exactly what Macrina had decided about her burial. When I asked her about it (for she happened to be present at our discussion) she replied weeping: 'For the holy one, the pure life was what she sought as adornment; for her, this was both the ornament of her life and the shroud of death. She had so little concern for dress that she owned nothing during her lifetime and stored none away for the present situation, so that, even if we desired it, there is nothing more to use than what is already here.' I said: 'Is there nothing in the storage closets to decorate the funeral bier?' 'What closets?' she replied. 'You have everything she possessed in your hands. Look at her dress, look at the covering of her head, her worn sandals. This is her wealth, this is her property. There is nothing beyond what you see put aside in hidden places or made secure in treasures houses. She recognized one storage place for private wealth: the treasury of heaven.[19] There she deposited everything and left nothing behind on earth.' I said to her: 'What if I brought some of the things I had got ready for the funeral? Would this be against her wish?' She replied that she did not think it would be. 'For,' she said, 'if she were alive, she would accept such a gift from you for two reasons: on account of your priesthood, which she always honored, and, on account of your kinship, she would not have thought that what belonged to her brother was not also hers. It was for this reason that she ordered her body to be prepared by your hands.'

When this was decided upon and it was necessary for the sacred body to be dressed in fine linen, we divided the various tasks among us. I told one of my attendants to bring in the robe. Vetiana, whom I have mentioned before, was arranging that holy head with her own hands when she put her hand on her neck and said looking at me: 'See the necklace the holy one wore.' And, at the same time, she unfastened the chain, stretched out her hand, and showed me an iron cross and a ring of the same material. Both of these worn on a thin chain were always on her heart. And I said: 'Let us make

---

19 Cf. Matt. 6.19,20.

this a common possession. You take the protection of the cross, and the ring will be enough for me,' for on the seal of the ring a cross was carved. Gazing at it, the woman said to me: 'You have made a good choice, for the ring is hollowed out and in it is hidden a piece of the wood of life. And thus the seal of the cross on the outside testifies by its form to what is inside.'

When the time came to cover the body with the robe, the injunction of the great lady made it necessary for me to perform this function. The woman who was present and sharing the great assignment with us said: 'Do not pass over the greatest of the miracles of the saint.' 'What is that?' I asked. She laid bare a part of the breast and said: 'Do you see this thin, almost imperceptible, scar below the neck?' It was like a mark made by a small needle. At the same time, she brought the lamp nearer to the place she was showing me. 'What is miraculous about that,' I said, 'if the body has a small mark here?' She said: 'This is left on the body as a reminder of the great help of God. At one time, there was a painful sore here and there was the risk that if it was not cut out it would develop into an irremediable illness if it should spread to places near the heart. Her mother begged her to accept the doctor's care and implored her many times saying that the art of medicine was given by God to man for his preservation. But Macrina considered worse than the disease laying bare part of the body to another's eyes, and one evening, after she had finished her usual tasks connected with her mother, she went inside the sanctuary and all night supplicated the God of healing, pouring out a stream from her eyes upon the ground, and she used the mud from her tears as a remedy for the disease. When her mother was earnestly distressed and asking her again to see the doctor, she said that there was a cure for her disease if her mother with her own hand would make the sign of the cross on the place. When the mother put her hand inside to make the sign of the cross on her breast, the sign of the cross worked and the sore disappeared. But this,' she said, 'is a small token and was seen then instead of the terrible sore, and remained to the end as a reminder, I suppose, of the divine consideration, a cause and reason for unceasing thanksgiving to God.'

When our work was finished and the body was adorned with what we had, the deaconess spoke again and said that it was not fitting that Macrina should be seen by the maidens dressed as a bride. She said: 'I have a dark mantle of your mother's which I think we should put over her, so that this holy beauty should not be made splendid by the extraneous adornment of the robe.' Her opinion prevailed and the mantle was put over her. But even in the dark, the body glowed, the divine power adding such grace to her body that, as in the vision of my dream, rays seemed to be shining forth from her loveliness.

While we were engaged in these activities and the maidens' psalm-singing, mingled with lamentation, resounded through the place, in some way the report spread about on all sides and all the people of the area began to rush in so that the vestibule was not large enough to hold them. There was an all night vigil with hymn-singing as is the custom in the case of the praise of martyrs, and, when it was finished and day dawned, a crowd of those who had hurried in from the entire countryside, men and women both, broke in on the psalmody with their cries of grief. Although my soul was distressed by my misfortune, I kept thinking, nevertheless, how it should be possible not to leave undone anything suitable for such an occasion. Separating the flow of people according to sex, I put the women with the choir of nuns and the men in the ranks of the monks. I arranged for the singing to come rhythmically and harmoniously from the group, blended well as in choral singing with the common responses of all. But as the day was advancing and the place was overcrowded by the multitude of people, the bishop of the region, whose name was Araxius (he was present with the full company of his priests), ordered the bier to be brought forward immediately, on the grounds that there was quite a distance to be covered and the crowd would prevent the swift movement of the funeral procession. At the same time, he ordered all the priests who were with him to escort the bier themselves.

When this was decided upon and the activity begun, I went to one side of the bier and called him to the other, and two of the others, distinguished in rank, took their position at the opposite end. I led the way slowly, as was fitting, and we proceeded at a moderate rate. The people crowded around the bier and could not get enough of that holy sight, so it was not easy for us to pass. There was a row of deacons and attendants on each side of the funeral train, all holding wax candles; it was a kind of mystical procession, the psalmody continuing from beginning to end harmoniously, as is sung in the hymnody of the three boys.[20] It was a distance of seven or eight stadia from the monastery to the House of the Holy Martyrs, where the bodies of our parents were at rest. We completed the journey with difficulty throughout most of the day, for the accompanying crowd and those who were always being added to our number did not allow us to proceed according to our estimate. When we were inside the gate of the House, we first put down the bier and turned to prayer, but the prayer was the starting point of lamentation for the people. When there was a lull in the psalm-singing and the maidens were looking at the holy face, as the tomb of our parents was being opened in which she was to be placed, one of them cried out saying that no longer would we look upon her divine face. The rest of the maidens joined her in her outburst and confusion drowned out the orderly and sacred singing. Everyone wept in response to the wailing of the maidens. We nodded for silence and the leader guided them to prayer by intoning the usual prayers of the Church and the people came to attention.

---

20 Cf. Dan. 3.51.

When the proper ceremony was finished, the fear of the divine command not to uncover the shamelessness of father and mother came upon me.[21] 'How,' I said, 'shall I ward off such a judgment if I look upon the common shame of human nature in the bodies of our parents, since they have surely fallen apart and disintegrated and been changed into a disgusting and disagreeable formlessness?' As I was considering this, and Noe's anger against his son was rousing fear in me, the story of Noe[22] indicated what ought to be done. Before the bodies came into view when the cover of the tomb was lifted they were covered from one end to the other by a pure linen cloth. When they were covered thus with the linen, the bishop I have mentioned and I lifted that holy body from the bier and placed it beside our mother, fulfilling the common prayer of both of them. For this they had asked from God all through their life, that after death their bodies should be together and that in death they should not be deprived of the comradeship they had had in their lifetime.

When everything was accomplished and it was necessary to go back, I fell upon the tomb and kissed the dust and retraced my steps, downcast and tearful, thinking of the good of which my life had been deprived. Along the way, a certain distinguished military man in charge of a garrison of soldiers in a district of Pontus, called Sebastopolis, met us graciously when I arrived there and, hearing of my misfortune, he was greatly disturbed (for he was connected with our family through kinship and association). He told me the story of a miracle connected with Macrina and, adding only this to my story, I shall come to an end. When I had stopped crying and we stood talking, he said to me: 'Hear what a great and substantial good has been removed from human life,' and, speaking thus, he began his tale:

'It happened that my wife and I were eager to visit the monastery of virtue (for that is what I think that place

---
21 Cf. Lev. 18.7.
22 Cf. Gen. 9.20 ff.

should be called) in which the blessed soul spent her life. There was with us our little girl who was suffering from an eye ailment resulting from an infectious sickness. It was a terrible and pitiful thing to see her as the membrane around the pupil was swollen and whitened by the disease. As we entered the monastery, we separated, my wife and I, for I went to the men's quarters where your brother Peter was Superior, and she went to the woman's quarters to be with the holy one. After an interval of time, we thought it was the hour for us to go home. We were getting ready to leave, but a kindly remonstrance came to us from both quarters. Your brother urged me to remain and share the monastic table. The blessed one would not let my wife go, and said she would not give up my daughter, whom she was holding in her arms, until she had given them a meal and offered them the wealth of philosophy. She kissed the child as one might expect and put her lips on her eyes and, when she noticed the diseased pupil, she said: "If you do me the favor of remaining for dinner, I will give you a return in keeping with this honor." When the child's mother asked what it was, the great lady replied: "I have some medicine which is especially effective in curing eye diseases." When a message came to me from the women's quarters about this promise, we gladly remained and disregarded the urgent necessity of starting on our way.

'When the feasting was over and grace said (the great Peter, having entertained and cheered us with special graciousness, and the great Macrina, having said goodbye to my wife with every courtesy), we started the journey home bright and happy. Each of us told his own story on the way. I spoke of everything I had seen and heard in the men's quarters, and she told everything systematically, as in a history, and did not think it right to omit the smallest details. She was telling everything in order, as if going through a treatise, and when she came to the point at which the medicine was promised, interrupting the narrative she said: "What have we done?

How did we forget the promise, the medicine for the eyes?" I was annoyed at our thoughtlessness and quickly sent one of my men back to ask for the medicine, when the child, who happened to be in her nurse's arms, looked at her mother, and the mother fixing her gaze on the child's eyes, said: "Stop being upset by our carelessness." She said this in a loud voice, joyfully and fearfully. "Nothing of what was promised to us has been omitted, but the true medicine that heals diseases, the cure that comes from prayer, this she has given us, and it has already worked; nothing at all is left of the disease of the eyes." As she said this, she took our child and put her in my arms and I, also, then comprehended the miracles in the gospel which I had not believed before and I said: "What a great thing it is for sight to be restored to the blind by the hand of God, if now His handmaiden makes such cures and has done such a thing through faith in Him, a fact no less impressive than these miracles." ' This was what he told me, and tears fell as he spoke and his voice was choked with emotion. This is the story of the soldier.

I do not think it is wise to add to my story all the other details we heard from those who lived with her and knew her life accurately, for most men judge the credibility of what they hear according to the measure of their own experience, and what is beyond the power of the hearer they insult with the suspicion of falsehood as outside of the truth. Therefore, I pass over that incredible farming phenomenon at the time of the famine when, as the grain was given out in proportion to the need, the amount did not seem to grow smaller, but remained the same as it was before it was given to those asking for it. And after this, there were other events more surprising than these; the healing of disease, the casting out of devils, true prophecies of future events, all of which are believed to be true by those who knew the details accurately, amazing although they are. But for the material-minded, they are beyond what can be accepted. They do not know that the distribution of graces is in proportion to one's faith, meager for those of little faith, great for those who have within themselves great room for faith. So, in order not to do harm to those who have no faith in the gifts of God, I have decided against enumerating the greater miracles, judging it sufficient to end my work about Macrina with what I have already related.

ON THE SOUL AND THE RESURRECTION

INTRODUCTION

THIS DIALOGUE BETWEEN ST. GREGORY and his sister, St. Macrina, during her last hours is reminiscent of Plato's *Phaedo* in which Socrates and his friends spend the last day of his life discussing the pertinent subject of the possibility of the soul's immortality. The fact that the role of protagonist is given to a saintly woman recalls the Platonic device in *The Symposium* where Socrates attributes his splendid insights into the nature of love to the instruction of the wise Diotima. St. Macrina's solicitude for her brother's state of mind creates a situation not unlike that in the first Book of *The Consolation of Philosophy* by Boethius. One is reminded also of another conversation between two saints, St. Augustine and his mother, recorded in the *Confessions*[1] as taking place shortly before St. Monica's death at Ostia. However, this work is most similar to a dialogue written in the second century by an opponent of Origen named Methodius, entitled *On the Resurrection,* in which a certain Aglaophon offers objections to the doctrine of the resurrection which Methodius himself resolves.

That St. Gregory was concerned with eschatological matters is evident from three other works written by him during the same period: his treatise *On the Creation of Man* (378), his *Sermon on the Resurrection* (379), and his *Catechetical Oration* (385). Father Daniélou, who has been particularly interested in this aspect of Gregorian thought,[2] has shown that,

---
[1] St. Augustine, *Confessions* 9.10.
[2] Cf. J. Daniélou, 'La résurrection des corps chez Grégoire de Nysse,' *Vigiliae Christianae* 7 (1953) 154-170; 'L'apocatastase chez Grégoire de Nysse,' *Recherches de science religieuse* 30 (1940) 328-347; *idem*, 'Notes sur trois textes eschatologiques de saint Grégoire de Nysse,' *loc. cit.*, 348-356.

although St. Gregory is in close agreement with Methodius' viewpoint, he has arrived at a more profound interpretation of it. St. Gregory agrees with Methodius in rejecting Origen's theory that it is a spiritualized body which will rise, since he maintains that the earthly body and the risen body are identical, being made up of the same unchanging elements which informed it from the beginning. Furthermore, he believes that the soul is never actually separated from these elements, even during the period between death and the resurrection. Origen held that the two bodies will have different natures; St. Gregory insists that the body will be the same, but the two states of the body different, the risen body being the last of a series of transformations which the body of man goes through from infancy to the resurrection.

Related to this speculation on the condition of the soul after death is the more controversial issue of *apokatastasis* which is also taken up in this dialogue. The word literally means a return to a former state of perfection, and the idea was a familiar one in Greek mythology and philosophy. In Christian literature, it was applied to the idea that there will ultimately be a restoration of all things in Christ. Origen's doctrine of *apokatastasis* was part of his belief that the souls would return to a purely spiritual condition at the time of the resurrection and it was condemned by the fifth Ecumenical Council. Although St. Gregory does not accept Origen's theory that it is a spiritualized body that will rise, he has been held by some[3] to come close to Origenistic teaching in his reluctance to accept the view that the punishment of sinners will be eternal. Early attempts were made to prove that certain passages in St. Gregory's writings relating to this question were interpolations, but this is seldom a satisfactory way of dealing with such problems. Daniélou thinks that *apokata-*

---

[3] e.g., H. Graef in the introduction to her translation of *The Lord's Prayer and The Beatitudes* (Ancient Christian Writers 18; Westminster, Md. 1954); W. Jaeger, *Early Christianity and Greek Paideia, op. cit.,* 89; E. V. McClear, 'The Fall of Man and Original Sin in the Theology of Gregory of Nyssa' (doct. diss.) (Woodstock, 1948) 206.

stasis in St. Gregory underlines what he calls the 'definitive character of the Incarnation, the social character of salvation,' and he concludes that 'our insufficient notion of eternity' makes it difficult for us to reconcile the notion of a universal physical *apokatastasis* with an affirmation of the eternal punishment of the damned.[4] J. Quasten comments that, in this matter, St. Gregory has 'simply erred in the attempt to conquer heights of speculation where but few mortals dare to tread.'[5]

As a statement of the doctrine of the resurrection, the dialogue belongs, strictly speaking, with St. Gregory's dogmatic treatises. However, it is included in this volume as an *addendum* to the portrait of his sister as an inspiring model of those pursuing the goal of the ascetic life and as a gesture of *pietas* to the distinguished scholar who devoted so many years of his life to making available a definitive edition of the works of St. Gregory of Nyssa.

---

4 'L'apocatastase chez Grégoire de Nysse,' *op. cit.*, 347.
5 J. Quasten, *Patrology* 3, *op. cit.*, 290.

ON THE SOUL AND THE RESURRECTION

AT THE TIME THAT BASIL, great among the saints, left the life of man and went to God and a common onset of grief descended upon the Churches, my sister and teacher was still alive and I hurried to her to tell her the sad news about our brother. My soul was sorrowful as I suffered the pain of this affliction and I was seeking someone to share my tears, someone whose burden of pain was equal to my own. As we met each other, the sight of my teacher reawakened the grief within me for she was already ill and close to death. She, however, like those who are skilled in the equestrian art, first, allowed me to be swept along for a little while by the violence of my grief and, after this, tried to restrain me, guiding the disorder of my soul with her own ideas as if with a bridle. She quoted the following apostolic saying:

Macrina: 'It is not right to grieve for those who are asleep, since we are told that sorrow belongs only to those who have no hope.'[1]

Gregory: And I, with my heart still seething with pain, asked: 'How is it possible for me to achieve this attitude, since there is a natural aversion to death in each person and no one can endure the sight of others dying and those who are dying themselves flee from it as much as they can? Also, since among the sentences for wrongdoing the most extreme penalty decreed by the laws is death, how can we come to think that the departure from this life is nothing even in the case of strangers, not to mention the case of the death of our close friends? Moreover, we see every human effort directed towards this,

---

[1] Cf. 1 Thess. 4.13.

namely, how to remain alive. Even houses are planned with this in mind so that our bodies will not be afflicted by excessive heat or cold. And what else is farming than a means of staying alive? Isn't concern for life altogether due to the fear of death? And what of the art of healing? Why is it so honored among men? Isn't it because through this art it seems possible to fight against death? Why do breastplates and shields and greaves and helmets and defensive weapons and walls and iron gates and trenches and such things exist if not because of the fear of death? Therefore, since death is naturally so fearful, how is it possible for us to believe the person who tells us not to grieve when someone has died?'

M. My teacher asked: 'What is it about death itself which seems especially fearful to you? Surely, the unanimity of the foolish is not enough to make you condemn it.'

G. I replied: 'Isn't this deserving of grief, to see someone who was recently alive and speaking suddenly without breath or voice or movement, bereft of all his physical perceptions, deprived of sight and hearing and all his other perceptive faculties? Whether you approach the body with fire or iron, or run it through with a sword, or attack it with ferocious animals, or cover it with earth, it responds in the same way to all as it lies there. When this change is seen the lifegiving principle, whatever it is, vanishes and disappears. Life is put out, as it were, no longer existing on the wick which was just now aflame and, having completely disappeared, it will not return. How can anyone endure such a change when he is dealing with something that is not evident? Hearing about the departure of the soul, we see what is left, but we do not know what has gone away, what its nature is, or where it has gone, and neither earth nor air nor water nor any of the elements indicates what force has left the body once it has gone out and the corpse is left behind already a prey to corruption.' As I was saying these things, my teacher shook her finger and interrupted me.

M. Isn't this what disturbs and distracts you, the fear that the soul does not last forever, but leaves with the dissolution of the body?

G. Then I, for I had not yet recovered from my grief, replied somehow rather boldly and without due consideration. I said that the divine words were like orders which force us to believe that the soul exists forever. We are not led to this point of view by any logic, but our mind slavishly accepts what is ordered because of fear and does not agree with what is said because of any voluntary impulse. As a result, our grief for those who have died increases, since we do not know exactly whether the life-giving principle exists in itself and where and how, or if it does not exist anywhere at all. The uncertainty of the real truth creates equal assumptions on both sides. Many have one opinion and many others the opposite and there are certain ones among the Greeks, not undistinguished in philosophy, who have these opinions and state them.

M. She said: 'Dismiss this pagan nonsense wherein the inventor of falsehood persuasively makes deceitful assumptions to the detriment of truth. Look at it this way, that to have this attitude towards the soul is nothing else than alienating yourself from virtue and looking only to the pleasure of the moment. Life viewed in this secular way is without hope which gives virtue its superiority.'

G. 'But how,' I said, 'can we arrive at some steadfast and unchanging opinion concerning the soul's immortality? I myself perceive that virtue is deficient unless some unequivocal belief on this subject prevails in us. How can virtue have a place among those who assume that the present life is the limit of existence and that there is nothing to be hoped for after that?'

M. My teacher replied: 'We must ask ourselves what would be a fitting starting point for a discussion on these matters. If you agree, let the defense of the opposing opinions be your responsibility. For I see that your thinking with regard to such a blow has been upset. After the opposition is set forth, the true argument can be examined.'

G. Since she ordered this procedure, I begged her not to think that I was offering the opposing arguments with conviction, but merely to establish our opinion firmly once the other had been demolished. I began: 'Those who support the opposing argument would say that the body being composite is entirely dissolved when the union of the elements in the body is dissolved. Each element, as is reasonable, inclines towards its own kind, the very nature of each of the elements, by some necessary attraction, returning to its own group. The elements of heat are thrust back to the hot, the earthy to the solid, and each of the rest go over to their own kind. But where will the soul be after this occurs? If someone says that it is in the elements, he will necessarily agree that it is the same as these. For a mixture of one nature with another cannot occur, and if it could, some completely variegated thing would appear made up of opposite qualities. However, what is variegated is not simple, but is looked upon as a synthesis. And everything composite is also by nature subjected to dissolution, for dissolution is the destruction of the composite. What is destroyed is not immortal; otherwise, the flesh would be called immortal although it is dissolved into the elements of which it is composed. But, if there is something else besides these, where does reason suggest that it is, since it is not found in the elements, and there is nothing else in the world in which the soul could be living suitably with its own nature? But what is nowhere certainly does not exist.'

M. And my teacher quietly groaned at what I had said. 'Perhaps it was such arguments as these that the Stoics and Epicureans presented to the apostle in Athens.[2] For I hear that Epicurus was brought around to this by his assumptions that the nature of reality is formed by chance and automatically,

---

2 Cf. Acts 17.18.

inasmuch as there is no providence governing things. Consequently, he also thought that human life was like a bubble brought together by some air of our body as long as the air wins out over what surrounds it, but what is left behind is annihilated by the blow of an atom. For, to him, the limit of reality was what is perceived and he made perception the measure of the comprehension of everything. He closed his eyes completely to the perceptions of the soul and was unable to recognize anything intelligible and incorporeal, just as someone kept in a little house is excluded from the sight of the wonders of the heavens, being cut off by the walls and roof from the sight of what is outside. There really are walls which prevent small-souled folk through their own fault from the contemplation of the intelligible. Such a person looks to the earth alone and to water and air and fire. And because of his smallness of soul he is not able to see whence each of these things exists, or in what or by what it is governed. Seeing a garment, one reasons that there is a weaver, and, because of a ship, one thinks of a shipbuilder, and at the sight of a house, the hand of the builder is in the consciousness of the beholder. However, some who see the universe are blind to what is made clear by it. As a result, these sophisticated and scornful persons are cited by those who philosophize about the disappearance of the soul, saying that a body is made of elements and that the soul cannot exist by itself unless it is one of these and exists in them. If our opponents think that the soul exists nowhere for this reason, that it is not of the same nature as the elements, they are expressing the opinion, first of all, that life in the flesh is soulless, since to them the body is nothing else than the coming together of elements. Moreover, they are not saying that the soul does exist among them bringing substance to life through itself, if, as they think, it is not possible for the soul to exist afterwards although the elements do. Consequently, they are teaching nothing else than that our life is dead. But if they do not doubt that the soul is now in the body, how do they teach that the soul disappears once the elements of the body have been dissolved? And then do they also dare to make the same assertions about the divine nature? For how will they maintain that the intelligible and immaterial and invisible which slips into the moist and the soft and the hot and the solid, holding reality together in its essence, is not related to these things in which it exists and is not able to be in them because of its difference from them? Therefore, let the divine itself, by which reality is governed, be entirely removed from their teaching.'

G. 'But,' said I, 'how could our opponents doubt this very thing, that all things are from God and fully governed by Him, or that there is something wholly divine underlying the nature of reality?'

M. She replied: 'It is more agreeable to remain silent on such questions and to consider their foolish and irreverent assumptions unworthy of a response, since the divine words forbid it saying: "Answer not a fool according to his folly."[3] But the fool, according to the prophet, is "the one who says there is no God."[4] But since it is necessary to discuss this, I will tell you my argument, my own and not that of someone else, a small point whatever it is, but the one that the Creator of reality gives us through the wonders of creation in which the eye becomes the ear, the wise and skillful argument being poured into the heart because of what is seen. For Creation declares the maker of the heavens,[5] as the prophet says, telling the glory of the Lord with unutterable words. Look at the harmony of everything, the heavens and the wonders beneath the earth, the elements so different from each other, woven together through some ineffable relationship for the same purpose, each contributing its own power to the permanence of all, not withdrawing from each other unmixed and un-

---
3 Prov. 26.4.
4 Cf. Ps. 52.2.
5 Cf. Ps. 18.2.

mingled because of their peculiar qualities, nor destroyed by each other being diffused through each other with their opposite qualities. Those whose nature it is to ascend are borne downwards, the heat of the sun coming down in rays, and the heavy bodies, being attenuated through the vapors, are lifted up so that water becomes a rising element contrary to its nature, carried through the air on the winds; ethereal fire goes earthward so that its depth has no heat and it pours the moisture of rain upon the earth and, although it is simple in its nature, it begets thousands of differences in seeds which are suitably rooted in all substances; and there is the swift revolution of the firmament and the reverse movement of the inner circles, the courses and meeting and harmonious spacing of the stars. Looking at these with the thoughtful eyes of the soul is one not clearly taught by what he sees that there is a divine power, skillful and wise, appearing in these things, going through everything, harmonizing the parts with the whole and completing the whole in the parts and governing everything with a single power, remaining in itself and being moved through itself and never ceasing its movement and never changing to a place other than where it is?'

G. 'But,' said I, 'how does the belief in the existence of God prove that there is a human soul? For the soul is not the same thing as God, so that if a person accepts the one he must altogether accept the other.'

M. She answered: 'It is said by the wise that man is a microcosm, encompassing in himself the elements by which he is made complete. If this is true, it is likely that we do not need any other support to strengthen our assumption about the soul. We assume that it exists by itself in a separate and particular nature within the bodily complex. For, as we know the whole world through sensual perception, we are led by this very activity of our senses to the notion of a thing and to a design beyond the senses and our eye becomes the interpreter of the all-powerful wisdom which is seen in everything and which, by itself, reveals that which encompasses everything in accordance with itself. Thus, looking at the cosmos within us, we have no small starting point for conjecturing as to what is hidden through those things that appear. But that is hidden which, being intelligible and invisible, escapes the observation of our senses.'

G. I said: 'Yes, it is possible to consider the wisdom which underlies everything through the wise and skillful logic seen in nature in this harmonious universe. But what knowledge of the soul can be derived from what the body reveals to those who are looking for the invisible in the visible phenomena?'

M. The virgin replied: 'The soul itself is an especially suitable teacher of opinions about the soul for those who desire to know themselves according to that wise precept, because it it is immaterial and incorporeal, acting and moving according to its own nature and indicating its own movements through the bodily organs. There is no less equipment in those who have become corpses through death; but, since the psychic power is not in them, it remains without movement and activity. There is movement when there is perception in the organs and the intelligible power goes through the body by perception as it seems best to it.'

G. 'What then,' said I, 'is the soul, if it is possible for its nature to be outlined with some reason so that some observation of what lies underneath may come to us through this delineation?'

M. My teacher answered: 'There are different points of view on this subject and each person defines it individually. Our opinion about it is this: the soul is a substance which is begotten, alive, intelligible, and, by itself, it puts into an organic perceptive body a life-giving power as long as the nature capable of receiving these things endures.' As she said this, she pointed to the doctor seated beside her for the purpose of curing her body and remarked: 'Testimony of what I have said is nearby. How does this doctor, by placing his fingers on the arteries, hear nature calling to him somehow through the sense of touch telling him its particular sufferings? The sickness is in the tension of the body; the illness arises from the inner organs and the tension extends as far as the inflammation. He also learns similar facts with his eye when he looks at the outward appearance of the patient, the wasting of the flesh, the internal distress, which the pale and bilious complexion indicates, and the expression of the eyes automatically revealing some sadness and depression. In the same way, hearing becomes the teacher of similar facts. He recognizes the disease by the frequent shortness of breath and the signs which accompany the breathing. And one might say that the doctor's sense of smell is not without help in diagnosing a disease hidden within the body, when he smells the patient's breath. But, you ask, isn't there some intelligible power present in each of the senses? What could the hand, by itself, teach us if the faculty of thought did not bring touch to an understanding of the object touched? What assistance could hearing separated from intelligence give us for a knowledge of what we seek, or the eye, or the nose, if each of these relied entirely on itself? This is the truest thing and well said: that the mind sees and the mind hears. If someone did not relay this truth to us, tell me how looking at the sun you could look upon it as you do when you learn from a teacher, so that you see it, not as it appears to the general public, but realize that it is of so great a circumference and a good deal larger than the earth? After you have followed a certain kind of movement with your mind, noting its temporal and spatial interludes and the causes of its ceasing, do you not have the courage to say that it is such and such a thing? And from the waxing and waning of the moon, you learn from its appearance that it is itself without a light connected with its own nature, that it goes around in a cycle near the earth, that it reflects the rays of the run, and does not give back its own rays, but reflects the sunlight from a smooth and shining surface.

Those who look at it thoughtlessly think that the light comes from the moon itself. This is shown not to be true from the fact that, when it is diametrically face to face with the sun, it illuminates the entire circle facing towards us, but, in the smaller place by itself, it goes faster around in the cycle in which it is and, before the sun revolves once in its course, the moon goes around in its own course more than twelve times.

'Therefore, it never happens that the element is filled with light, for that which goes around many times in a short period never remains continuously opposite that which goes around in a long time for any consistent period. When its position is directly opposite the sun, all of the moon on our side is illuminated by the sun's rays, and when the sun is placed indirectly, the hemisphere of the moon being cut off from the beams, the part of the moon on our side is necessarily in shadow, the light passing to the other side away from the part that is not able to look upon the sun towards the part which is present to it, until, going directly beyond the solar cycle, it receives the beam as a bastard light, and thus the hemisphere shining around from above it makes the part on our side invisible because, by its own nature, it is completely dim and obscure, a thing which is spoken of as a complete diminution of the element. But if it enters the orbit of the sun again in its own natural course of movement and from the side again faces the beam, what was without light before begins to light up, the beam going over from the illuminated part to the part recently dark. Do you see what the sense of sight teaches us and that it could not provide us with the contemplation of such things by itself unless there were something which sees through the eyes and uses what is known by the senses as guides and, in this way, penetrates from the visible to the invisible?

'Why is it necessary to add illustrations from geometry which through sensual forms lead us to what is beyond the senses, or countless other illustrations which bring us through our bodily activities to a comprehension of the intelligible essence hidden within us?'

G. I said: 'But if there is a common matter for the sensual nature of the elements, as well as a great individual difference in each form of the matter (there are contrary movements among them, one going upwards, another downwards; the form is not the same and there is also a difference in quality), what if someone should say that there is some power belonging to these which, according to the same argument, activates these intellectual visions and movements from a natural individuality and force? For example, we see many things activated by those who make machines. By technically arranging material, they imitate nature, showing a likeness, not only in form, but also in movement, and the mechanism resounding phonetically simulates the voice. Yet we do not envisage any intelligible power activating the arrangement, the form, the sound, the movement in what results. What if we should say also in connection with the mechanical instrument of our nature that there is no intelligible essence individually infused, but that some kinetic power lies within the nature of the elements in us and it is such an activity which creates the effect that is nothing else than some compulsive movement caused in connection with what is desired? How does this help to prove either the existence or the nonexistence of an intelligible and incorporeal essence of the soul itself?'

M. She replied: 'This example does help our argument. Every contrived contradiction brought against us contributes not a little to the steadfastness of what is perceived by the mind.'

G. 'What do you mean?'

M. She said: 'I mean that to know how to use and arrange lifeless material so that the skill invested in instruments results in an object by which movement and sound and arrangement and other such things are simulated is proof of the existence of something in man which by nature, through its theoretical and inventive power, conceives these inventions and prepares the mechanism by its intelligence. It leads the inventor to activity through skill and demonstrates an intelligence by his use of the material. First, he realizes that air is needed for projecting the sound. Next, he figures out how the air is to be contrived for the instrument. According to the nature of the elements, there is no void in things. Although what is light is considered a void, when it is compared to what is heavier, air by itself, in keeping with its own substance, is solid and full. A vessel is wrongly said to be empty, when it is empty of water, for it is, none the less, full of air, as every intelligent man knows. Proof of this is that when an amphora is put into a pool, it is not immediately filled with water. It floats about at first, the intercepted air keeping it hollow on the surface, until, pushed by the hand of the person drawing the water, it submerges and then takes the water into its opening. This shows that it was not empty even before it took in the water. Here, one sees two elements at war over the opening of the vase, the water forcing its way and flowing into the opening under pressure, and the air kept back in the hollow being forced out through the same opening around the water in the opposite direction and flowing upwards. The water lashed into foam by the force of the air makes a gurgling sound. The technician notes these things and figures out how the air can be put into the mechanism, taking into account the nature of the elements. Making a hollow box out of thick wood, sealing the air in it on all sides, he prevents it from rushing out; then, he puts water into the opening of the box, having decided on the right amount; and next, he makes a passageway for the air to a pipe which has been inserted transversely. The air pushed out by the water becomes breath and, striking the pipe, it creates a sound. Isn't it clear from this that there exists in many persons something other than what is seen, something which creates these instruments

through the power of thought because of some immaterial and intellectual faculty of man's nature? Using material in this way, he brings into view the power of thought which is within him. According to the opposing argument, that such wondrous works could be imputed to the nature of the elements, such machines would come into being automatically. Bronze would not wait for the craftsman's skill to take on the form of a man, but would do so naturally. Air would not need a pipe for the production of sound. It would resound by itself, moving and flowing by chance, nor would the passage of water upward through a channel take place by technical force contrary to its nature, rather it would run towards the machine entirely by itself carried upwards by its own nature. But none of these things does happen and each thing is produced by technical skill according to what seems the best method. The technical skill is a kind of stable intelligence working towards a goal by means of material, and thought is the special movement and activity of the mind. So you see that the argument offered in opposition to us actually demonstrates the existence of something beyond the visible, namely, the mind.'
G. 'I myself agree that the visible and invisible are not the same thing. However, I do not see what we are looking for in this argument. Nor is it clear to me, yet, what we must think the invisible thing is, except that the argument taught that it is not material. I do not know, yet, what it is fitting to say about it. What I want to learn is, not what does not exist, but what does exist.'
M. She said: 'We learn much about many things when we say that something does not exist, interpreting the very essence of whatever we are investigating. For example, if we say that someone is not wicked, we prove that he is good. Or if we call someone "unmanly," we recognize that he is a coward. We could cite many other examples of how, through the negation of bad qualities, we gain a better understanding

of something or we form a worse opinion of someone, suggesting what is bad by the withholding of what is good. Following our present argument, you will not be cheated of an idea pertinent to our investigation. What we are seeking is an essential definition of the mind. The person accepting our idea that the mind exists because of the activity it produces would, in learning this very fact, discover that it is not anything grasped by the senses, it is not color, or arrangement, or resistance, or weight, or quality; it does not have dimension or position in space, nor any of the other qualities connected with matter, if, indeed, there is anything besides these things.

G. After she enumerated these things, I objected: 'If all of these things are removed from our discussion. I do not see how what we are seeking will not also be blotted out. In my opinion, we have not yet discerned what a zeal for understanding can be applied to apart from these qualities. For everywhere in our search for reality, by examining what we seek with an inquiring intelligence, we are like blind men led through the walls to a gate. We perceive either color or arrangement or one of the other qualities just enumerated by you. When it is a question of something that is none of these things, we are led by our smallness of soul to decide that nothing else exists.'

M. Then, she broke in impatiently: 'How ridiculous! What is the purpose of this low and mean judgment of reality? If everything not known through the senses is excluded from reality, the person agreeing to this would not admit the very power governing everything and encompassing reality. Having learned the incorporeal and invisible character of the divine nature, he will deduce from what we say that it does not exist at all. Moreover, if a definition of being does not come from non-being, how is the human mind saved from being used up in the dispersal of the bodily properties?'

G. I said: 'With this train of thought, we are exchanging one absurdity for another. The argument leads us to believe that our mind and the divine nature are the same thing if each of them is known by the discarding of what is perceived by the senses.'

M. My teacher replied: 'Don't say that, for it is an irreverent argument. But as you have learned from the divine voice, say that one is similar to the other. What is made as an image is in every way similar to its archetype, intellectual if the archetype is intellectual, incorporeal, weightless, without dimension. But, in keeping with the peculiar nature of the image, there is something different from the archetype, for it would not be an image if it were identical with it in all respects. The created nature shows this in the same features in which the archetype is seen in its uncreated nature. Just as when a small fragment of glass happens to be exposed to a ray, the entire circle of the sun is seen in it, not appearing in it in conformity with the sun's size; as the smallness of the fragment receives the reflection, so, in the smallness of our nature, the images of those ineffable peculiarities of the Godhead shine forth. Consequently, the argument does not cut us off from a comprehension of the essence of the mind, since the subject has been clarified by our investigation; nor, again, does it lead us to equate the small and mortal with the unseen and incorruptible nature (of God), but it does affirm that its being is intelligible since it is an image of what is intelligible. Nevertheless, the image is not the same as the archetype. Therefore, just as through the unspeakable wisdom of God appearing in all things we do not doubt that there is a divine nature and power in all being, so all things remain essentially themselves, and yet, if anyone should demand an account of the divine nature, the essence of God would be very far away from what is demonstrated and known in each thing in created nature, and yet it is agreed that the divine nature is present in these despite the difference. So it is not at all incredible, and the essence of the soul, although it is something else in itself (whatever it is conjectured to be), is not prevented from existing, despite the fact that those things contemplated in the universe under the heading of elements do not come together in it according to the logic of its nature. For, as has been said before, in the case of living bodies in which there is substance resulting from the mingling of the elements, there is, according to the logic of being, nothing in common between the simple and invisible essence of the soul and the coarseness of the body. Nevertheless, it is not doubted that the vital energy of the soul is present in the elements, diffused with a logic that is beyond human comprehension. Therefore, when the elements in the body are resolved into themselves, that which links it together through its vital energy does not perish.

'Just as when the composite form of the elements still exists and each is given life, the soul entering equally and similarly all the parts that make up the body, one would not say that the soul is firm or resistant, being mixed with earth or the moist or the cold or the quality contrary to the cold, although it is in everything and sends the vital force into each of them; so, also, when the composite body is dissolved and goes back into its individual parts, it is not at all unreasonable to think that the simple and uncomposite nature is present in each of the parts even after the dissolution, and that, once joined to the composite elements through some ineffable logic, it remains always with these elements with which it was mingled and is, in no small way, severed from the union in which it once existed. For when the composite is dissolved, the uncomposite runs no risk of being dissolved with it.'

G. And I said: 'No one disputes the fact that the elements come together and are separated from each other and that there is a constitution and dissolution of the body. However, since it is known that there is a great deal of difference between each of these elements, which are heterogeneous among themselves, depending on their position and their qualitative differences and peculiarities, inasmuch as these elements come together in subjection to each other, it follows that this intellectual and undimensional nature which we call the soul must be attached to what it was yoked to. But if these are separated and go off wherever the nature of each takes it, what will happen to the soul once its vehicle is dispersed on all sides? Like a sailor whose vessel has been destroyed in a shipwreck, not being able to cling at the same time to all of the different parts of the ship scattered in all directions over the sea, he will take hold of whatever part he happens upon and leave the rest to the waves; in the same way, the soul, not being prepared by nature to go in separate ways when the elements separate, if it is reluctant to be separated from the body and clings entirely to one of the elements, it will be separated from the others and the sequence of the argument does not lead us to consider it immortal on account of its existing in one any more than to think it mortal on account of its not existing in many.'

M. 'But,' she said, 'the intelligible and undimensional does not contract and expand. In accordance with its own nature, it is present equally invisible and incorporeal at the joining and separating of the elements in the body. It is not shut in by the conjunction of the elements or abandoned when the elements go off to those related to them by nature, even if there is a great difference to be observed in the heterogeneity of the elements. There is, indeed, much difference between that which is light and goes upwards and the heavy and the earthy, between the hot and the cold, the moist and its opposite. Nevertheless, it is no trouble for the intelligible nature to be present in each, since it is not affected by the opposition of the elements, for, while these are thought to be apart from each other, depending on their position and particular qualities, the undimensional nature does not suffer by being joined to things that are apart. Even now, it is possible to contemplate the sky in our thought and to reach the boundaries of the universe in our curiosity, and the contemplative faculty of our soul is not distended by such distances. Therefore, the soul is not prevented from being equally present in the elements of the body, both when they are mingled with each other and when they are separated from each other. For, just as when gold and silver are melted together a certain technical skill is observed in the melting process, and if later the one metal is melted away from the other the artistry remains no less in each, that is, the material is divided but still is not cut apart with the matter, how can that which is indivisible be broken up into parts? According to the same argument, the intelligible nature of the soul exists in the union of the elements and is not separated when they are dissolved. It remains in them and is not cut apart or extended by their separation. Nor is it broken up into bits and pieces in relation to the number of the elements. This is characteristic of a bodily and dimensional nature, whereas the intelligible and undimensional nature is not subject to dimensional effects. Therefore, the soul is present in those elements in which it once dwelt, there being no necessity for withdrawing it from its union with them. What, then, is so terrible about the invisible being changed from the visible and why is your mind so set against death?'

G. Then I, reverting to the definition she had given for the soul in our previous discussion, said that her argument did not prove sufficiently for me the powers observed in the soul. 'That argument says that the soul is an intelligible essence and puts a vital power into the organic body by activating the senses. For the soul is not only active in connection with knowledge and theory, activating the faculty of intelligence, nor does it control only the senses in its natural operation. There is also perceived in its nature much movement connected with the desiring faculty and the spirited faculty and, since each of these is present in us specifically, we see its movement proceeding energetically in many various ways. It is possible to observe the many activities to which the desiring faculty leads and also the many activities caused by the spirited faculty and there is no body connected with either of these since they are completely in the realm of intelligence. But the definition says that the soul is something intelligible so that one of two absurdities results from the sequence of the argument: either the spirit and will are other souls within us and one perceives a multiplicity of souls instead of one, or the soul within us is not capable of thought. For the intelligible harmonizes equally with all things so that all of these faculties indicate souls in us or each of them equally partakes of the peculiar nature of the soul.'

M. She replied: 'You have rightly inquired into this subject already investigated by many others, namely, what must we think of the desiring and spirited faculties; are they part of the essence of the soul and present in it from the beginning, or something additional which come to us later. Everyone agrees that they are present in the soul, but what we think of them is not so accurately known that we can have a firm opinion about them and many people have widely different opinions about them. If secular philosophy, which treats these subjects technically, were able to reveal the truth to us, it would be strange for us to propose a discussion about the soul. For the secular philosophers' speculation about the soul proceeds freely in accordance with what appears to be so, but we do not have this freedom to say whatever we wish about it since we rely on Holy Scripture as a rule of dogma and as law. Therefore, we necessarily accept only what lies within the scope of what is written. Consequently, we disregard the Platonic chariot and the team of horses yoked to it, each going at his own pace, and their charioteer and all the details with which Plato sets forth symbolically his philosophy of the soul.[6] Nor do we care what the philosopher after him said, the one who, after technically inquiring into phenomena and the evi-

---

6 Cf. Plato *Phaedrus* 246 ff. The philosopher mentioned in the next sentence is Aristotle; cf. his *De anima* 2.2.

dence at hand, declared that his investigations proved the soul to be mortal. Rejecting all those before and after him in time, those who have written in prose and in poetry, we base our argument on the inspired scripture which decrees that there is nothing in the soul which does not reflect the divine nature. For the one who says that the soul is "the image of God"[7] affirms that what is alien to God is outside the definition of the soul. So, if some quality is not recognized as part of the divine nature, we cannot reasonably think that it is part of the nature of the soul. We accuse those forms of argument which strengthen our beliefs, through dialectic and syllogism and analysis, of being weak and suspect for revealing truth. It is clear to everyone that the dialectical method is equally effective for subverting truth and accusing an opponent of falsehood. Even truth itself, when it is advanced with such artfulness, often becomes the object of suspicion on the grounds that cleverness in such matters can mislead us and even divert our mind away from truth. However, if someone brings forward an argument which is extemporaneous and devoid of such circumlocutions, we say that it may be credible and apply to it the theory about these subjects set forth in scripture. What are we saying? That man, this logical man, has been testified to as being capable of intelligence and knowledge and reason on a higher level and that the definition given by scripture would not be applicable to our nature if we conceive of anger and desire and such qualities as being essential to it.

'In any case, you would not give an essential definition of anything by speaking of the general rather than the specific. So, if the desiring and spirited elements are common to both the logical and illogical nature, you are not reasonably distinguishing between the general and the specific, and such a definition of our nature is irrelevant and worthless. How could part of a nature undermine the definition, since every

---

[7] Gen. 1.27.

definition of essence looks to what is proper to the subject? Whatever is outside of the specific difference is rejected as being alien to the definition. Surely, it is agreed that activity connected with anger and desire is characteristic of an irrational nature. But what is characteristic of something is that which is peculiar to it. Because of this, it is necessary to reason that these faculties are not present among those by which human nature is specifically defined. When a person notes the faculties of perception and nutrition and growth in us, he does not, for this reason, reject the given definition of the soul—for one faculty is present in the soul and the other faculties are not; so, also, a person observing activities in us related to anger and desire will not reasonably quarrel with our definition on the grounds that it defines our nature inadequately.'

G. I said to my teacher: 'What knowledge should we have of these matters? I do not see, yet, how it is fitting for us to reject what is present in us as being alien to our nature.'

M. She replied: 'Don't you realize that reason is fighting against these faculties and that the soul is eager to be separated from them as far as possible? There are certain persons who have been very successful in this battle. For example, it is said of Moses that he was superior to anger and desire. History testifies that he was the "meekest" of men[8]—an incapacity for anger is shown through mildness and an aversion to wrath—and that he desired none of the things the desiring element in many people is directed towards. This would not have been so if these qualities had been natural to him and logically in keeping with his essence, for it is not possible for that which is unnatural to remain in the essence. Moses, you see, was true to his essence and not involved in desire and anger which are an addition to our nature and not our nature itself, for nature is truly that in which being has its essence. These qualities are alien to us so that the eradication of them is not only not harmful, but even beneficial to our nature.

---

8 Cf. Num. 12.3.

Therefore, it is clear that these qualities belong to what is considered external, the affections of our nature and not its essence, for nature is that which is.

'The ordinary man thinks of anger as a boiling of the blood around the heart. Others look upon it as the desire to avenge injury. As we understand it, it is an impulse to harm someone who annoys you. Nothing of this is pertinent to the definition of the soul.

'And if we define the term "desire" by itself, we say that it is a longing to fulfill some need or the enjoyment of some pleasure or grief over something beyond our reach or an habituation to a pleasure which we are not, at the moment, enjoying. All of these are indicative of the meaning of desire, but they are not suitable for a definition of our nature. All the other qualities that are regarded as being connected with the soul, those that are in opposition to each other, for example, cowardice and courage, pain and pleasure, fear and contempt, and the like, each of which appears to be related to the desiring and spirited faculties, belong to a particular nature with its own definition. Boldness and contempt indicate a certain emphasis of the spirited impulse, whereas the habituation to cowardice and fear indicates some diminishing and remission of the same impulse. Grief derives its material from both faculties. The languishing of the spirit, because of our inability to take vengeance on those who have offended us, produces grief, and the despair of not having what we desire and the deprivation of what is agreeable to us creates this gloomy disposition in our consciousness. And what is regarded as the opposite of pain, I mean the sensation of pleasure, is, likewise, divided between anger and desire, for pleasure is the guiding force of each of these. All of them are connected with the soul, but they are not the soul. They are like warts on the thinking part of the soul and they are considered parts of it because of being joined to it, but they are not what constitutes the essence of the soul.'

G. I said to the virgin: 'We see that no small contribution is made to this idea by men conspicuous for their virtue. Daniel, for example, was praised for his eagerness,[9] Phineas was pleasing to God because of his anger,[10] we are told that "fear is the beginning of wisdom,"[11] and we learn from Paul that "the sorrow according to God worketh unto salvation,"[12] and the Gospel legislates "contempt for dangers"[13] and the admonition "be not afraid of dangers"[14] is nothing other than a description of courage which is put into the category of goods under wisdom. In these passages, scripture shows that it is not necessary for us to think of these qualities as base passions, for they would not, then, be included under the heading of the attainment of virtue.'

M. My teacher responded: 'It seems that I myself am responsible for some confusion in not making a distinction which would impose some suitable order upon our theorizing. Now, then, as far as possible, we will devise a plan which will prevent the occurrence of such contradictions as our discussion proceeds. We are maintaining that the power of the soul to contemplate and to make distinctions and to speculate is proper to its nature and that, because of these capabilities, it preserves in itself the image of the divine grace. Since reason conjectures that the divine also, whatever it is by nature, has its existence in these activities of observing everything and distinguishing the good from the bad, but whatever lies on the margin of the soul, inclining towards each of the extremes according to its own peculiar nature, which we need when we take a step towards the good or its opposite, for example, anger or fear or any of the other impulses in the soul without

---

[9] Dan. 10.12.
[10] Num. 25.11.
[11] Prov. 9.10.
[12] Cf. 2 Cor. 7.10.
[13] Although this idea occurs in the New Testament, the vocabulary which St. Gregory uses here is not Biblical but Platonic. Cf. Plato's discussion of courage and the legislation in the ideal state about 'the things that are to be feared' (περὶ τῶν δεινῶν; *Rep.* 429). For the Christian, the Evangelist is the legislator (ὁ νομοθέτης).
[14] Cf. Luke 21.9.

which human nature cannot reflect, these we consider externals because they are not perceived in the beauty of the archetype. Meanwhile, let our proposition on these matters be stated as in a gymnastic school so that we may avoid the abuse of those who listen with evil intent. Scripture describes the divine impulse towards the creation of man in a certain orderly sequence. History tells us that when everything was created man did not immediately come into existence on earth, but that the irrational creatures and their seed preceded him. I think that in this way scripture shows that the life-giving power mingles gradually with the corporeal nature, entering first into the things which lack sensation and advancing after this to the sensual and then rising to the intelligible and logical. Therefore, of the things in existence, some are entirely corporeal and others completely intelligible. The corporeal is soulless and the other has a soul. I mean that it is the soul which participates in life. Some of the living things are endowed with sensation and some are not. Again, of those with sensation some have reason and some do not. Since the sensual life could not exist apart from matter nor the intelligible be in the body if it were not attached to the sensual, it is said that man was finally created for this, that he might encompass every vital form envisaged in plants and animals. To plant life belong nourishment and growth and it is possible to observe this in plants, nurture being taken up through the roots and given back through the fruits and leaves. The sensual belong to the irrational. But the thinking and logical is unmixed, having its own nature perceived in itself. Just as nature has a faculty which attracts what is necessary for material life—when this is present it is called appetite—but we say that this is characteristic of plant life since it is necessary to see in plants certain naturally activated impulses in their coming to complete growth and in their fertility, so also the faculties peculiar to the irrational nature are mingled with the intelligible nature. Anger belongs to these and fear and all of those impulses which are in conflict within us except the logical and thinking power which is the only special feature in us, being, as it has been said, the image of the divine character. But since, according to our previous discussion, it is not possible for the power of reason to be present in the corporeal life except through the senses, and since perception comes under the heading of the irrational, existence of our soul comes about through its one essential feature and its relation to the qualities joined to it. Such qualities in us are called emotions and they have not been allotted to human life for an evil purpose. For if that were the case and such compulsions to sin had been included in our nature, the Creator would be the cause of evil. Such faculties of the soul exist because of the need to choose good or evil. Think of how iron, forged through the judgment of the craftsman, is formed in keeping with his intention and becomes either a sword or a farming implement. Therefore, if reason, which is the special ingredient of our nature, is in control of the faculties imposed upon us externally, then, as scripture has made clear through the symbol of man being ordered to rule over all irrational things, none of these faculties within us is activated towards the service of evil—fear engenders obedience, anger courage, cowardice caution; the desiring faculty fosters in us the divine and pure pleasures. However, if reason lets go of the reins like a charioteer who has become entangled in his chariot and is dragged along by it, being pulled wherever the irrational impulse of the team carries him, then, our faculties are turned towards emotions such as are seen among the irrational animals. Since reason does not by nature control the movement of animals, through their passions, they destroy each other being dominated by rage, and the powerful carnal impulses do not operate for their own good, reason being overcome by the resulting confusion. Their activities of desire and pleasure are not concerned with any lofty matter nor are they directed with any logic toward anything advantageous. So, also, in us, unless our faculties are directed by reason towards what we need, when emotions govern the mind, man goes from the intellectual and the godlike to the irrational and the foolish, and he is ruined by the onrush of such affections.'

G. Very much impressed by what she said, I replied: 'Your speech has been so direct and spontaneous and cohesive that any intelligent man would be convinced that you are correct and that you deviate in no way from the truth. But since the syllogism is enough to convince those skilled in the technical means of demonstration, whereas for us it is agreed that of all the technical conclusions the more trustworthy are those which appear also in the sacred teachings of scripture. I think we must now ask if the inspired teaching agrees with what we are saying.'

M. She answered: 'Who would contradict the statement that truth resides only in that which bears the seal of the testimony of scripture? If then, it is necessary for us to draw some support for our opinion from the teaching of the Gospel, it would not be amiss to consider the parable of the weeds.[15] We are familiar with the whole story. In it, the master of the house sowed good seed, but, while the watchmen were asleep, the enemy sowed worthless seed in with the nourishing crop, putting weeds in the midst of the grain. The plants grew up together, for it was not possible for the seed mixed in with the grain not to grow along with it. Because the roots of the two were joined, the steward of the farm forbade the servants to pull up the weeds, fearing that they would pull up the useful plants along with the useless. We think that here, with the good seeds, scripture refers to the impulses of our soul, each of which, if it works only for good, produces entirely a harvest of virtue. However, when sin is sown in among these in connection with our judgment of the good, that which is completely good in its own nature is obscured by the treacher-

---

15 Cf. Matt. 13.24 ff.

ous seed growing with it. The desiring element, although it is not by nature related to the good (for the sake of which it is sown in us), grows and increases, but it belongs to the brutish and irrational seed. That is to say, our uncritical desire for the good directs our impulses irrationally. And, likewise, the seed of anger is not directed towards courage, but arms itself for battle on the side of its own kind, namely, the irrational. The power of love stands apart from the intelligible and runs riot in the enjoyment of the senses, and the other emotions in the same way produces worse shoots instead of better ones. For this reason, with the same foresight, the wise farmer allows the useless sprout attached to the seed to continue to exist, so that we will not be deprived of the better ones, desire within us being completely compounded with the useless sprouts. If human nature should experience this eradication, what would draw us to a union with celestial things? If love is taken away, how shall we be joined to God? If our anger is quenched, what weapon shall we have against the Adversary? The farmer permits the adulterous seeds to be in us, not in order for them to dominate the more honorable ones, but in order that the arable land (thus he refers to the heart), through the natural power in it, may dry up some of the seeds and make others fruitful and productive. If this does not occur, he turns over to the fire the job of separating the crop. Therefore, if anyone uses these faculties with right reason, keeping them within his power and not coming into theirs, he will be like a certain king who used the assistance of a great horde of subordinates and easily achieved what he desired to do in keeping with virtue. However, if he comes into their power, they are like slaves rising against their master and he will be carried off into slavery, ignobly surrendering to their slavish insolence. Once he becomes the possession of those subject to him by nature, he will be reduced to anything the power of those in control forces him to. If this is so, we shall declare that in themselves these faculties are neither a virtue nor an evil. Whether they are good or not depends upon the use to which they are put. When the activity is for the better, then, it is material for praise, as, for example, the desire of Daniel and the anger of Phineas who rightly lamented his grief. When the activity inclines towards the worse we call it passion.'

G. As she paused for a moment after this explanation, I reflected on what had been said in an earlier portion of our discussion where we affirmed that it was not impossible for the soul to exist in the scattered elements once the body was dissolved. I said to my teacher: 'But what about that popular word "hell" which occurs so often in everyday life and in our literature and others? I mean the place everyone thinks the soul passes into as if into a receptacle. You would not say that the elements are hell would you?'

M. My teacher replied: 'It is clear that you have not paid close attention to the argument. In speaking of the transition of the soul from the seen to the unseen, I did not think I was omitting what we wanted to learn about hell. For it seems to me that this word, which occurs in the profane writings and in ours to designate the place where the souls exist, means nothing else than a change into the unseen and the invisible.'

G. 'And how,' I said, 'do certain people say that there is a place below the earth and that it takes in the souls and entertains them as if it were an inn capable of receiving such a nature, drawing to itself those who have flown away from human life?'

M. My teacher answered: 'But our opinion is not harmed at all by this notion. For, if what you say is true, that the celestial pole is continuous and indissoluble, encompassing everything in its own circle, and the earth is in the middle with everything suspended around it, and the movement of everything in the circle is going around that which is established and fixed, it is entirely necessary that whatever each of the elements has in the region above the earth will exist also in the opposite region, since the same essence goes around the entire bulk of the earth. Now, when the sun appears above the earth, the shadow is cast over its lower parts, since the circuit of the beam cannot encompass the entire spherical form at the same time. Since the sun exists at a kind of midpoint with relation to the sphere, when it embraces one part of the earth with its rays, the part directly opposite will necessarily be in darkness. Thus darkness comes around continuously, together with the course of the sun, to the section directly opposite the sun's rays, so that the lower and upper parts of the earth are alternately in light and darkness. Likewise, we should not doubt that whatever is seen in connection with the elements in our hemisphere is also in existence in the other one, since one and the same complex of elements is present in every part of the earth. I think we need not agree or disagree with those who maintain that it is necessary to believe that there is a place below the earth set apart for the souls freed from the body. As long as the objection does not interfere with what we agreed upon before, concerning the existence of the soul after its life in the flesh, our discourse will enter no controversy concerning the place. We assume that it is characteristic only of bodies to exist in a place and that the soul which is incorporeal is not required by nature to be contained in one.'

G. I said: 'But what if our opponent cites the apostle who states that, in the restoration of the universe, all creatures endowed with reason look to the One who governs the universe when he says in his epistle to the Philippians[16] that "every knee will bow before him of those in the heavens and on the earth and below the earth"?'

M. My teacher replied: 'We shall stand by our opinion even if we hear people saying these things about the existence of the soul and even if we have the opponent on our side, and as we said before, we shall not argue about the place.'

G. 'But, even if we disregard the word referring to place, what

---
16 Cf. Phil. 2.10.

answer should we give to those inquiring into the meaning of what the apostle has said?'

M. She said: 'It does not seem to me that the divine apostle is making a distinction about place when he uses the words "in the heavens, on the earth, and below the earth." But since there are three classes of beings endowed with reason, one which has from the beginning been given life apart from the body which we call the angelic, one intermingled with the flesh which we call the human, and one released from the body through death, I think that the divine apostle in the depths of his wisdom is looking at every condition observed among souls and indicating an ultimate harmony on the side of the good when he refers to the angelic and incorporeal as being "in heaven," those intermingled with the body as being "on earth," and those separated from the body as being "below the earth." And if someone wishes to mention some other nature among logical beings and to call them "demons" or "spirits" or something similar, we shall not disagree with him. For there is a belief, stemming from common opinion and the tradition of scripture, that there is some incorporeal nature which is opposed to the good and harmful to human life. Because these creatures have rejected the better portion of their own will and have defected from the good, they are thought of as representing the opposition in themselves and it is they whom the apostle numbers among those "under the earth." By this, he means that when evil is blotted out by the long period of the ages nothing will be left except the good beings, and that among them, there will be agreement in the lordship of Christ. If this interpretation is true, we need not think of a subterranean place in connection with the phrase "below the earth," since the air is diffused about the earth from all sides in such a way that it is understood that no part is deprived of it.'

G. While my teacher was explaining this, I was demurring somewhat. I said: 'I have not yet grasped what we are seeking, and somehow I do not agree with what has been said. I beg you to return to the point in the discussion where we deviated from what we had agreed upon. I think that those who are very much opposed to us will not easily be deterred by what we have said from believing in the destruction and non-existence of the soul after the dissolution of the body, nor will they assert that it cannot exist anywhere in the universe because its nature is essentially different from the elements. For even if the intelligible and immaterial nature of the soul does not conform to them, it is not prevented from existing in them. This assumption is confirmed for us in two ways: by the fact that, at present in this life, the soul is in the body although it is something different from the body by nature, and from the fact that the argument shows that the divine nature, although it is something entirely different from the sensual and material essence, nevertheless, pervades each aspect of being, and, by mingling with everything, it contains in essence what exists. For these reasons, it is logical for us to think that the soul is not cut off from existence when it migrates from the life in which things are formally visible to the invisible. But,' I said, 'once the union of elements has taken on (because of their mingling with each other) a form with which the soul has become familiar, when this form disappears, as is likely because of the dissolution of the elements, how will the soul follow along, since what it knows no longer remains?'

M. She, after a brief hesitation, said: 'Allow me to fashion an argument by analogy, to clarify what we have proposed, even if what I say does not seem to be pertinent. Imagine that in the art of painting colors could not only be mixed as they usually are, but that those already mixed could be separated from each other and that each color could return to its original hue. In that case, if the white and the black or the red and the gold, or any other shade mixed to match the color of the object being painted, should be separated from its mixture with another color and should become itself again, we would say that the appearance of the color is no less known to the artist and that he does not forget the red or the black even if the various colors which entered into the mixture return to their natural state. He recalls how the mixture of the colors was achieved and he knows that if one of the colors is washed out the original shade recurs. And if it is necessary for him to produce a similar effect again, the preparation of the mixture will be easy because of his previous experience. Now,' she said, 'if this analogy is pertinent to our argument, we must find out how to apply it to our proposition. Let the soul in the argument correspond to the art of painting and let the nature of the elements correspond to the colors. Let the mixing of the various different colors and their being resolved again into their individual shades correspond, according to our hypothesis, to the union and dissolution of the elements. Then, just as we said in our analogy that the painter is not ignorant of the color he had produced, even after it is dissolved into the individual colors, and he knows the red and the black and any other quality which produced the mixture, he knows what was in the mixture, what it has become, and what will occur again if the colors are mixed again with each other in the same way. Thus the soul knows the individual elements which formed the body in which it dwelt, even after the dissolution of those elements. Even if nature drags them far apart from each other and, because of their basic differences prevents each of them from mixing with its opposite, the soul will, nevertheless, exist along with each element, fastening upon what is its own by its power of knowing it and it will remain there until the union of the separated parts occurs again in the reforming of the dissolved being which is properly called "the resurrection." '

G. And I said: 'You seem to me, in passing, to give excellent support to the doctrine of the resurrection. It should be possible through these arguments to persuade those who are reluctant to accept it because they do not think it is possible for the elements to come back together again and produce the same man.'

M. My teacher replied: 'You are quite right. One hears people advancing this argument, asking how, since the dissolution of the elements according to their kinds is complete, the element of heat in a person, once it has mingled generally with its own kind, can be withdrawn again for the purpose of reforming a man. For, they would say, unless the very same element returns the result would be a similar being and not the individual himself, that is to say, another person would come into being and such a process would not be a resurrection, but the creation of a new man. But, if the original is to be reconstituted, it is necessary for it to be entirely the same, taking up its original nature in all the parts of its elements.'

G. 'Therefore, as I said, such an opinion about the soul would be a sufficient rebuttal to this objection. Even after the dissolution of the elements in which it existed from the beginning, the soul, like a guardian of what is its own, remains in them and, even when it is mingled with the general mass, it does not give up its individuality in the subtlety and mobility of its intellectual power. It does not deviate in the delicate diffusion of the elements, but joins the mass with its own constituents, and, having gone along with them, when they are poured back into the universe, it remains in them always, wherever or however nature arranges them. And if, through the power which governs all things, the dissolved parts are allowed to be united again, then like different ropes suspended from one starting point, they all follow along at the same time. In the same way, through the unique force of the soul, when the different elements are drawn together and when what was once the cord of our body is reconstituted by the soul, each part is folded again into its former accustomed place and embraces what is familiar to it.'

M. My teacher said: 'The following analogy could also be added reasonably to those already examined as proof that the soul has no difficulty in distinguishing from among the elements what is her own and what is alien to her. Let us assume as a hypothesis that some clay exists for the making of pots, a large amount of it, some already prepared to be made into vases and the rest about to be. Let us design all the vases in different shapes, making one a wine jar, another an amphora, another a plate or a bowl or any other useful container. For the sake of argument, imagine that all the vases do not belong to one person, but that each is owned by a different person. As long as they remain intact, their owners recognize them and, even if they are broken, they are still identified by their owners, one fragment as belonging to a particular jug and another to a particular cup. And even if the clay of the fragments is mixed in with the unused clay, the owner still recognizes the parts already worked. In the same way, each man has his own form resulting from the union of elements. Molded from a common material, each being has its own individual form which differs greatly from the others in the same genus. When the dissolution occurs, the soul, which is the owner of the vase, recognizes its own in what remains, and it is not separated from it in the mass of the fragments even if the material of the elements is mixed with the unused matter. It always recognizes its own, what it was like when it had its form, and, even after the dissolution, recognizing the specific features surviving in the remains, it will not be in error about what belongs to it.'

G. Accepting what she said as being very much to the point, I replied: 'It is good for these things to be said and to be believed. However, if someone brings up a passage in the Gospel where our Lord refers to those in hell in order to argue against what we have said here, how can we be prepared to answer?'

M. She said: 'Scripture directs its story more to the bodily aspect of man, offering many suggestions by which the person who examines them is prepared for a more subtle theory. The one[17] who separates the evil from the good by "a great gulf" and speaks of a beggar bringing a drop of water on his finger to the man in torment and suggests the bosom of the patriarch as the place of rest for the individual who has been hard pressed in this life, after he has described the dead as having been put into a tomb, in no small way leads the attentive reader away from ordinary reasoning. What kind of "eyes" does the rich man lift up in hell, having left the eyes of his flesh in the tomb? How does that which is without a body "feel" the flame? What kind of "tongue" does he want to have cooled by a drop of water, since he does not have his fleshly tongue? What fingers bring him the drop? The bosom of rest itself, what is it? Since the bodies are in the tomb and the soul is not the body and not made up of parts, it would be difficult to adjust the details of the story to the truth as it is perceived by ordinary reasoning. One would have to transfer each of the details to a theoretical level so that we would not think of the gulf which separates what ought not to be mixed as a space of earth. What trouble would it be for the incorporeal and the intellectual to fly over the gulf, even if it were very large, inasmuch as the intellect is timeless and exists wherever it wants to exist?'

G. I said: 'What, then, are the fire or the gulf or the other things which are mentioned, if they are not what they are said to be?'

M. 'It seems to me,' she said, 'that the Gospel wishes, through each of these details, to indicate some opinions concerning what we are seeking in connection with the soul. The patriarch says to the rich man: "You had your share of goods during your life in the flesh," and similarly he says concerning the beggar: "This man fulfilled his duty by his experience of hardship during his life." By the gulf separating the one

---

17 Cf. Luke 16.19 ff.

from the other, Scripture seems to me to set forth an important belief. This, in my opinion, is what it means. In the beginning, the life of man was simple. I mean by this that it was conceived of only in connection with the good, and not as being mixed with evil. The first law of God testifies to this. It gave man full enjoyment of all the beauties of paradise and forbade him only that which was by nature an opposite, that is, evil mixed with good, and it imposed death as punishment upon the transgressor. Man, of his own accord and of his own free will, gave up his lot unmixed with evil, and took for himself a life which is a mixture of opposites. However, divine providence did not leave us without a means of correcting our ill-advised choice. When death came as a necessary consequence for the transgressors, human life was divided into two parts. One part is spent in the flesh, and the other part after this is spent outside of the body. Nor are they of equal duration; one being very short in time, and the other extending to eternity. Through God's kindness, man was given the freedom to choose whichever of the two he wishes. I mean the good and the bad, or what is in accord with a brief and fleeting life and what is in accord with those unending ages whose boundary is infinity. The good and the bad are spoken of equivocally and each of them is divided according to a double notion. I mean according to mind and sensation. One group considers as belonging to the good whatever seems pleasant to the senses, and the other group believes that only that which is in the world of thought is good and is to be called good. The one group is devoid of reason and is unconcerned with the better, and these, through their indulgence in the life of the flesh, squander the share of the good which is owed to their nature and save nothing at all for the life after this. The others, managing their own lives with discerning reason and wisdom and enduring in this short life things not agreeable to the senses, are providing the good for the life to come, so that a better lot stretches out before them in the eternal life. This, in my opinion, is the gulf, which is not an earthly abyss, that the judgment between the two opposite choices of life creates. Once one has chosen the pleasure of this life and has not remedied this bad choice by a change of heart, he produces for himself a place devoid of good hereafter, digging this unavoidable necessity for himself like some deep and trackless pit.

'And it seems to me that Scripture uses the "bosom of Abraham," in which the patient sufferer finds rest, as a symbol of the good state of the soul. For this patriarch was the first of men recorded to have chosen the hope of things to come in preference to the enjoyment of the moment. Bereft of everything he had in the beginning of his life, living among strangers, he sought a future prosperity through present affliction. Just as we use the word "bosom" when referring figuratively to a part of the outline of the sea, it seems to me that Scripture uses the word "bosom"[18] as a symbol of the immeasurable goals towards which those who sail virtuously through life will come when having departed from life, they moor their souls in this good bosom as in a quiet harbor. On the other hand, for the others, the deprivation of those things which seem good to them becomes a flame penetrating their soul, which requires as comfort some drop from the sea of good things that wash about the holy ones, but does not get it. Looking at the words, tongue and eye and finger and the other terms related to the body, if you consider them closely, you will agree that they fit in very well with our conversation about the soul. For as the union of the elements creates the substance of the entire body, so, also, is it likely that the nature of the parts of the body is completed from the same cause. If the soul is present to the elements of the body when they are mixed again with the universe, it will not only know the sum of those that have

---

[18] The word used here in Luke 16.26 for 'bosom' is κολπός, and 'bosom' or 'lap' is its proper meaning.

run together in the common mass and be present in them, but it will not even fail to recognize the individual constitution of each of the parts among the elements from which our members are produced. Therefore, it is not unlikely that the soul exists both in the complex of the elements and in the individual elements as well. And thus anyone who looks at the elements, which by some power make up the members of the body, and thinks that Scripture says that the finger and the eye and the tongue and all the other parts are connected with the soul even after the dissolution of the whole, will not be in error.

'If, then, the individual parts lead the mind away from the corporeal in our interpretation, we surely ought not to think that what is referred to as "hell" is a place, but a state of life, invisible and incorporeal, to which Scripture teaches us that the soul leads.

'And from the story about the rich man and the begger, we learn another teaching which will be very pertinent to our investigation. It presented the rich man as passionate and flesh-loving and, when he saw the inevitability of his misfortune, he was concerned with what he would have beyond the earth in keeping with his class. When Abraham told him that no provision was made for those living their life in the flesh and that this was amply set forth for them in the law and in the prophets, the rich man still continued to plead that this unexpected proclamation be reported to the rich by one brought back to life from the dead.'

G. I said: 'What teaching is there in this?'

M. She replied: 'While the soul of Lazarus was concentrating on its present existence and not distracted by any of the things he had left behind, the rich man, even after death, clung to the carnal aspect of life which he did not put aside although he was no longer living. He was still thinking of flesh and blood. It is clear that he was not yet free from fleshly inclinations from which people of this kind must be separated. I think,' she said, 'that with these facts the Lord teaches that those living in the flesh must somehow be separated from it through a life of virtue, and be freed from the habit of it, in order that after death they may not be in need of a second death to purify them from the remains of the fleshly glue.

'When the chains (so to speak) around the soul are broken, its ascent to the good is light and free, since no bodily weight is dragging it down. But if anyone is entirely preoccupied with the things of the flesh and uses every movement of the soul and all its energy for his fleshly desires, he will not be separated from experiences involving the flesh, even when he is out of it. Just as those who spend a long time in evil-smelling places, even if they come to a place where the air is fresh, are not free from the unpleasantness they encountered because of their extensive sojourn there, so, when the lovers of the flesh move into the invisible and finer life, they cannot be drawn away entirely from the carnal odor. Consequently, they are in great distress, their souls having become wooden as a result of this condition. It seems, somehow, that this assumption agrees with what is often said about the shadowy phantoms of the departed which are seen in the vicinity of tombs. If this is true, the soul is guilty of an excessive inclination towards the life of the flesh, so that, even when it is pushed out of the flesh, it is unwilling to flee from it entirely. Neither is it willing to concede the fact that a change has occurred which renders it formless, but it still retains its form after the form has been dissolved and, although it is outside of the form, it longingly wanders about material places and returns to them.'

G. But I, holding back a little and returning to an earlier part of our conversation, said: 'It seems to me that there is a certain conflict between what we are saying and what we investigated before in connection with the emotions. On the one hand, these movements of the soul were thought to be active in us because of our affinity to irrational animals—I mean the emotions we enumerated earlier in our discussion: anger and fear and desire and pleasure and such things. But it has also been said that the good use of these emotions is a virtue and that evil comes about because of their abuse. Furthermore, we pointed out how each of them contributes to the virtuous life and we stated, in particular, that we are led to God through desire, being drawn up to Him from below as if by a choir. Somehow, it seems to me that there is a conflict here.'

M. 'What do you mean?'

G. I said: 'Since every irrational impulse in us is removed after purgation, the desiring faculty will no longer exist, but, if this is so, there will be no inclination towards what is better, since the soul will no longer have a desire for the good.'

M. She said: 'To this, we reply that the faculty of contemplation and of making distinctions is characteristic of the godlike portion of the soul, since, by these, we comprehend even the divine. When, either because of our effort here on earth or because of our purgation afterwards, our soul is freed from its association with the emotions, we shall in no way be impeded in our contemplation of the beautiful. The beautiful, by its very nature, is somehow attractive to everyone looking at it. If the soul is freed from all evil, it will exist entirely in the realm of the beautiful. But beautiful is the divine to which the soul will be joined on account of its purity, uniting with what is proper to it. If this occurs, there will no longer be a need for any movement based on desire to lead us to the beautiful. The one who lives in darkness has a desire for the light. If he comes into the light, the enjoyment of it follows upon the desire and the power of enjoying makes the desire useless and foolish. Nor, as far as our own participation in the good is concerned, will there be any penalty if the soul, freed from such impulses, turns back upon itself and sees itself clearly (that is, what its nature is) and looks towards the archetype because of its own beauty as if looking into a mirror and image. It is truly possible to say that in our soul's imitation of the nature above it, there is complete assimilation to the divine. The nature beyond thought, far removed from what is seen in us, leads its own life in some other manner and not as we do in our present life. Man, because it is his nature to be always in movement, is borne wherever the onset of choice takes him, for the soul is not affected in the same way by what comes before and what comes later. Hope is the guide in our motion forward and memory follows upon the motion effected by hope. If hope leads the soul to what is beautiful by nature, the motion of choice imprints a bright track upon our memory; but, if the soul is defrauded of what is better, hope having deluded it by some false image of beauty, shame follows upon what has happened. In this way, civil war is set up in the soul and memory fights with hope on the grounds that it has led the soul astray. The feeling of shame clearly reveals the state of mind, and the soul, remorseful because of what has happened, reviles the ill-advised impulse with penance as if with a whip and courts forgetfulness in its battle against grief. But the nature of the beautiful, because it is impoverished, always aims at what is needed, and the desire for what is lacking constitutes the desiring disposition of our nature which either makes a mistake because of the vagueness of the truly beautiful or happens upon it by chance. However, the nature which is beyond thought and which supersedes all power needs none of the things which are thought of as being connected with the good, being itself the fulfillment of the goods, nor does it exist in the beautiful because of its participation in some beauty, being itself the nature of the beautiful, whatever the mind considers the beautiful to be. Nor does it contain in itself the motion of hoping, since hope is activated only towards what is not present. The apostle says: "Why does a man hope for what he has?"[19] Nor is memory needed for knowing anything be-

---

19 Cf. Rom. 8.24.

cause there is no need of memory when something is seen. Therefore, since the divine nature is superior to every good and the good is altogether pleasing to the good, because of seeing itself, it desires what it has and has what it desires and takes into itself nothing from the outside. But outside of the divine nature, nothing exists except evil which (although this is paradoxical) has its existence in not existing. For what is the origin of evil if it is not the deprivation of being? What actually exists is the nature of the good. Consequently, that which does not exist in reality exists entirely in non-being. When the soul, separated from all the emotions, becomes godlike and goes beyond desire, existing in that towards which its desire tended, it no longer has in itself any place for hope or memory. For it has what it had hoped for and, because of its concentration on its enjoyment of the good, it drives memory from its thought. And thus it imitates the life beyond, being informed by the characteristics of the divine nature, so that none of the other things is left in it except the disposition to love and to attach itself naturally to the beautiful. For this is what love is: a state of mind directed towards what is pleasing to the mind. When the soul, having become simple and uncomplex and entirely god-like, discovers the good that is truly simple and incorporeal, the only thing in existence which is absolutely delectable and loveable, it clings to it and mingles itself with it through its affectionate movement and activity. It conforms itself to that which is always comprehended and discovered and, once it has become, through its similarity to the good, identical with the nature of what it participates in, desire is no longer present in it because there is no need of any of the goods. Consequently, the soul in this state of abundance expels from itself the desiring motion and disposition which existed only when what was desired was not present. The divine apostle led the way in such an idea when he predicted the end and overthrow of all the things we desire (even those which aim at what is better) and found love alone to be without limit. For he says: "Prophecies will disappear and knowledge will be destroyed, but charity never fails,"[20] which is equal to saying that love is always the same. And when he says that faith and hope remain with love,[21] he again places love above these and rightly so. For hope motivates a person as long as he is not enjoying what is hoped for. In the same way, faith is a support of the uncertainty of what is hoped for. This is the way he defines it: "Faith is the substance of things to be hoped for."[22] When what is hoped for arrives, the other emotions desist, and what remains is the activity connected with love which finds nothing to succeed it. On this account, love is first among all the activities connected with virtue and all the commandments of the law. If, therefore, the soul ever attains this goal, it will need none of the others, having reached the fullness of its being, and it seems that it alone preserves in itself the character of the divine blessedness. And knowledge becomes love because what is known is, by nature, beautiful. Wanton satiety does not touch the truly beautiful. And, since the habit of loving the beautiful is never broken by satiety, the divine life, which is beautiful by nature and has from its nature a love for the beautiful, will always be activated by love. Nor does it have a limit of its activity of love, since we assume that beauty has no limit which would cause love to cease when beauty comes to an end. The beautiful comes to an end only through its opposite. Its nature is not to accept anything inferior and it continues to an unending and boundless good. Since all nature is attracted to what is related to it and a human being is somehow related to God, containing within himself imitations of the archetype, the soul is necessarily attracted to the divine and related to it. It is entirely and in every way necessary for what is related to God to be preserved. If the soul happens to be light and simple, with no material heaviness pressing

---

20 Cf. 1 Cor. 13.8.
21 Cf. 1 Cor. 13.13.
22 Heb. 11.1.

it down, its approach to what is attracting it is pleasant and easy. However, if it is held down by the nails of a passionate attachment to material habits, it is likely to have the experience of bodies crushed in the ruins of earthquakes. Let us assume, for the sake of discussion, that not only are they oppressed by the ruins, but that they are also pierced by nails and pieces of wood imbedded in the mass of ruins. It is likely that bodies lying like this until they are rescued by their relatives will be mangled and torn apart and they will suffer every kind of grave injury. The ruins and nails will crush them because of their power to drag them along. It seems to me that the soul has the same experience when the divine power, because of its benevolence, draws what is its own out of the irrational and material ruins. In my opinion, God does not inflict these painful circumstancees on those who have sinned when He lays claim to them or draws them to Himself because He hates them or blames them for their evil life. He, who is the source of all blessedness, draws them to Himself for a higher purpose. The feeling of pain comes of necessity to those who are being drawn up. Just as those who, by means of fire, purify gold mixed with matter, not only melt the impure matter, but also melt the pure gold along with the counterfeit, and when the counterfeit portion is consumed, the pure gold remains; so, also, when evil is being consumed by purifying fire, it is entirely necessary for the soul immersed in the evil to be in the fire until the alien and earthly and counterfeit elements scattered through it are destroyed. Or, imagine there is a rope smeared with mud and someone begins to draw the rope through a narrow hole from above; the rope will follow along, but the mud, scraped off by the violent tugging, will not go through the hole and it will be the cause of the rope's not slipping through easily and of the violent straining as it is pulled from above. Apply this analogy to the soul. Weighted down by material and earthly passions, it struggles and strains when God draws what is His own to Himself. The alien part is somehow scraped off in the process, and this is what brings about the terrible and intolerable pain.'

G. I said: 'It seems, then, that the divine judgment does not inflict punishment upon those who have sinned, but, as your argument proves, only acts in separating good from evil and in drawing them to a share of blessedness. And it is the tearing off of the evil attached to the good which causes the pain to the one being drawn up to God.'

M. My teacher replied: 'Thus it is my opinion that the pain is measured by the amount of evil in each person. For it is unlikely that the person deeply involved in forbidden evils and the person who has fallen into minor transgressions will undergo the same pain in the process of being purified of their bad habits. That painful flame will be applied to a greater or lesser degree in proportion to the amount of matter adhering to each one and as long as that which nourishes it is in existence. If a person has much earthy stuff clinging to him, his purging flame will necessarily be of long duration; but, if the flame is applied to someone with a smaller amount, there will be a remission of its more violent and fierce activity proportionate to the lesser evil. It is altogether necessary for evil to be removed entirely from that which exists and, as we said before, that which does not exist in being does not exist at all. Furthermore, since it is the nature of evil not to exist apart from choice, when all choice resides in God, evil will disappear completely because there will be nothing left to contain it.'

G. 'But,' said I, 'of what use is this good hope to anyone thinking of how terrible it is to endure pain even for one year? Also, if the intolerable pain is extended over an endless period of time, what consolation is there in a hope to come for one whose punishment is measured throughout all eternity?'

M. My teacher said: 'It means that we must take thought

ahead of time either to safeguard our soul so that it is entirely unmixed with and free from the defilements of evil, or, if that is impossible because of the weakness of our nature, we must see to it that, as far as possible, our deviations be in minor matters and ones easily remedied. For the teaching of the Gospel[23] tells us of a debtor who owed ten thousand talents and one who owed five hundred denarii and one who owed fifty and one who owed a pence, which is the smallest coin. And it tells us that the just judgment of God pertains to all and the necessary repayment corresponds to the amount of the debt so that not even the smallest is overlooked. However, the Gospel says that the payment is not made in money, but that the debtor is "delivered to the torturers until he pays all the debt," which is nothing else than saying that the payment must be made through torture. The debt owed is participation in the troubles of life since he foolishly chose pleasure unmixed with pain. Once he has put aside everything that is alien to him, namely sin, and is relieved of the shame of being in debt, he becomes free and is at liberty. Freedom means being independent and without a master. It was given to us in the beginning by God, but it was obscured by the shame of our debts. All freedom is essentially the same and identical with itself. Consequently, everything that is free is in harmony with whatever is similar to itself. But virtue knows no master. Therefore, all freedom, being without a master, consists in virtue, and since the divine nature is the source of all virtue, those who are free from vice will exist in it, in order, as the apostle says: "that God may be all in all."[24] This saying seems to me to reinforce clearly the idea we investigated earlier when God is referred to as being all things and in all things. Our present life is lived by us in varied and multifarious ways. We partake of many things, such as time, air, place, eating and drinking, the light of the sun, lamplight, and the many other necessities of life, and

---

23 Cf. Matt. 18.23 ff.
24 1 Cor. 15.28. The next sentence refers to Macrina's discussion on p. 203.

God is none of these. However, the blessedness we look forward to requires none of them and, instead of these, the divine nature will become everything to us imparting itself harmoniously to every need of that life. This is clear from sacred pronouncements which tell us that God becomes a place to those who are worthy and a home and a garment and nourishment and drink and light and wealth and a kingdom and every idea and name we have for what makes up the good life.[25] But the one who becomes everything exists in everything. Here, Scripture seems to me to be describing the complete disappearance of evil. For if God will exist in all being, clearly evil will not exist in it. If anyone supposes that evil also exists, how can we maintain that God exists in everything? For the removal of evil limits the idea of the inclusion of everything. But the one who is in everything will not be in that which is not.'

G. I said: 'What are we to say to those who are dejected by misfortune?'

M. My teacher answered: 'Let us tell them this. You foolishly rant and rave against a necessary series of events because you are ignorant of the good towards which each feature of the universal economy aims, and of the fact that everything must be identified with the divine nature in a certain arrangement and sequence in keeping with the artistic wisdom of the one who established it. The rational nature came into being for this purpose, that the wealth of divine goods might not be idle. Receptacles with the faculty of choice were constructed like vases by the wisdom that sustains all things in order that there would be some place capable of receiving these goods, a place that always becomes larger because of what is additionally poured into it. For participation in the divine good is such that it makes larger and more receptive that in which it exists. It is accepted by the recipient for the purpose of increasing power and size so that what is being nourished

---

25 These terms are not exact Biblical *testimonia*, but a convenient way of referring to a number of ideas which recur in the New Testament.

always grows and never ceases to grow. Since the source of all goods flows continuously, the nature of the one who has a share in them converts everything that flows into it to its own size because nothing that is taken in is superfluous or useless. At the same time, it becomes much more capable of attracting what is better and more spacious. The two are reciprocal; the capability increases as it is nourished by the abundance of goods, and the nourishing agent abounds with the increased growth. Therefore, it is likely that those whose increase is not limited in any way will achieve such magnitude. Once this has been put before us, do you still complain because of the course arranged for us, as our nature proceeds to its particular good? It is impossible for our road towards these goals to be otherwise, without our being burdened. I mean without our soul being harassed by this heavy and earthy load. Only after we are purged of the sympathy we had with it in this life are we able to be joined in purity to what we are similar to. But, even if you have become accustomed to your body and the separation from what you love grieves you, do not be without hope. You will see this bodily garment which is now dissolved by death woven again of the same elements, not according to its present crass and heavy construction, but with the thread resewn into something more fine and delicate, so that what you love will be present to you and restored to you with a greater and more lovable beauty.'

G. I said: 'It is clear that somehow, as a consequence of what we have been saying, the dogma of the resurrection has come into our discussion, a dogma which seems to me to be true and worthy of belief from the teaching of Scripture and not to be doubted. However, since the weakness of human thought relies somehow on more accessible arguments for such a belief, I think we should not leave this point without consideration. Let us see, therefore, what we ought to say.'

M. My teacher said: 'Those outside of our philosophy have widely differing opinions about the resurrection and, although they do not agree with us completely, neither do they fail to have such a hope. Some of them insult the human race by the idea of the community of animate beings, declaring that man and animal have the same soul in turn, that the soul changes bodies, always going on to what is pleasing to it, a bird, a fish, or a land animal after man, and that it returns from these to human form again. Others extend such nonsense even to trees, so that they think a life of wood is suitable for the soul. To others, it seems that the soul is always going from one human form to another and that human life goes on all the time with the same soul, that is, that the same souls now reside in these human forms and again in others continuously. We, starting from the dogmas of the Church, are content to accept from the philosophers only what indicates that they agree with our opinion that there is a resurrection. When they say that the soul chooses to enter certain other bodies after being separated from these, they do not dissent from our hope that we shall live again. When our argument is that the soul is made up of the atoms of the universe, we seem to agree with those outside of the Church, for they do not think that there is any kind of body not resulting from a coming-together of the elements. There is this difference, that we say that the same body provides a frame for the same soul, whereas they think that the soul changes over into rational and irrational and non-sentient bodies, all of which are agreed to be made up of parts of the universe. They disagree with us in not thinking that the bodies are not made up of the same elements that the soul was attached to in the beginning. In any case, let testimony be given from secular philosophy that it is not unlikely that the soul exists again in the body.

Now is the time to examine the inconsistency of their point of view and, from our conclusion based on right reason, to clarify the truth as far as we can. What is their argument along these lines? Those who make the soul migrate to different natures seem to me to confuse the peculiarities of nature and to mix everything up, confusing the rational, the irrational, the sentient, and the non-sentient, if, indeed, these do exist in each other and are not separated from each other by some natural barrier. For they say that the same soul endowed with reason and intelligence is clothed in such a covering that now it creeps with the serpents or flies with the birds, or inhabits a beast of burden or a carnivorous animal or a fish, or that it changes over into non-sentient beings, putting out roots and becoming a tree or sending forth branches and producing thorns or fruit that is nourishing or poisonous. This is nothing else than thinking that everything is identical and that there is one nature in all things mingled with itself in a confused and disorderly unity and that there are no individual traits distinguishing one thing from another. The person who says that the same thing is in everything would have it that everything is one, in which case apparent differences would not prevent the mingling of things that have nothing in common. It would be necessary, even if something poisonous or carnivorous is seen, to think that, whatever it is, it is of the same species and related to oneself. And the person who sees the human element in plants will not look upon hemlock as being alien to his particular nature, nor will the grape which is cultivated for fostering life be unsuspected, since it is produced by a plant. Furthermore, plants provide us with the grain by which we are nourished. How will he cut down the grain; how will he press the grape or dip up a weed or pick a flower or hunt birds or light a fire when it is not clear whether he is lifting his hand against his relatives or ancestors or fellow-tribesmen, and whether it is through the body of these that the fire is kindled, the pot heated, or the food cooked? To the person thinking that the soul of man becomes a plant or animal, no sign is given as to which plant or animal was originally a man and which was not. Assuming this, a person will be equally disposed toward all things, so that he will necessarily either act harshly towards the men living in those forms of nature or he will be kindly disposed towards those of the same nature as himself and have the same attitude to everything that is animate, even if it happens to be a serpent or a wild animal. If he extends his theory to the wood of trees, he will think that trees are a race of men. What sort of life will such a man have, reverencing all things because of their kinship to each other or being cruel even to men since they are no different from the rest of nature? Certainly, such an argument must be rejected because of what we have said and there are many other logical reasons for rejecting this assumption. I have heard from those having such opinions that certain souls are supposed to have existed in a certain state before they came to live in bodies, whirling about in accordance with the movement of the universe because of their delicacy and mobility, but that because of some inclination towards evil, they entered into bodies; first of all, into human bodies, then, because of their association with the irrational emotions, being dispossessed of their human dwelling, they degenerated to the life of plants and non-sentient beings, so that naturally light and mobile thing which is the soul, first of all, became heavy and downward in its motion, inhabiting human bodies because of evil; then, when its reasoning power was quenched, it dwelt among the irrational animals, and from there, when the gift of the senses was taken away, it went down into the non-sentient life of the plants, but after that, it rose up again through the same levels and was restored to its celestial abode. Even for those moderately skilled in judging such ideas the argument is refuted by its inconsistency. If the soul is pulled down by evil from its heavenly life to a material life, and then, because of virtue ascends again to heaven, the argument fails to show which life is preferable, the material or the heavenly one. A certain cycle exists going through the same stages, and the soul, wherever it is, is always unstable. If it is borne down from its incorporeal existence to the corporeal and from this to the non-sentient and from there it ascends again to the incorporeal, nothing more than an indistinct confusion of evils and goods is conceived of by those advocating this idea. The heavenly sojourn in blessedness will not persist if evil fastens upon those living there, nor will the material be divorced from virtue if they think that the soul runs back again to the good and from there begins a life in accordance with evil. If the soul, flitting about in heaven, is interwoven with evil and, after being dragged down because of it into the material life, is again thrust up from there to its sojourn on high, then, these affirm that the material life is purged of evil; but the fixed celestial circuit is the beginning and cause of evils for the souls if, sprouting wings through virtue, they are borne through the air, and then, when they lose their wings through evil, they fall to the ground and become earth-bound and are mixed with the crassness of matter. The absurdity of such an idea is not confined to the conflict of the opinions. Sometimes, these people do not even remain steadfast in their opinion. If they say that the heavenly is unchangeable, how can corruptibility have a place in it? If nature below is subject to change, how can lack of incorruptibility be achieved there? They mix the unmixable and unite those things which have nothing in common, seeing the unchangeable in the corruptible and the incorruptible in the changeable, nor do they hold even to this. They send the soul down from that state because of evil, and then bring it back to the secure and immortal life as if forgetting that the soul, weighted down by evil, had been mixed with the nature below. So the criticism of life here and praise of the celestial life are confused and mixed up, the one being criticized because, in their opinion, it leads to the good, and the other (which we assume to be the better) because it gives the soul an opportunity to incline to the worse. Every false and unstable opinion on these matters should be excluded from the true dogmas.

'Furthermore, let us not follow those who deviate from the

truth in thinking that souls change from female bodies to the life of the male, or that the souls of men exist later among women, or that souls go from one man's body to another, or one woman's body to another. The former idea is rejected, not only because, being contradictory, it is unreliable and fallacious, but because it is irreverent. They hold that nothing comes into existence without evil being present in its nature from the very beginning. If, as they maintain, neither men, nor plants, nor animals are born unless the soul descends into them from on high, but this fall comes about through evil, they make evil the source of everything. How can it happen at the same time that man is born from marriage and that the fall of the soul coincides with an eagerness for marriage? And this is even more illogical, if many irrational animals come together in the spring, to say that spring causes evil to be born, so that simultaneously the souls filled with evil fall through some celestial motion and the womb of the animals become pregnant. And what could be said of the farmer who plants shoots in the ground? Would his hand bury the human soul along with the plant, since the soul would lose its wings as a result of the farmer's energy in planting? There is the same absurdity in the other theory of those who think that the soul concerns itself with the physical intercourse of those who are married, or watches for the birth of children in order to enter into their bodies. If a man forgoes marriage and a woman frees herself from the necessity of having children, will that prevent evil from burdening the soul? Is it marriage, then, which gives the evil on high its opportunity against souls or, even apart from marriage, does evil fasten upon the soul? The soul, in that case, is homeless, floating about in mid-air having come down from the heavens and having found no body to receive it. Then how do they think that there is a divine principle governing reality if they argue that the beginning of human life is due to this chance and to the irrational descent of souls? It is altogether necessary for what happens later to agree with what happened in the beginning. If life begins through some automatic coincidence, its continuation will also be a matter of chance. In vain do such people attribute the universe to the divine power if they say that things in the world are not born through the divine will, but attribute the beginnings of things to some evil coincidence on the grounds that human life would not occur if evil did not give life an opportunity. If life begins in this way, it will clearly proceed according to its beginning. For no one would say that beauty comes from evil or its opposite from good. The fruit is expected to correspond to the nature of the seed. Therefore, this very automatic and coincidental movement of all life will lead the way and there will be no providence in the universe. Reasonable forethought will be useless; nothing will be gained by virtue; to be free from evil will count for nothing. Everything will be subject to coincidence and life will be no different from ships at sea without ballast, changing anchorage from good to bad and bad to good according to the concurrence of the automatic waves. No gain can come from virtue if nature has its beginning in the opposite of virtue. If our life is determined by God, it is agreed that it cannot begin with evil. If we are born through evil, we shall live entirely and altogether according to it. Punishments and rewards for merit in the after-life will be shown to be nonsense, as will whatever else is believed to be connected with the removal of evil. If man is born of evil, how could any deliberate impulse towards the good life be present in a man, since his nature, as they say, has its beginning in evil? Just as none of the irrational animals tries to speak like a man, but use their own natural voices and do not think it a penalty not to have been given the gift of speech; in the same way, those for whom evil is considered the beginning and cause of life would not have a desire for virtue since it would be beyond their nature. However, to those whose soul is purified by reason, the virtuous life is a matter of zealous desire. Therefore, on account of this, it has been clearly shown that evil is not older than life and that nature does not have its first beginnings in it, but that the wisdom of God, which governs everything, is the beginning of our life. Our soul was born in a manner pleasing to the Creator and, then, the soul itself of its own volition, with its faculty of choice, chose what it wanted to be and became that.

'Let us understand the argument from the analogy of the eye which has the power to see by nature, but the power of not seeing by choice or because of disease. Sometimes, what is unnatural could occur instead of the natural: someone might voluntarily close his eyes or be deprived of sight through disease. Thus it is also possible to say in connection with the soul that its constitution comes from God and that, since no evil is known to be in the divine, the soul itself is outside of evil. However, once it has been born, it is led by its own judgment to what seems good to it. Either it closes its eyes to the beautiful by choice or the eye of the soul is harmed by a conspiracy of the enemy which is involved in our life and the soul lives in the darkness of deceit, or it is cured of the disease which causes the darkness and purely looks again towards the truth.

'But when and how will anyone say the soul is born? An inquiry into how each thing comes into being must be removed entirely from our discussion. It would not be possible for reason, investigating the constitution of the visible, to understand it through the usual things that man perceives through his senses. This is not considered comprehensible by the prophets and holy men. "For," says the apostle, "by faith we understand that the world was fashioned by the word of God; and thus things visible were made out of things invisible."[26] He would not have said this, as I think, if he had thought that what was being sought was understandable through logic. What the apostle wants us to believe is that

---

26 Heb. 11.3.

the world itself (whatever the world is in which all things seen and unseen are envisaged) and everything in it were framed by the divine will. The "how" we should leave unexamined, for there are so many difficulties in the way of such an inquiry that I do not think anyone investigating this will succeed. For how can that which is moved and has dimension and composition come from what is simple and without dimension? From the supreme being? Because of the diversity of things, it is not agreed that that is the source of being. But what other source is there? Our argument recognizes nothing outside of the divine nature. The argument about different first principles would be rent asunder if anything should be thought outside of the efficient cause by which the professional philosophers explain creation. Since, therefore, there is one cause of whatever exists, but it is not of the same genus as the supreme nature which brings all things into being, both theories are equally absurd: the one that maintains that all creation is derived from the nature of God, and the one that says all things are made of some other essence. Either the divine is thought to be in the peculiarities of what comes into being through creation and God belongs to the same genus, or some nature materially different from the divine is to be introduced instead, and this will be equated with God in connection with the unborn in the eternity of being. The Manichaeans and certain Greek philosophers, agreeing with these notions, have adopted this fantasy as their dogma. Therefore, to avoid the absurdity of each of these theories, we shall accept the apostle's suggestion and not meddle with an investigation of how each thing comes into existence. Only this much shall we affirm, that when the divine will wishes it, a thing comes into being and the divine wish is realized and, once this has occurred, the divine will never revokes what it has wisely and skillfully effected. Moreover, substance is the essence of the will.

'Since there are two kinds of being, that of the mind and that of the body, the creation of intelligent beings does not preclude the incorporeal nature, but is closely connected with it, embracing the invisible and the intangible and whatever is without dimension, and if anyone suspects that this is related to the divine nature, he is not in error. On the other hand, the corporeal creation is looked upon as being made up of characteristics which have nothing in common with the divine. This puzzles our reason which cannot understand how the visible comes from the invisible, the firm and resistant from the intangible, the limited from the unlimited, the measured from the unmeasured, and the other qualities we include when we refer to the bodily nature. Concerning these, we say only this, that none of them exists by themselves—figure, color, weight, dimension, quantity, or anything included under the term "quality," but there is a reason for each of them and, when they come together, the result is the unified body. Since the qualities which make up the body are comprehended by the mind and not by the senses, and since the mind is divine, what trouble is it for the mind to cause those things which it comprehends, the coming together of which results in our bodily nature? But let these questions be examined elsewhere. What we were asking was this: if our souls do not exist before our bodies, when and how do they come into being? Scripture has dismissed our meddlesome query about the "how" because it is impossible to know. So it is left for us to investigate the question of when the souls begin to exist in the light of our previous investigations.

'If it is granted that the soul exists in some state before the body, it is altogether necessary for us to think that there is some validity to those dogmatic absurdities about the souls entering bodies because of evil. But no intelligent man would suppose that the birth of souls occurs later or earlier than the formation of bodies, since it is clear to all that none of the things without a soul have the power of moving within themselves. Furthermore, there is nothing controversial or ambiguous about the growth or motion of what is nurtured in the womb. We must conclude, therefore, that the soul and the body have a single beginning. And just as the earth, which receives a shoot from the farmer and produces a tree, does not give it the power to increase, but only the opportunity to increase; so, also, can we say that what is taken from man for the producing of a human being is also itself in the same way a living thing, the animate coming from the animate, and the nourished from the nourished. And if the short span of the shoot does not allow it to contain all the activities and movements of the soul, this is not surprising. The grain in the seed does not become an ear of corn as soon as it appears (how could it?), but when the earth supplies it with suitable nourishment, it becomes a stalk of grain without changing its nature in the clod of earth, showing itself and perfecting itself through the energy derived from the nourishment. Just as in the growing shoots the growth continues gradually until the plant is perfected, in the same way in the case of the human being, the power of the soul also appears in accordance with the condition of the body. First of all, it is present in what is being formed within the womb through the process of being nourished and growing, and after that, it brings the faculty of perception to the creatures which are coming into the light. Then, after the plant has grown, it moderately displays the power of reason. It does not cause it to grow instantly and entirely, but each step occurs in keeping with the springing up of a plant in its normal progress of growth. Since what is plucked from animate beings for the producing of an animate constitution cannot be without life—for mortality means the absence of a soul and since absence does not precede a state of being—we learn from this that there is a common entrance into existence for both parts of a human being: the one does not precede the other, nor does the other come later. Moreover, reason necessarily foresees an end to the increase in the number of the souls sometime, in order that nature which is always being poured into new beings and never ceases to move, may not flow forever. We think the reason it is necessary for this nature of ours to be stabilized is this, that since all intelligible nature consists in its own fulfillment, it is likely that sometime mankind will come to an end. It is not alien to the intelligible nature not to seem inexhaustible. The very fact that new beings are being born suggests that nature is becoming used up. So, when mankind reaches the point of its own fulfillment, the flowing movement of nature will stop, having reached its necessary end, and some other conditions will descend upon life, different from the present one which consists of coming into being and passing away, and when there is no birth, there will necessarily be no death. If we say that synthesis causes a thing to be born and synthesis precedes dissolution, it would altogether follow that if synthesis does not come first dissolution will not occur. Therefore, the life after this being stable and without dissolution promises to be changed neither by birth nor corruption.'

G. As my teacher was explaining this, it seemed to many of those sitting around that our discussion had reached a fitting conclusion, but I was afraid that, if she succumbed to the illness she was already suffering, there would be no one to answer for us the objections proposed by the outsiders to the doctrine of the resurrection. So I said: 'Our discussion has not yet touched upon the most crucial point in what we are seeking in connection with the dogma. Divinely inspired Scripture, in both the New and Old Testaments, says that when our nature has completed its planned sequence, in keeping with the periodic movement of time, this flowing motion will stop going forward in its succession of births. When the sum of everything no longer goes on to a greater increase, the whole complement of souls will return, the unseen and the scattered to the composite and the visible and the same elements will run back to each other in the same arrangement. Such a condition of life is called the resurrection by the divine teaching of Scripture, and this entire movement of the elements is synonymous with the end of the world.'

M. She said: 'What have we forgotten in our previous discussion?'

G. I replied: 'The very dogma of the resurrection.'

M. She said: 'And yet much of what we have said just now pertains to this in a rather indirect way.'

G. I answered: 'Don't you realize what a host of objections will be brought against this hope by our opponents?' And, at the same time, I tried to tell her what arguments were invented by quarrelsome persons to refute the idea of the resurrection.

M. She said: 'It seems to me that first we should run through briefly the scattered references to this dogma in Sacred Scripture and conclude our discussion there. Well, then—when David made the creation of the universe, his theme in the one hundred and third Psalm, I heard him singing this towards the end of it: "If you take away their breath, they perish and return to their dust. When you send forth thy spirit, they are created, and you renew the face of the earth."[27] Here he is saying that the power of the spirit which is active in all things gives life to what it is present in and takes life away again when it departs. Since he is saying that with the departure of the spirit there is a failure of life and with the presence of the spirit a renewal of what has failed takes place, and since, according to the order of reason, failure precedes renewal, David, in proclaiming this grace with prophetic spirit, is announcing to the Church the mystery of the Annunciation. And elsewhere this same prophet says that the God of all, the Lord of creation "hath shone upon us" for the appointing of "a solemn day, with shady boughs." Here, with the term "shady boughs," he is referring to the feast of tabernacles[28] which is thought to go back to the Mosaic tra-

---
27 Ps. 103.29,30.
28 Cf. Lev. 23.39-43. For a history and exegesis of the feast of tabernacles and its eschatological symbolism, cf. J. Daniélou, *Primitive Christian Symbols* (London 1964) 1-24.

dition where the lawgiver is predicting the future prophetically, I think. Although it is always taking place, it has not yet taken place. The truth is made clear figuratively by the symbol of something taking place, but the true feast of tabernacles has not yet taken place. For this reason, according to the prophetic word, the God and Lord of all has shone upon us in order to appoint for human nature a feast at which the dissolved tabernacles will be reformed through the coming together again of the elements of our bodies. The term "shady boughs" in its own way signifies the putting on of a covering and the adornment connected with it. The wording of the Psalm is as follows: "The Lord is God and he has shone upon us. Appoint a solemn day with shady boughs, even to the horns of the altar."[29] This seems to me to proclaim that one feast is appointed for all creation endowed with reason, the inferior and the superior making up a chorus in an assembly of the good. In the symbolic temple not everyone is allowed within the outer portico, the Gentile and the foreigner are barred from the entrance, and of those who do enter, not all are permitted to go farther inside unless they have been purified by a purer way of life and certain ablutions. And again, the inner part of the temple was not accessible to all of these since it was customary for the priests alone to be inside the veil according to the demand of the ritual. The hidden and innermost part, where the altar was placed, was decorated with horns and the priests themselves could not enter there except for the one in charge of the priesthood, who once a year on a traditional day went in to offer some remote and mystic sacrifice. Therefore, if such distinctions were made in this temple, which was used as the image and symbol of the mind, observation of the body teaches this, that not all reasonable nature comes near the temple of God, that is to a confession of the great God, but those who have erred because of false assumptions are outside

---

29 Cf. Ps. 117.27.

of the divine precincts. And of those who are within because of their confession, those are more honored than the others who have been purified ahead of time by ablutions and purifications, and those who have been consecrated excel to such a point that they are worthy of the more esoteric rites. In order to explain the point of the symbol, one can learn that Scripture teaches this: that some of the faculties endowed with reason are situated, as it were, at the altar in the approach to the godhead, whereas some of them, being considered outstanding, have advanced as far as the horns, and others hold first or second rank near them according to some kind of protocol. Moreover, because of the evil present in it, mankind was dismissed from the divine protection and is only permitted inside when it has undergone purifications. But, since these intermediate obstacles, by which evil kept us away from the place within the veil of the temple, are going to be done away with when our nature is reconstituted through the resurrection and all corruption caused by evil will be annihilated, then, a general feast will be established around God by those who have been clothed through the resurrection and there will be one and the same joy for all. No longer will there be different degrees of participation for the reasoning nature. Those now excluded because of evil will be inside the approaches to the divine blessedness and the altar with the horns, that is, they will unite themselves to the exceptional faculties of the supramundane beings. This is what the apostle states more directly when, in interpreting the harmony of everything with the good, he says: "Every knee will bow of those that are in heaven and on earth and under the earth, and every tongue will confess that the Lord Jesus Christ is in the glory of God the Father."[30] Instead of horns, he speaks of the angelic and celestial beings and, with the other words, he refers to those created after them, i.e., to us, and he says that one harmonious feast will prevail for all. The

---

30 Cf. Phil. 2.10,11.

feast is the confession and recognition of true reality. It is possible,' she said, 'to collect many other passages of Holy Scripture which confirm the dogma of the resurrection. Ezechiel,[31] with prophetic spirit, has surpassed all time and space and with his power of prediction has stood at the very moment of the resurrection. Seeing the future as already present, he has brought it before our eyes in his description. He saw a plain, large and boundless, and a large mound of bones scattered haphazardly upon it. Then, sorting themselves out through the divine power "the bones came together each one to his own joint." Then, they were covered by sinews and flesh and skin for which the Psalm used the symbol of the "shady boughs" and a life-giving spirit roused all that lay there. And why should one mention the apostle's descriptions of miracles involving a resurrection since these are at hand for anyone to read? Scripture tells us[32] how, at a certain command and sound of trumpets at a given moment of time, all who are dead and lying in the grave will be transformed into an immortal nature. But we shall pass over the passages in the Gospels since they are known to everyone. For not by word alone does the Lord say that the dead will rise. He Himself caused a resurrection beginning with the wonder-working of those nearer us whose testimony cannot be discounted. First of all, He showed His life-giving power in the case of fatal illnesses where he drove out disease by His order and His word.[33] Next, he awakened the child who had just died.[34] Then, he restored to his mother the young man who was being carried to his burial, causing him to rise from the funeral couch.[35] After this, he brought Lazarus back from the dead after he had been in the grave four days, calling him back by word and command.[36] His own body, pierced by nails and a lance,

---

[31] Cf. Ezech. 37.1 ff.
[32] Cf. 1 Cor. 15.52.
[33] Cf. Matt. 8.2,3.
[34] Cf. Matt. 9,18-25.
[35] Cf. Luke 7.11-15.
[36] Cf. John 11.17-44.

he brought back after three days and he retained the traces of the nails and the wound caused by the lance as proof of his resurrection.[37] I do not think it is necessary to go through these since there is no doubt about them among those who have inherited what has been written.'

G. I said: 'But this is not what we are looking for. Many of our listeners will agree with the scriptural proofs and our previous discussions that there will be a resurrection and that man will be subject to a just judgment. It remains for us to see if what is hoped for is related to our present existence. For, if our human bodies return to life in the same condition in which they left it, then, man is looking forward to endless misfortune in the resurrection. What is more pitiful than bodies bent down and deformed by extreme old age? The flesh is withered by time, the skin, dry and withered, stretched over the bones because of the lack of natural moisture, the sinews are contracted so that the whole body is an absurd and pitiable sight, the head bent down to the knee, the hand shaking involuntarily and unable to perform its natural function. Or, again, the bodies are wasted by chronic diseases, differing only from skeletons in that they are covered by a thin and wasted skin. And there are those swollen with dropsy and those afflicted with epilepsy. What word could bring before the eye the horrible mutilation, the putrefaction which, as it progresses, feeds upon all the organs and the senses? And those crippled in earthquakes or in wars or from some other cause and live for some time before death in this wretched condition, or those deformed from birth—what could one say of them? And what are we to think of babies newly-born who are exposed or suffocated? If they are brought back to life, will they remain in the same state of infancy? What could be more wretched? Or will they come to a mean point in age? With what kind of milk will nature nourish them? If in all circumstances, the same body is to be brought back to life for

---

37 Cf. John 20.27.

us, all we are anticipating is misfortune. But, if it is not the same, will it not be someone else who has been awakened rather than the one lying there? For, if a child has died and a grown man rises, or vice versa, how can one say that the person himself has risen since the person who has died will be changed by the difference in age? Anyone seeing the grown man instead of the child, or the young man instead of the old one, will see one person substituted for another, the whole instead of the mutilated, the sleek instead of the emaciated, and so forth. Unless the body is brought back to life as it was when it was mingled with the earth, the dead person will not have risen, but the earth will have been formed again into another man. What does it mean to me if someone else comes back to life? How could I recognize myself not seeing myself in myself? For I would not be truly I if I were not identical with myself in all details. Just as in our present life if I remember a certain person—let us assume for purposes of discussion that he is growing bald, has prominent lips, a small nose, pale skin, greyish eyes, white hair, and a wrinkled body—if, in looking for such a one, I come upon a young man with long hair, an aquiline nose, dark skin, and all the other features of his body different, when I look at him will I think I am seeing the former one? But why should we waste time with minor objections and neglect more valid ones? Who does not know that human nature is like a stream which is always moving from birth to death and that it ceases to move when it ceases to exist? But this movement is not an exchange of place, for nature does not go beyond itself, but it goes forward through change. But change, as long as it is what it is said to be, never remains the same, for how could what is changed remain the same? Just as fire in a lamp always seems to be the same, since the continuous movement always shows it joined to itself, but, in truth, it is always changing and never remains the same—the moisture extracted by the heat is inflamed and, being enkindled, changes into smoke, and the movement of the flame is always activated by the power of change which transforms what is underneath into smoke—so it is not possible for anyone touching the flame to touch it twice in the same spot since the change occurs so quickly that it does not wait for the second touch, even if one is as fast as possible. The flame is always new and fresh and going in relays and it never remains the same. There is a similar process connected with the nature of our body. That part of our nature which flows in and out and is always proceeding and moving because of changing movement stops when it ceases to live. As long as life continues, there is no stop, for it is either increasing or decreasing or forever going from one state to another. If someone is not the same as he was yesterday, but becomes someone else through the process of change, when the resurrection brings our body to life, a kind of all-inclusive man will come into being so that nothing of the resurrected person will be missing in the risen person, the newly-born, the infant, the child, the adolescent, the man, the father, the old man, and all the stages in between.

'Since both temperance and incontinence are exercised through the flesh and, for reasons of piety, people sometimes endure harsh tortures and at other times shrink from them, doing both because of bodily sensation, how is it possible for justice to be preserved through judgment? The person who has sinned purges himself afterwards through penance and it sometimes happens that he falls again into sin. His body alternates between being pure and impure and he is not in either state perpetually. Which body will be punished for intemperance? The one shriveled in old age or near to death? But this body was not responsible for the sin. Or the body stained by passion? But where will the old man be? Either he will not rise and the resurrection will not have occurred, or he will rise and the body which deserves punishment will escape.

'Shall I mention another objection brought forward by

those rejecting our point of view? They say that there is no part of our body without it natural function. Some parts are the life-giving cause and power without which life in the flesh could not be sustained, e.g., heart, liver, brain, lungs, stomach, and the rest of the internal organs; others are allotted to sensory movement, others to action and locomotion, others to the succession of activities that follow. If our life after this is to consist of the same thing, the change will amount to nothing. If it is true, as it certainly is, that there is no provision for marriage in the life after the resurrection and that our life then will not depend on eating or drinking, what use will the parts of the body be, since in that life we no longer expect these activities for whose sake the parts of the body now exist? If for the sake of marriage there are parts which pertain to marriage, when marriage no longer exists, we will have no need of those parts. Or of hands for work or feet for running or a mouth for eating or teeth for chewing food, or internal organs for digestion or the intestines for elimination. When these activities do not exist, how or why will the organs exist which came into being because of them and will not be necessary if none of these functions are going to be performed in the life after this? The after-life consists of other things and one would no longer speak of a resurrection if the individual parts did not rise with the body because of their uselessness in that life. On the other hand, if a complete resurrection occurs, the one bringing it about wills what is vain and useless for our life then. However, it is necessary to believe that there is a resurrection and that it is not futile. Therefore, we should direct our attention to preserving the reasonableness of all the details of the dogma.'

M. As I was enumerating these arguments, my teacher said: 'You have tried nobly to attack the dogma of the resurrection by means of the so-called art of rhetoric. You have circumvented the truth with such persuasively destructive arguments that a person not examining the truth of the mystery would feel that the objections are reasonable and the suggested doubts not unjustified. But,' she said, 'this is not the truth, even if we are unable to match the rhetoric in word. The true reasoning on these matters is stored in the hidden treasures of wisdom and will come into the open only when we have experienced the mystery of the resurrection; then there will no longer be any need for a verbal statement of what is to be hoped for. But as for those speculating at night about the light of the sun, what it is, the splendor of its beam as it comes forth makes a verbal description unnecessary, so any speculation touching on our future condition amounts to nothing once we experience what has been expected. However, since we must not dismiss any objections offered by our opponents let us continue the discussion on these points.

'First of all, we need to know the scope of the dogma of the resurrection and why it has been spoken of by the holy voice and believed. In order to provide a comprehensive definition, we shall say this: the resurrection is the restoring of our nature to its former condition. At the beginning of life, whose creator was God, there was neither old age, as is reasonable, nor infancy nor sickness resulting from disease, nor any of the other bodily miseries. For it is not likely that God would create such things. Human nature was something divine before humanity inclined itself towards evil. All of these ills came to us with the introduction of evil. There is no need for life without evil to be involved in what comes about because of evil. For just as someone is chilled if he encounters cold weather or becomes tan if he is exposed to the heat of the sun's rays, but if neither of these situations occurs, he does not become chilled or grow darker and no one would reasonably ask why something should happen if there is no cause for it to happen, so our nature, once it is involved in the disease of sin, necessarily suffers the consequences of sin. But when it returns to undiseased blessedness, it will no longer be affected by the consequences of evil. Consequently, whatever of the irrational life was mixed with human nature which was not in us before mankind fell into the disease of sin, when we leave sin behind, we shall necessarily also leave with it whatever accompanies it. And no one would rightly seek in that life what came to us as a result of evil. Just as one who is wearing a torn garment takes it off and no longer connects the ugliness of what he has discarded with himself, so we shall be when we have put off that dead and ugly garment made of the skins of irrationality. I here equate the word "skin" with the aspects of the animal nature with which we clothe ourselves when we become accustomed to sin. Among these are sexual intercourse, conception, child-bearing, sordidness, the nursing and nurturing of children, elimination, the process of growing up, the prime of life, growing old, disease, and death. If that skin no longer envelops us, how can those things connected with it continue to exist in us? Since another state of being is hoped for in the life to come, it is foolish to attack the idea of the resurrection with arguments that have nothing to do with it. For what does being fat or thin, or ill or healthy, or anything else coincident with the changing nature of our bodies have to do with an anticipated existence so different from the fluid and transitory course of this life? The logic of the resurrection requires one thing only, that a man come into existence through birth, or, rather, as the Gospel says, that 'a man be born into this world';[38] the length or brevity of his life or the manner of his death, whether it is thus or so, have no relevance to an inquiry into the resurrection. However we conjecture this to have been, it is all the same, and the differences provide neither help nor hindrance as to the resurrection. Having begun to live, man must continue to live always, once his dissolution, which was caused in the meantime by death, has been put to rights in the resurrection. But the how or the why of his dissolution,

---

[38] John 16.21.

what has that to do with his resurrection? But this is something else again, whether anyone has lived a life of pleasure or pain, or virtue or vice, or whether he was worthy of praise or blame, or has had a life of wretchedness or happiness. All of these things and others like them are determined by the length of a man's life and the kind of life he led. In order to form a judgment of those who have lived, it would be necessary for a judge to investigate a man's experience; the indignities he has suffered, the sickness he has had, his old age, his prime, his youth, his wealth and his poverty; how each man has conducted himself in the various circumstances of the life allotted to him, whether he has been the recipient of goods or of evils in a long life, or whether he was deprived of these from the beginning, having ceased to live before he reached maturity. However, when God through the resurrection brings man's nature back to its original condition, it will be vain to speak of such matters and to think of God's power being kept back from its goal. For Him, the one goal is this, the perfection of the universe through each man individually, the fulfillment of our nature. Some of us are purged of evil in this life, some are cured of it through fire in the after-life, some have not had the experience of good and evil in life here. God proposes for everyone a participation in the goods in Himself which Scripture says: "eye has not seen, nor ear heard, nor has it entered into the mind of man."[39] In my opinion, this is nothing else than existing in God Himself, since the good which is beyond hearing and seeing and the heart would be the very thing which is superior to the universe. The different degrees of virtue or vice in our life will be revealed in our participating more quickly or more slowly in the blessedness we hope for. The extent of the healing will depend on the amount of evil present in each person. The healing of the soul will be purification from evil and this cannot be accomplished

---

39 1 Cor. 2.9.

without suffering, as was shown in our previous discussion. We can recognize how empty and superfluous the objections are by looking closely into the depths of apostolic wisdom. In clarifying the mystery about these things for the Corinthians (and perhaps they presented the same arguments to him as those now brought forward by those opposing the dogma for the purpose of disturbing the faithful), he reproved the boldness of their ignorance by his own authority and said: "But you will say to me: How do the dead rise again? Or with what kind of body do they come? Senseless man, what thou sowest is not brought to life unless it dies. And when thou sowest, thou dost not sow the body that shall be, but a bare grain, perhaps of wheat or something else. But God gives it a body, even as he has willed."[40] It seems to me that here he is refuting those who ignore the particular standards of nature and assess the divine power in the light of their own strength, thinking that God can do only as much as man can comprehend, and that what is beyond us also exceeds the power of God. The person who asked the apostle how the dead rise again practically rejects the coming together again of the scattered elements and, since this is impossible and there is no other body left for the reunion of the elements, he says this as skilled dialecticians do and draws what appears to be a logical conclusion: viz., if the body is a union of elements, but it is impossible for this union to occur a second time, what sort of body will the risen ones use? What seems to be contrived by them through some technical philosophizing, the apostle calls the foolishness of those who do not recognize the excellence of the divine power in the rest of creation. He does not mention the higher wonders of God which might lead his listener into difficulty, e.g., What is a heavenly body and where does it come from? What is the sun—the moon—or what appears among the stars—or what is the aether, or the air, or water, or earth? Instead, he convicts our ad-

---

40 1 Cor. 15.35-38.

versaries of carelessness with arguments more familiar to us. He asks whether farming does not show the foolishness of the person who estimates the divine power according to his own measure, where the bodies come from which are grown from seeds, what brings them to the point of germination? He asks if this is not death, since death is the dissolution of what has consistency? For the seed does not germinate unless it is dissolved in the earth, rarefied, and made porous, so that it is mixed with the moisture nearby and thus changes into root and sprout, and it does not stop there, but changes into a stalk with sections in-between which are surrounded by chains, as it were, so as to be able to hold the grain in an upright position. Where were the things connected with the grain before the dissolution in the earth occurred? Of course it comes from the seed, for if the seed had not existed before, the grain would not have come into being. Therefore, just as the grain comes from the seed, the divine power produces it from that very thing and it is not entirely the same as the seed or entirely different from it. Thus, the apostle says that the mystery of the resurrection is presignified for us in the miracles performed in the seeds. The divine power in its surpassing excellence not only gives back the seed, but adds many great and more wonderful features with which nature is magnificently adorned. For he says the resurrection of the dead "is sown in corruption and rises in incorruption; what is sown in weakness rises in power; what is sown in dishonor rises in glory; what is sown a natural body rises a spiritual body."[41] For as the seed, after it is dissolved in the soil and leaves behind its quantitative deficiency and qualitative peculiarity of form, does not give up being itself, but remains itself although it becomes a stalk of grain which differs very much from itself in size and beauty and variety and form; in the same way, human nature also lets go in death all the peculiar characteristics it acquired through its sinful disposition. I

---

41 1 Cor. 15.42-44.

mean dishonor, corruption, weakness, differing ages, but it does not give up being itself although it changes over into a spiritual and sinless condition. This is characteristic of the psychic body that, through some flux and movement, is always being changed from the state it is in into something else. None of the beauties we now see, not only in men, but also in plants and animals, will be destroyed in the life to come. The word of the apostle seems to me to support in every detail our opinion about the resurrection and to show what our definition stated, that the resurrection is nothing but the restoration of our nature to its original state. We learn this from Scripture which tells us that in the beginning of the world, the earth first produced grass and then came the seed and, when this fell into the earth, the same species was born again as had grown in the beginning. This is what the divine apostle is saying about the resurrection. We learn not only this from him, that man is changed into something more magnificent, but that nothing else is hoped for than for him to be what he was in the beginning. For the grain did not come in the beginning, but the seed from it, and, after this, the grain grew from a seed; and the sequence, as it is described, shows clearly that the entire blessedness sprouts up for us and there is a return to our original grace. In the beginning, we also are grain, in a sense, and afterwards we are burned by the fire of evil. The earth which receives us in death, when we are dissolved in the spring, gives back in place of a seed or ear of corn this bare grain of the body, large and strong and straight, reaching to the sky, adorned with incorruptibility and other tokens befitting the divine. For the apostle says the corruptible must put on incorruptibility. But incorruptibility and glory and honor and power are recognized as the particular features of the divine nature. They existed formerly in what was made in the image of God and they are hoped for again. The first grain was the first man, Adam. But when nature was multiplied by the introduction of evil as in the harvest of the grain, men were deprived of the form of their prototype and, after being mixed with earth, through the resurrection we grow again in keeping with our pristine beauty, countless numbers of us having been produced. The virtuous life will be distinguished from the evil life by the fact that those of us who cultivated virtue will grow immediately into a perfect plant, while those whose virtues became faded and deformed through evil, having "fallen on the horns"[42] as the saying goes, even if we are born again through the resurrection, will be harshly treated by the judge and will not be strong enough to return to the form of the original plant and become what we were before our fall into the earth. The farmer's task is the gathering of the weeds and thorns which grow along with seed. These cause the nourishing power to be diverted and the real seed to be undernourished and undeveloped and choked by the unnatural sprouts. After he has pulled out every bastard and alien growth and burned it, then, the plants will be well nourished and come to fruition as the result of much care. After a long period of time, they will assume again the form which they received from God in the beginning. Blessed are those who come immediately to a complete perfection of growth. We say this, not because there will be some visible corporeal difference between those who have lived good or bad lives or because we think one will be imperfect in body and the other perfect, but it will be like the difference between one who lives in chains and one who is free, a question of pleasure and pain. That I think is the kind of difference we must expect between the good and bad in the time to come. For the perfection growing again from the seed is said by the apostle to include incorruptibility and glory and honor and power. Nor will a deficiency in such bodies mean that they will be mutilated. There will simply be a deprivation or alienation of each of them from what we considered to be

---

42 This agricultural metaphor refers to those who have been stubborn and inflexible in their adherence to evil. Cf. Plato *Laws* 853D.

in the category of the goods. Since we must be one of the two in the antithesis, either good or bad, it is clear that if anyone is said not to be on the side of the good this indicates that he is on the side of evil. Surely, in evil there is no honor or glory or incorruptibility or power. So there must exist in an evil person the antithetical qualities of weakness, dishonor, corruption, and any of the other qualities we have spoken of before. The passions of the soul resulting from evil are hard to drive out since they are mixed with it and have grown with it and become one with it. However, once such souls have been purified by fire and sanctified, the other qualities will enter into them in place of the evil ones, namely, incorruptibility, life, honor, grace, glory, power, and whatever else we conjecture to be discerned in God and that image of Him which is human nature.'

GENERAL INDEX

Aaron, 8, 60, 61.
Abel, 150-151.
Abraham, 234-235.
Adam, xv, 43-46, 49, 85, 129, 270.
adultery, 52, 134, 138.
Aglaophon, 195.
Alexandria, 82.
Altaner, B., ix n.
angels, 51, 171, 179, 180, 227, 259.
anger, 57, 219, 221, 224, 237, *passim*.
Annunciation, mystery of, 257.
Antioch, xii, 163, 173.
apokatastasis, 196-197, 226-227, 267.
Araxius (bishop), 186-187.
Araxius (senator), 183.
Arianism, ix, xii, 174, 178.
Aristotelian concept of virtue, xiv, 4, 32, 55.
Aristotle, 216 n.
Armenia, 168.
art of painting, 37, 68, 85, 98, 110-111, 165, 228.
ascetic life, xi, xiii, xvi, xviii, xix, 3, 80, 95, 161, 171, *passim; see, On Virginity*, 3-75; *On Perfection*, 93-122; *Life of St. Macrina*, 161-191.
Athens, xi, 201.
Aubineau, Michel, xxi n.
Augustine, St., 195.

Baptism, xvii, 129, 139.
Basil of Caesarea, father of St. Gregory of Nyssa, x, 165-167, 178.
Basil, St. (the Great):
Bishop of Caesarea, 173; brother of St. Gregory of Nyssa and St. Macrina, ix-xiii, 161; death, xii, 173, 198; education, xi, 167; founder of monasticism in the East, ix-xii, *passim;* opponent of Arianism, ix, xii; portrait of, xi, 3, 7, 72; Reference to his works:

275

Letters, x; *Address to Young Men on Reading Greek Literature*, xi n.; *On the Hexaemeron*, xii; *Rules*, xiii, xviii, xix, 3.
beauty (the beautiful), 8, 36-42, 237, *passim*.
body, 67-68, 201 ff.; *see* dualism and *On the Soul and the Resurrection*, 198-272.
Boethius, 195.

Caesarea, x, 173.
Cain, 151.
Campbell, J. M., ix n.
Campenhausen, H. V., ix n.
Cappodocian Fathers, ix; *see* St. Basil, St. Gregory of Nazianzus, and St. Gregory of Nyssa.
Cavarnos, John P., xxi.
change, 26-27, 94, 122, 141, 262-263.
charity, xvii, 140 ff.; *see* love.
Cherniss, H., xiii, xiv.
choice, xv, 88, 233, 238, 244, 252.
Christ, xv, 11, 36, 41, 73, 74, 84, 93 ff., 96, 101-107, 112, 118, 120, 121, 260, *passim*; Archetype, xv; Bridegroom, 51, 53, 64, 179; High Priest, 75; King, 84, 97, 119; Logos, 105-107, 114; paschal victim, 104; Prototype, 110-111; head of the Church, 111; only-begotten, 113; Mediator, 116-118; Savior, 143; miracle-worker, 260; *see* analysis of some thirty epithets in St. Paul, 96 ff.
Christian, 79-80, 93; his true nature, xiv-xvi; *see*, *On What It Means to Call Oneself a Christian*, 81-89; *On Perfection*, 95-122; *On the Christian Mode of Life*, 127-158.
Chrysaphius, 168-169.
Constantinople, xi, xii.
contemplation, 4, 27, 39, 176, 237.
Corinthians, 268.
courage, 57, 220.
creation, 43, 203, 221, 243, *passim*; *see* also God as Creator.

Daniel, 74, 220, 225.
Daniélou, S.J., Jean, ix, xiii, xiv, xvi, xix, 3, 122, 195, 196-197, 257.
David, 37, 40, 132, 134, 137, 257.
death, 14 ff., 19, 43, 48, 49, 104, 166, 176, 198 ff., 233.
desire, 6, 40, 57, 88, 99, 103, 219, 224, 237, 239.
devil, 83, *passim*; Adversary, 150, 156, 169, 180, 224; Belial, 117; craftsman of evil, 148; inventor of evil, 87; inventor of falsehood, 200; serpent, 47, 87-88; slanderer, 181; tempter, 142.
Diotima, 195.
dove, symbol of the Holy Spirit, 40.

INDEX

dualism, xiii, 47, 62-63, 99, 100, 103, 137, 171, 233, 235, 253 ff.

Egypt, xi, 25.
Egyptians, 26, 60.
Elias, 5, 8, 28-29.
Emmelia, mother of St. Gregory of Nyssa, x, 161, 164-173.
emotions, 88, 222-223, 237, *passim*.
envy, 13-14, 20, 22, 25, 52, 134.
Epicureans, 201-203.
Epicurus, 201-203.
Eunomius, xii.
eschatology, 196 ff.; *see, On the Soul and the Resurrection*, 198-272.
evil, 8, 20, 43, 44, 47, 87-88, 239, 242, 250-251, 265.

faith, xvii, 129, 130, 191, 240.
fall (of man), 43-47, 233; *see also* man.
fasting, xviii, 71, 153.
fear (of God), 147-148, 158.
Flaccilla (Empress), xii.
freedom, 32, 59, 233, 243.

glory, 9, 39, 105, 118, 122, 135-136, 149, 150, 157-158, 203.
God, 54; Archetype, 110; Creator, 45, 57, 202-204, 222, 252, 257, 265; existence of, 203-204; love of, 44, 80, 127; equated with perfect virtue, 55; incorruptible nature of, 212; source of all blessedness, 241, 251; source of all reality, 203, 243-244, 253; will of, 131, *passim*.
grace, xvii, 68, 125, 130, 131, 141, 151, 155, *passim; see also* synergia.
Graef, H., 196.
greed, 20, 22, 25, 52, 58, 134.
Gregory of Nazianzus, St., ix, xi, xvi.
Gregory of Nyssa, St.:
philosopher and theologian, ix, xvi; mystic, ix, xvi; family of, ix ff., *see* his *Life of St. Macrina*, 161-191; details of his life, xi-xii, 161, 173, 178; spiritual development, xvii - xviii; influenced by Greek philosophic thought, xi, xiii, xiv, xv, 80, 84, 126, 143; his use of the Bible, xv, xvi, 84, 126; works of, xii ff.; *Ascetica*, xviii-xxi; *see* introductions to each treatise; References to works not contained in this volume: *Encomium of St. Basil*, xii; *Against Eunomius*, xii, xx; *On the Creation of Man*, xii, 195; *On the Hexaemeron*, xii; *On the Life of Moses*, xiii, 126; *On the Psalms*, xiii, 126; *On the Canticle of Conticles*, xiii, xix, 126; *Letters*, xx; *Panegyric on St. Gregory Thaumaturgus*, 161; *Sermon on the Resurrection*,

195; *Catechetical Oration,* 195; *On the Lord's Prayer,* 196 n.; *On the Beatitudes,* 196 n.
Gregory Thaumaturgus, St., 161.
grief, 14, 57, 88, 169, 173, 175, 182 ff., 219.
guidance, 68-71.

habit, 34-36, 69, 70.
hagiography, 161.
Harmonius, 79, 93.
Harvard Institute for Classical Studies, xx-xxi.
hell, 180, 225 ff., 231.
honor, 22-24, 39, 135, 149; *see also* glory.
hope, 57, 238-240.

Iliad, 165.
Illyricum, 61.
immortality, 103, 129, 176, 195 ff., 200 ff.; *see, On the Soul and the Resurrection,* 198-272.
Incarnation, 197.
Iris River, x, xiii, 168.
Isaac, 33.
Israel, 60.

Jaeger, Werner, ix, xiii, xv, xvi, xviii-xxi, 82, 125, 196 n., *passim.*
Janson, H. W., 82.
Jerome, St., xii.
Jerusalem, 61, 163.
John, St. (the Apostle), 134, 136.

John, St. (the Baptist), 5, 8, 28-29.
judgment, 261, 263, 267.
justice, 57-58, 144, *passim.*
Keenan, Sister Mary Emily, xiv.
Krabinger, J. B., xxi.

Lampadium, 183-186.
Lazarus (the beggar), 232-235; resurrected by Christ, 260.
Logos, 105, 106, 107, 122.
love, xvii-xviii, 35-36, 126, 140-152, 239-240, *passim.*
Lucian, 79, 82.

McClear, E. V., 196 n.
Macarius, 125.
'Macarius Letter,' 125-126.
Macrina (the elder), grandmother of St. Gregory of Nyssa, x, 164.
Macrina, St., sister of St. Gregory of Nyssa: life of, x ff.; *see, The Life of St. Macrina,* 161-191; *On the Soul and the Resurrection,* 195-272; embodiment of the ascetic ideal, xviii-xix.
man, 22-23; fall of, 44-46, 233; the image of God, xv, 42-43, 80, 85-127, 272, *passim;* free to choose, 233, 238; individuality of, 231; inventive power of., 208-209; a microcosm, 204-205; a thinking animal, 42, 98, 217, 221-222.

Manichaeans, 253.
Mariam (sister of Aaron), 8, 60-61.
marriage, 12 ff., 166, 250; joys of, 13 ff.; disadvantages of, 14-20, 31, 49-50; not to be despised, 31-33; a consolation for death, 46; two kinds (physical and spiritual), 62 ff.; no marriage after death, 264.
Mary, immaculate, 11; Mother of God, 49, 61.
Mary (Magdalene), 116.
medicine, 20, 67, 69, 185, 189-190, 199, 205-206.
Melchisedech, 151.
memory, 238-239.
Meridier, L., 3.
Methodius, 195, 196.
Minotaur, 93, 99.
miracles, 185, 189, 190-191, 260.
moderation, 32, 58, 66, 68, 73, 138, 169.
monasticism, ix, xiii, xvii, 3, 126; *see* the ascetic life.
Monica, St., 195.
mortification, 8, 63, 66, 104.
Moses, 60, 74, 75, 85, 138, 218, 258.
Musurillo, H., 3.

Naucratius (brother of St. Gregory of Nyssa), 168-169.
Neocaesarea, xi.
Newman, Cardinal, J. H., ix, x.
Nicodemus, 47.

Noe, 188.

obedience, 157-158.
Olympius, 93, 161, 163.
Origen, 195-196.
Ostia, 195.

pagan literature, xi, 79, 82, 165.
paideia, xiv.
pain, 241-242.
Paradise, 181.
Paul, St., xvii, 47, 64, 74, 94, 96, 101, 104, 105, 109, 111, 120, 121, 134, 148, 220.
Pelagian controversy, 125.
perfection, xiv-xvii, 80, 86; *see, On Perfection*, 93-122.
Peter, St. (brother of St. Gregory of Nyssa), x, xi, 171-173, 189.
philosophical life (equated with the ascetic life), xi, 80, 126, 143-145, 154, 163, 167, 171-173, *passim*.
philosophy (Greek), xiv, 65, 69, 79, 84, 196, 200, 216, 245 ff., 253.
Phineas, 220, 225.
Pius XI, Pope (Achille Ratti), xx.
Plato, xi, xiii, xiv, xv, xvii, 4, 94, 195, 216, 220, 222, 271; works referred to: *Laws*, 271 n.; *Phaedo*, 195; *Phaedrus*, xiv, 4, 216 n.; *Republic*, 4, 220 n.; *Symposium*, 4, 195.
pleasure, 24, 28, 36, 46, 54, 65-66, 219, *passim*.

Polack, H., xxi.
Pontus, ix, 168, 178, 188.
poverty, 168, 171.
prayer, xvii, xviii, 34, 96, 102, 137, 142, 151-154, 171, 172, 174, 178, 180, 181, 187, 190.
pride, xviii, 22, 137, 143.
priesthood, 74-75.
prudence, 57-58.
Pulcheria, Princess, xii.
purgation, 237, 241 ff., 245, 263, 267, 272.

Quasten, J., ix n., 197.

Rebecca, 33.
Red Sea, 26.
resurrection, xi, xix, 51, 115, 156, 180, 229-272.
Reuben, 113, 115.

Sebaste, xii.
Sebastopolis, 188.
self-control, 8, 63, 65, 66, 68, 171.
service, 145-146, 178.
sin, 44, 134, 265-266, *passim.*
slavery, 26, 54, 59, 103-104, 168.
Socrates, xiv, 195.
Sodom, 25.
Solomon, 64, 165.
soul (focus of the ascetic life), xix, 8, 28; birth of, 252-254; darkened by sin, 44; faculties of, 45, 57-58; immortality of, 195-196; nature of, 205-215; perceiver of beauty, 38-40; purity of, 51-52; temple of God, 137, *passim; see, On the Soul and the Resurrection,* 198 ff.
Spirit, Holy, xvii, xviii, 10, 31, 40, 48, 128 ff., 137, 140-144, 149, 152, 157, 175-176, *passim.*
Stoics, 201.
superiors, xvii, 145-147, 154.
synergia, xvii, 11, 80, 125-126, 131.

Tabernacles (feast of), 257-260.
thanksgiving, 177, 178.
Thecla, 164; *see* St. Macrina.
thought (power of), 88, 210 ff.
Trinity, 5, 10, 106, 128.
truth, xvii, 26, 127, 223.

Valens (Arian emperor), xii, 178.
vanity, 23, 25, 71, 147, 171.
Vetiana, 183-184.
virginity, defined, 4; a life of, 4-6; equated with the incorruptible, 9 ff.; a safe fortress, 35; goal of, 42; stronger than death, 48; not confined to the body, 4, 51; *see, On Virginity,* 6-75.
virtue, xiv, 6 ff., 10, 21, 55, 56, 60, 132, 271, *passim;* Aristotelian idea of, xiv, 4, 32, 55, 67.
virtues, xiv, xvii, 4, 45, 52, 103, 119, 149, 151, *passim.*

Wilamowitz-Moellendorff, Ulrich von, xx.
wisdom, 58, 64, 101, 102, 220, *passim*.

women, community of, 168, 170, 174; *see, Life of St. Macrina*, 161 ff.

INDEX OF HOLY SCRIPTURE

(BOOKS OF THE OLD TESTAMENT)

Genesis
 1.26, 27: 127.
 1.27: 42, 85, 217.
 3.14: 88.
 3.16 ff.: 46.
 3.24: 180.
 4.4, 5: 151.
 9.20 ff.: 188.
 14.18: 151.
 25.20: 33.
 27.1: 33.
 29.32: 113, 115.
Exodus
 14.21 ff.: 60.
 15.20: 60.
 19.15: 74.
 19.22: 74.
Leviticus
 18.7: 188.
 19.19: 138.
 23.39-43: 257.
Numbers
 12.3: 218.
 25.11: 220.
Deuteronomy
 6.5: 143, 148.
 22.9-11: 138.
 32.39: 100.
1 Kings
 9.16: 98.
 10.1: 98.
 12.1 ff.: 98.
Job
 2.8: 175.
 7.5: 175.
Psalms
 4.8: 152.
 5.7: 134.
 8.6: 97.
 17.26, 27: 72.
 18.1: 40.
 18.2: 203.
 18.9: 54.
 18.13, 14: 137.

21.26: 135.
22.2: 107, 180.
23.1: 22.
23.3: 133.
23.4: 133.
24.17: 50.
27.3, 4: 134.
33.3: 135.
43.4: 132.
46.8: 22.
50.12-14: 133.
52.2: 203.
54.7: 40.
55.2, 3: 52.
57.3: 134.
57.4: 116.
62.6: 152.
68.2, 3: 60.
68.3: 34.
72.28: 54.
73. 13, 14: 180.
83.3: 152.
89.10: 22.
93.9: 113.
103.15: 107.
103.29, 30: 257.
112.9: 48.
115.2: 37.
117.27: 258.
118.4: 23.
118.5: 23.
118.6: 133.
118.80: 133.
118.119: 120.
118.127: 56.
118.157: 52.
123.4: 26.
126.1: 132.
138.8-11: 87.

Proverbs
  2.4, 5: 148.
  3.18: 73.
  4.6: 64.
  4.8: 64.
  4.18: 41.
  4.23: 137.
  9.10: 220.
  11.22: 56.
  15.19: 71.
  16.5: 137.
  20.6: 44.
  26.4: 203.
Ecclesiastes
  1.4: 23.
  4.9: 70.
  4.10: 70.
Canticle of Canticles
  1.7: 180.
Wisdom
  1.4: 53, 116.
Sirach (Ecclus.)
  24.20: 152.
Isaia
  25.8: 50.
  26.18: 61, 62.
  41.25: 64.
  52.5: 86.
  60.8: 60.
Ezechiel
  37.1 ff.: 260.
Daniel
  3.51: 187.
  7.10: 75.
  10.12: 220.
Zacharia
  5.7: 60.
Malachia
  3.20: 103.

(BOOKS OF THE NEW TESTAMENT)

Matthew
  2.36 ff.: 143.
  3.12: 66.
  5.8: 75, 116, 132.
  5.11, 12: 156.
  5.14: 41.
  5.15, 16: 103.
  5.16: 135.
  5.19: 69.
  5.28: 65.
  5.48: 86, 132.
  6.1 ff.: 158.
  6.2: 158.
  6.5: 158.
  6.16: 158.
  6.19: 88.
  6.19, 20: 184.
  6.24: 63.
  7.6: 56.
  7.13: 131.
  7.14: 146.
  7.18: 32.
  8.2, 3: 260.
  9.6: 181.
  9.18-25: 260.
  10.16: 55.
  10.22: 131.
  11.12: 131.
  11.29: 111.
  12.42: 157.
  12.50: 50.
  13.13: 131.
  13.24: 223.
  13.47 ff.: 60.
  16.18: 180.
  18.23 ff.: 243.
  20.28: 147.
  21.42: 97.
  22.12: 117.
  22.37: 35.
  23.11: 145.
  23.12: 147.
  23.25: 149.
  24.35: 23.
  25.1 ff.: 154.
  25.40: 158.

Mark
  12.10: 97.
  2.10: 181.
  3.35: 50.
  9.34: 147.
  9.40: 157.
  10.43: 145.
  10.45: 147.
  12.30: 35.

Luke
  1.33: 97.
  1.42: 172.
  3.17: 66.
  6.22, 23: 156.
  6.26: 135.
  7.11-15: 260.
  10.3: 55.
  10.27: 35.
  12.33: 88.
  13.24: 131.
  14.11: 137, 147.
  14.28: 56, 109.
  15.9: 45.
  16.15: 136.
  16.19 ff.: 232.
  16.22: 180.
  16.26: 181, 234.
  17.21: 44, 152.

18.1: 153.
18. 6-8: 139.
18.7: 153.
18.14: 147.
19.3 ff.: 129.
20.17: 97, 108.
21.9: 220.
21.19: 131.
23.34: 111.
23.42: 181.
23.53: 108.
John
  1.9: 41, 103.
  1.13: 50.
  1.29: 117.
  3.5: 114.
  3.6: 47.
  3.17: 97.
  4.13 ff.: 97.
  5.29: 116.
  5.44: 136, 149.
  6.56: 108.
  7.12: 84.
  8.32: 26.
  8.34: 59.
  11.17-44: 260.
  12.35: 25.
  12.36: 41.
  12.46: 41.
  13.15: 110.
  14.6: 84.
  14.9: 106.
  14.23: 11.
  16.21: 266.
  20.17: 116.
  20.27: 261.
Acts
  3.15: 114.
  4.12: 84.
  11.26: 119.
  17.18: 201.
  23.6: 166.
Romans
  1.28-32: 136.
  3.25: 96, 105.
  5.3: 156.
  6.11: 176.
  7.14: 47.
  8.2: 104.
  8.6, 7: 103, 104.
  8.10, 11: 176.
  8.12: 110.
  8.16: 149.
  8.24: 238.
  8.29: 97, 113.
  9.5: 109.
  10.8: 68.
  11.33: 105.
  11.36: 107, 113.
  12.1: 104, 128.
  12.1, 2: 74.
  12.2: 104, 128, 131.
  12.2, 3: 132.
  12.12: 151, 153.
  13.12: 103.
  13.13: 103.
  14.17: 54.
  14.23: 120.
  15.19: 61.
1 Corinthians
  1.24: 84, 96, 101.
  1.30: 54, 96, 103.
  2.8: 97, 118.
  2.9: 89, 267.
  3.9: 34.
  3.10: 108.
  3.11: 97.
  3.12: 56.

3.16: 116.
3.17: 137.
4.15: 61.
4.16: 111.
5.7: 96, 104, 142.
5.8: 142.
5.12: 31.
6.9, 10: 53.
6.15 ff.: 112.
6.18: 51.
7.25 ff.: 6.
7.32, 33: 36, 63.
7.34: 133.
9.9, 10: 12.
9.24: 131.
10.3: 97, 107.
10.4: 97, 107, 108.
10.11: 30, 60.
11.1: 134, 144.
11.28: 108.
12.26: 52.
12.31: 140.
13.3: 140.
13.4-8: 141.
13.8: 240.
13.13: 240.
15.20: 97, 114.
15.28: 243.
15.35-38: 268.
15.42-44: 269.
15.52: 115, 180, 260.
2 Corinthians
 1.4: 152.
 3.18: 122.
 4.2: 103.
 4.5: 147.
 4.16: 62.
 5.4: 23.
 5.16: 11.
5.17: 114, 141.
6.4: 131, 157.
6.6: 64.
6.7, 8: 24.
6.14: 53, 100.
6.15: 118.
6.16: 116.
7.10: 220.
9.15: 110.
10.18: 149.
12.2-4: 47.
12.4: 105.
12.9, 10: 157.
13.3: 96.
13.13: 143.
Galatians
 2.20: 96.
 3.13: 180.
 3.28: 64.
 4.19: 61.
 5.1: 59.
 5.17: 73, 103.
 5.22: 64.
 6.15, 16: 141.
Ephesians
 1.5: 117.
 1.15-19: 140.
 2.3: 114.
 2.14: 96, 102.
 2.15: 102.
 2.16: 102.
 2.20: 108.
 3.14-19: 140.
 3.16: 102.
 4.13-15: 130.
 4.16: 112.
 5.2: 104.
 5.23: 111.
 5.27: 9, 142.

6.6: 145.
6.12: 118.
6.14-16: 142.
6.17: 142.
6.18: 142, 153.
Philippians
  1.23: 18.
  2.6: 106.
  2.10: 226.
  2.10, 11: 259.
  3.8: 20.
  3.13: 144.
Colossians
  1.15: 97, 109, 113.
  1.18: 97, 113, 118.
  1.27: 109.
  1.28: 132.
  1.28, 29: 139.
  3.2: 110.
  3.5: 104.
1 Thessalonians
  1.5: 129.
  4.13: 198.
  5.5: 114.
  5.17: 153.
  5.23: 121, 129, 143.
1 Timothy
  2.5: 97, 116.
  2.15: 48.
  4.2: 31.
  6.15: 84.
  6.16: 84, 96, 103, 105.

2 Timothy
  2.5: 121.
  2.26: 31.
  3.17: 99.
  4.7, 8: 177.
Titus
  2.13: 97, 109.
Hebrews
  1.2: 97.
  1.3: 96, 105, 106.
  2.7: 97.
  2.7-9: 117.
  2.14: 180.
  2.15: 180.
  4.14: 96, 104.
  6.8: 66.
  7.2: 84, 97, 118.
  7.4: 151.
  11.1: 240.
  11.3: 252.
  12.1: 131.
  12.1, 2: 144.
James
  4.4: 116.
1 Peter
  1.8: 110.
  1.24: 23.
  2.22: 110, 115.
1 John
  3.3: 134.
  3.15: 136.

www.ingramcontent.com/pod-product-compliance
Lightning Source LLC
Chambersburg PA
CBHW032028290426
44110CB00012B/717